D0609524

OXFORD STUDIES IN
SOCIAL AND CULTURAL ANTHROPOLOGY

Editorial Board

A MARKET OUT OF PLACE?

OXFORD STUDIES IN
SOCIAL AND CULTURAL ANTHROPOLOGY

Oxford Studies in Social and Cultural Anthropology represents the work of authors, new and established, that will set the criteria of excellence in ethnographic description and innovation in analysis. The series serves as an essential source of information about the world and the discipline.

Gariūnai Market scenes

A Market out of Place?

Remaking Economic, Social, and Symbolic Boundaries in Post-Communist Lithuania

PERNILLE HOHNEN

OXFORD
UNIVERSITY PRESS

OXFORD
UNIVERSITY PRESS

Great Clarendon Street, Oxford OX2 6DP

Oxford University Press is a department of the University of Oxford.
It furthers the University's objective of excellence in research, scholarship,
and education by publishing worldwide in

Oxford New York

Athens Auckland Bangkok Bogotá Buenos Aires Calcutta
Cape Town Chennai Dar es Salaam Delhi Florence Hong Kong Istanbul
Karachi Kuala Lumpur Madrid Melbourne Mexico City Mumbai
Nairobi Paris São Paulo Shanghai Singapore Taipei Tokyo Toronto Warsaw

and associated companies in Berlin Ibadan

Oxford is a registered trade mark of Oxford University Press
in the UK and in certain other countries

Published in the United States
by Oxford University Press Inc., New York

British Library Cataloguing in Publication Data
Data available

Library of Congress Cataloging in Publication Data
Data applied for
ISBN 0–19–926762–6

1 3 5 7 9 10 8 6 4 2

Typeset in Ehrhardt by
Cambrian Typesetters, Frimley, Surrey
Printed in Great Britain
on acid-free paper by
Biddles Ltd,
Guildford and King's Lynn

PREFACE

This is an important book. Through a detailed ethnography of a Lithuanian market place in the mid-1990s, Pernille Hohnen shows us how the period of historical transition manifested itself in a liminal space, where ethnicity and gender were laid open for contestation alongside economic structures and legal norms. The historical uncertainties of the moment were literally embodied in the transactions of traders as centred on the market place but by no means confined to it. Through anthropological participant-observation, among other things implying helping out as a saleswoman at a particular stall, Pernille Hohnen gives us a vivid picture of the social life of the market place, but also—by implication—of life in transitional Lithuania. Incidentally, this sheds new light on the notion of transition itself. Precisely because of its attention to detail and to the local voices the book is bound to become an important source for future studies in the political and economic transformation of the former Soviet Union.

The empirical focus is on a specific market place where petty traders, large-scale entrepreneurs, and groups of racketeers compete for gains in the gap between past socialist ruling and future capitalist economy. The legal uncertainties concerning travel and trade open up new routes of import; traders go to China, India, Turkey, and Poland and bring back items for local consumption. The global extension of the local market is astonishing, not least for the personal ingenuity invested in an uncertain business where one can only learn the hard way. The legal ambiguities are accompanied by a moral ambivalence as far as trading on the market goes: both would-be traders and their environment tend to evaluate the market place as somehow beyond civilized society. While criminality and aggression are certainly conspicuous at the market place—barring certain areas from the lone ventures and questioning of the anthropologist— there is also a remarkable will to make the market *work*. One cannot help being impressed by the reflections on their trade and its conditions made by the traders themselves.

The book demonstrates the value of anthropology as complementary to economics when it comes to studying the market. Where economists in general have focused on the market *principles*, and thus primarily dealt with the formation of prices and profit, anthropologists studying market *places* engage with the concrete exchanges and transactions between people, and thus show the social and cultural aspects of trade. This helps us to realize that people are never simply victims of history but are also actively engaging and transforming it through their actions. By giving a voice to the Lithuanian traders and making us party to their deliberations and choices, Pernille Hohnen has contributed significantly to our sense of human agency, not as the prerogative of the few, but as an inherent element in what it means to be human.

Kirsten Hastrup
Professor at the Institute of Anthropology
University of Copenhagen
January 2003

ACKNOWLEDGEMENTS

During my periods of fieldwork in 1994 and 1995, many people in Lithuania were facing very difficult times. In the course of conversations with traders in the Gariūnai market outside Vilnius, some of whom were highly qualified people with university degrees, I often wondered how I myself would have felt and what I would have done if I had suddenly found myself unemployed and without the possibility of earning a living in any way formerly known to me. It is difficult to imagine the kind of chaos that such a situation must have presented. On the other hand it is easy to imagine how soon it could have led to apathy and passivity.

I was therefore impressed not only by the Gariūnai traders' energy and initiative but also by the humour and wit they displayed in attempting to come to terms with their difficult situation.

I particularly remember a day in the market when the rain was pouring down. I was sharing an umbrella with a Thermos flask vendor—an engineer from Azerbaijan—because I was trying to interview him. Suddenly he decided we needed some champagne, and off he went to the nearest kiosk and bought a bottle! He made no complaints about the situation, but just tried to make the best of it. I am not sure I could have done the same thing if I had been in his shoes.

Although many market traders (including Irena, who generously allowed me to join her at her stall in the market) naturally felt they were the victims of forces over which they had no control, they certainly did not behave like victims. I am grateful for the chance to witness such a positive attitude to life and, hopefully, learn from it. I sincerely wish that in the long run their efforts may bear fruit.

I should also like to thank the many Lithuanians outside the market who devoted their time and energy to helping me in various ways. I am particularly grateful to Aušra Šapranauskienė, who worked with me as my fieldwork assistant and interpreter, and to Vytis Čiubrinskas of the department of History and Ethnology of Vilnius University, who shared his insight and time with me. Furthermore, I am most grateful to Gintaras Steponavičius, Dalia Jurgaitytė and Natalija Kasatkina for allowing me to benefit from their knowledge and networks of contacts.

I am grateful to Karen Fog Olwig, my supervisor at the Institute of Anthropology, Copenhagen University, for her valuable suggestions and patience. I would also like to thank Kirsten Hastrup for her support and encouragement at a crucial moment in the course of my work. Finally, I am grateful to my fellow Ph.D. students for their interest and critical observations.

I am particularly indebted to Steven Sampson at Lund University, who supported my project from the very outset. He has not only shown a continuous interest in it but also spent a considerable amount of his free time with our small group of Danish anthropology students when we were struggling to make sense of the situation in Eastern and Central Europe at the time. His support has been crucial to my studies.

Outside anthropological circles I should like to thank Dalia Barauskaitė Mikkelsen, my Lithuanian teacher at Copenhagen University, who became a good friend, and also her sister, Jūratė Barauskaitė, who joined us in Denmark and later in Lithuania, looking after my daughter and killing the mice in our apartment while I was in the market. Last but not least, I would like to thank my father-in-law, David Hohnen, who has let me benefit from his life-long experience with Danes writing English and has turned the manuscript into a comprehensible English text.

Finally, I am grateful to the Danish Research Council for the Humanities and the Danish Research Council for the Social Sciences for financial support as well as to The Danish National Institute of Social Research for granting me time to make the final revisions of the manuscript.

I am well aware that many of my informants in Lithuania may not agree with the conclusions I have reached. To some extent anthropology always involves deconstructing local knowledge and meaning. If by writing this book I have hurt the feelings of any of those involved I can only apologize deeply. I present it as my version of a slice of reality, but it is of course by no means the only one.

Pernille Hohnen

CONTENTS

1

Conceptualizing 'Transition'

To say that society and history are products of human action is true, but only in a certain ironic sense. They are rarely the products the actors themselves set out to make. (Ortner 1984: 157)

INTRODUCTION

Tremendous changes have taken place during the last fifteen years all over the former 'Eastern bloc', i.e. the former Soviet Union and Eastern Europe. These changes are by far the most important European political events in the second half of the twentieth century. However, the road to democracy and market economy has proved to be more difficult and involved more hardship, poverty, political conflicts, and civil wars than was anticipated by either Eastern or Western Europe when the Berlin Wall was pulled down in 1989.

The present book is primarily an empirical study of how some of these changes have come about and been experienced by people in the now independent republic of Lithuania. Originally intended as a study of changing economic practice, it has grown into an analysis of the changing moral economy and the social and symbolic confusion that has proved to be a part of the economic and political changes. Although the changes in the economic field therefore form an important part of the analysis, their importance has also been as a vehicle for understanding the changing social structure, meanings, symbols, and terminology, which at first glance may seem irrelevant to an economist. Thus, although 'the transition' has usually been presented as a rapid, systemic, economic, and political change from socialism to capitalism, the analysis shows that it had much broader connotations of social and cultural crisis. Moreover, the very conceptualization of these specific historic changes as 'transition' is analytically problematic as it 'freezes' the present into a phase of 'liminality' (Turner 1969), an intermediate phase, as compared with a stable past and the prospects of a predetermined and stable future. As emphasized by several anthropologists working in the region, this is largely inadequate, since it reflects at most an idea of 'textbook capitalism' (cf. Burawoy and Verdery 1999) rather than empirical evidence of the economic, cultural, and political situation of countries in the region. In addition, as the quotation from Ortner above signals, social and cultural changes are much less of a planned project, and with the time that has elapsed since the beginning of 'the great transformation' it has become clear that the policies—such as 'shock therapy', based on the idea of a rapid substitution of 'capitalism' for 'socialism'—have resulted in the long run in very different paths of remaking, unmaking, or reforming socialism into various versions of market economies (Burawoy and Verdery 1999; see also Buchowski 1994; Bridger and Pine 1998; Humphrey 2002).

Wedel (1992), much in line with Ortner, finds that the outcome of 'transition' may be highly unintended, but it is not unregulated. Everybody aims for a legal, open, and stable free market, but in practice their conduct results in a reconsolidation of former black-market structures such as tax evasion and short-term speculation. More recently, Wedel has added another dimension to this discussion by questioning Western aid to Eastern Europe and showing how this has added to, rather than weakened, illegal networks and corruption (Wedel 2001). The economic field in post-Communist Lithuania moreover appears contested and rapidly changing as different social actors (and groups) struggle for influence. A market does not just establish itself, although its mechanical autonomy is often implicit in neo-classicist economic theories (cf. Preston 1992). As Friedland and Robertson (1990) have demonstrated, the 'birth' of the Western market in seventeenth-century England was created by a particular group of merchants, and its form was very much the result of a struggle between various economic agents.

Verdery (1991 and 1996) has suggested that the term 'transition' may be used as an indication of change *from* a certain system, since it is now possible to theorize on what such a system (of socialism) entailed, but one has to be very careful when discussing what the outcome of such changes will be. Verdery proposed, along with Humphrey (1995a), that so far the development may generally be characterized more as a movement towards 'feudalism', i.e. the emergence of local chiefdoms, than towards a modern Western-style democracy. Others have suggested a development of bazaar economies (Gerner and Hedlund 1994), 'merchant capitalism', or even new forms of socialism:

What we are observing is not the development of capitalism, but the restructuring of the Soviet system from below, subordinating capital and the commodity to the reproduction of the existing social relations of production. (Clarke quoted in Humphrey 1995a: 9)

Lately, the differences between various paths of development have become so apparent that Humphrey and Mandel (2002) question the very idea of a common condition inherent in the concept of 'post-socialism'. At the same time, however, they do suggest that 'the 1990s represented a critical period that does have a certain unity' (ibid. 3).

In the present study I shall attempt to shed more light on some regularities of this particular period of unity in the 1990s—and also on the specific conditions shaping the process of transformation in Lithuania—by analysing the establishment of a specific open-air market called Gariūnai on the outskirts of Vilnius in 1990. Since this type of market was formerly forbidden it may be regarded as a very visible symptom of the political and economic changes. Moreover, it has a

very bad reputation in Lithuania as a whole, being regarded as shameful, uncivilized, and criminal. My analysis has three principal aims. First, to trace the making
of the market by looking at changing routines and changing concepts of trade, in
the course of which I shall illuminate the process of establishing a new economic
field. Second, to add a more phenomenological perspective by regarding the negative moral evaluations of the market, the social stigmatization of market traders,
and the influence of such evaluations on social identity as a parallel research theme.
Third, by focusing on such processes of institutionalization and marginalization, it
is my aim to contribute to a wider understanding and conceptualization of 'the
transition'. I suggest that the rapid social and cultural changes may be regarded as
processes of spatial, social, and symbolic reterritorialization.

By selecting this market place, which is clearly bounded in time (and space), I
have in a sense opted for a view on 'the transition' as a distinct period in the history
of Eastern Europe. However, such boundaries become somewhat illusive as my
analysis of the market in practice and its image develops. My decision to focus on
an apparently bounded place therefore also helps to frame processes of boundary-
remaking and boundary-trespassing. It is by relating the moral reactions to the
market place with the remaking of social and cultural boundaries in various
domains that I shall attempt to illuminate the changing moral landscape epitomized by the market. A characteristic feature when moving within the domain of
morality is that what appears to challenge the normative order is not the transformation of existing practices or categories as such. The 'moral outcry' becomes
specifically loud when existing practice suddenly takes place in a different (and
therefore often inappropriate) social space.

OPEN-AIR MARKETS, CROSS-BORDER TRADE, AND THE QUEST FOR CHEAP
CONSUMER GOODS

Open-air markets have existed as an integral part of the retail sector in most states
in Eastern and Central Europe during the socialist period. They formed a part of
the second economy and an essential part of the State redistributive system in most
countries, not only in the 'liberal states' of central Europe such as Poland and
Hungary, but also in the Soviet Union (Wedel 1986, Shlapentokh 1989, Shelley
1990, Fisher-Ruge 1993, Czako and Sik 1999). Especially during the perestroika
period, and the opening of borders in the 1980s, increased trading activities
resulted in a large number of such small markets (Sik and Wallace 1999).
According to the predictions of macro-economists it was believed that the second
economy (including open-air markets) would disappear along with the development of market economy, but this has not happened. On the contrary, there has
been a tremendous expansion of these markets all over the former Soviet Union
and Eastern Europe. From an institutional point of view it has been argued that as
existing arrangements, especially Comecon, were dismantled and subsidies and
other grants were withdrawn, shuttle traders bringing in cheap consumer goods

from Asia and China filled the 'institutional void' (Sik and Wallace 1999: 699). The same vacuum may be said to have appeared regarding the national redistributive channels. As Burawoy and Verdery phrase it: 'Because socialism was a system organized around state-controlled redistribution, dismantling those channels produces a relative vacuum of mechanisms for exchange and distribution . . .' (Burawoy and Verdery 1999: 3).

This vacuum has to some extent been filled by individual traders, operating either alone or in small family networks, who have established new channels of supply and redistribution of consumer goods. These activities, termed 'shuttle trading' or 'trading tourism', where most merchandise is purchased abroad and sold at open-air markets, are estimated to have a tremendous economic importance in most post-socialist countries. Vaknin (2002) writes that according to the 27 March 2002 issue of the *East West Institutes Russian Regional Report*, the value of Chinese goods shuttled into the borderlands of the Russian Far East is around 50 million US dollars a month. The far-ranging consequences of this trade is also emphasized by Humphrey (1999), who suggests that in 1996, around 41 per cent of Russia's working population was engaged in international shuttle trade or services linked to that trade. All over the region, open-air markets have developed as places where commodities can be sold, and they form a continuum from largely disorganized street corners to a number of very large bazaars such as that in the Warsaw Stadium (Sik and Wallace 1999).

Along with the expansion of both the number and size of open-air markets, they have also changed in character. During the socialist period, traders would sell a range of products that were difficult to obtain—merchandise that had been acquired either via relations in other countries or by pilfering at the workplace. At the time traders would offer merchandise such as cheap coffee, cigarettes, spirits, and sweets, and selling would take place at the existing food markets (Sik and Wallace 1999). The new open-air markets, the large bazaars, have usually outgrown the old food markets and are often placed at some distance from the main city. Furthermore, traders have ceased to offer food products and are mainly selling clothes and related items. At present, shuttle traders in the open-air markets provide cheap consumer products for the millions of citizens in the former socialist countries, who, although exposed to new forms of consumer-bound social status systems, are by and large unable to afford the fashionable Western status symbols. Shuttle traders and the establishment of the large open-air markets have provided the possibility of buying cheap substitutes for the symbols of social status within the new social system (ibid.)

Despite the fact that these markets seem to have become a more permanent part of the new market economies, selling in the market has not developed into a socially and morally acceptable activity. On the contrary, open-air markets are still seen as dangerous and immoral places, yet, as the present study of Gariūnai shows, marginalization and condemnation have taken on new forms along with the shifting contextualization of trading.

The present study will therefore examine social and cultural changes at several levels, although its starting-point is the emerging economic field. I shall trace Lithuanian trading practices back to black-market activities in Soviet society and show how these form a basis for the emerging market by becoming increasingly routinized and institutionalized while also including new ways of reproducing traders' moral position at the edge of society. Increased institutionalization as well as growing formalization does not necessarily lead to social acceptance. My study of the market place points rather to a reproduction of the interdependency between formal and informal economic activities, not only economically but also culturally. Market behaviour is still constitutive of non-market behaviour (and vice versa) and the images of the market place as 'marginal' and 'dirty' form an important part of the symbolic reconstruction of Lithuanian society.

THE MARKET AND SOCIETY

Although the Gariūnai market is huge and provides tens of thousands of people with a daily income, it has—along with other non-food markets in Lithuania—a very bad reputation. The criticism I heard was levelled at various aspects: the market was 'uncivilized' and dominated by racketeers and thieves; traders just stood there, never did any real work; incomes were not declared, therefore trade was black; the market was considered non-Lithuanian, and especially dominated by Poles and Russians; it was outdoor and dirty (one's shoes got dirty), and finally, goods were of poor quality and traders were believed to be cheating. A gradual impoverishment of the market had further added to its bad reputation; profits were diminishing, while at the same time, as mentioned above, new groups in the population were entering it. Many teachers, technicians, and even a few artists (many of them women) have recently begun trading. This development has further influenced the status of the market. But although all the points of criticism of the market hold elements of truth, the process of marginalization, symbolically as well as economically, seems to be more complex and in addition highly political: there is indeed more to it than dirty shoes.

Traders usually explained that the market began as *talkučkė*, which refers to an 'illegal place for speculation' in Soviet society. In the late 1980s and 1990s, along with the opening of borders between countries in Eastern and Central Europe, shuttle trading intensified, and traders of this kind started to 'colonialize' the main food market in Vilnius. Around 1990, the Vilnius city council moved this trade away from the centre of the city, first to an area near the airport and then to Gariūnai, 10 km from the centre of Vilnius. This development reveals not only how the market was first established but also that during the process it was removed from the centre of the city and re-established far outside it. But although the attitudes towards trading as 'speculation' can be viewed as a 'remnant of socialist discourse', one needs to look at the ways in which such attitudes are being reproduced in order to reveal the role of the market in the contemporary restructuring of Lithuanian society. For example, why are some forms of trade, although also illegal during Soviet times, becoming widely accepted today while Gariūnai has become perhaps even more socially stigmatized than before?

IN SEARCH OF LOCAL MEANINGS

The establishment of the Gariūnai market and negative moral evaluations of it may be regarded analytically as a specific event and as such, according to Sahlins, directly linked to the symbolic order of society:

> An event is not just a happening in the world; it is a *relation* between a certain happening and a given symbolic system. And although as a happening an event has its own 'objective' properties and reasons stemming from other worlds (systems), it is not these properties *as such* that give it effect but their significance as projected from some cultural scheme. (Sahlins 1985: 153)

In order to illuminate the moral condemnation of new and recontextualized forms of trade I have therefore attempted to include an analysis of at least part of the particular 'cultural scheme' that has invested them with significance. However, such an investigation has not been without problems, mainly because of the sparse ethnographic accounts of Lithuanian culture during the Soviet period. The present book is primarily based on fieldwork. Although part of the purpose of data-collecting has been to investigate the present by relating it to the past, the historical scope for analysis is fairly brief. There are several reasons for this, the most important being that by focusing on practice it seems most relevant to investigate the relatively short span of time within which the basis for such practice has been generated. In a Bourdieu framework, this would be termed the social conditions during which present *habitus* has been generated (Bourdieu 1992). The historical period investigated is therefore generally confined to the later half of the Soviet era. I am aware of a discrepancy here, because Lithuanian representations of self and nationhood are heavily influenced by a sense of their long-term history and national tradition.[1] When relevant, I have therefore included a few references to this 'Lithuanian tradition'.

Another reason why I have found it necessary to base most of my observations on my own data relates to the fact that very little material about 'everyday life' or 'social life' in Lithuania, either as a Soviet republic or after independence, has been collated so far.[2] The available material on Lithuania can be classified more or less as follows: a fair amount of factual historical work, written by dissidents or journalists focusing on political resistance, etc. (cf. Vardys 1965, Senn 1990, Lieven 1993, Misiunas and Taagepera 1993 (1983)); some recent factual accounts of the

---

[1] See, for example, Roepstorff 1996.

[2] There may be more such accounts in Lithuanian. To my knowledge, however, the social science tradition in Soviet society was concerned more with statistical analysis than with anything resembling participant observation. Social anthropology did not exist as a science in the Soviet Union.

political and economic situation after independence (Nørgaard *et al.* 1994), a fair amount of statistical work dealing with people's opinions on various subjects carried out by Lithuanian sociologists (cf. Alisauskienie and Bajaruniene 1993, Taliūnaitė 1996, Kanopiene and Juozeliūniene 1996). Finally, I must mention a Lithuanian ethnological tradition for studying regional traditions, material culture, and mythology (cf. Greimas 1992 and 1993). This material has been useful in various ways in forming an idea of the chronological history of Lithuania and factual knowledge of the country's geography, economy, folklore, and so forth, but it has given little insight into the lives of people during and after Sovietism. How people have dealt with their lives, what they have believed in, and how they felt about socialism has not been a major concern in any of these writings. Hardly any research has been published on issues such as social identities, social interaction or topics of gender relations, family, childbearing, or forms of communication.[3] Generally, questions about people's everyday lives have not featured very strongly in research on Lithuania, yet they represent crucial knowledge if one wishes to understand the 'cultural schemes' mentioned above.

THE ANTHROPOLOGY OF SOCIALISM

As Eastern European anthropology has been virtually non-existent until recently, the field has been dominated by 'Western' anthropologists. According to Sampson (1991), Hann (1994b), and Kurti (1996), the region as a whole has moreover received little attention from them and has thus remained marginal within the anthropological field. One reason for this may be the difficulty in obtaining permission to do fieldwork in most socialist countries. Yet the high degree of industrialization in socialist Eastern Europe combined with anthropology's weak methods of studying complex societies has probably also influenced the lack of interest, and much anthropology of the 1970s and 1980s has actually been community studies in rural areas (for a review see Hann 1994b). Eastern Europe and the former Soviet Union, situated between the Occident and the Orient, might have been viewed as confusing rather than as contributing to anthropology's theory-making because the prevalent us/them dichotomies have fitted poorly here (cf. Boym 1994). Eastern Europe is highly industrialized and urbanized, and at the same time without many of the conditions normally associated with Western-style modernism and post-modernism. It is not my intention here, however, to review the anthropology of Eastern Europe and the Soviet Union, but rather to discuss some characteristics that I have found in the material upon which my own conclusions are partly based.

First, there is a general focus on socialism as the common denominator within this region. This has resulted in a preoccupation with certain topics such as underground economy, political rituals, life on collective farms, political dissent, and

---

[3] Here I am speaking specifically about the Lithuanian situation.

other matters. However, a range of topics such as self and person, identity, communication and symbolism, which elsewhere are key areas of anthropological analysis, are absent.[4] Instead, there is often a preoccupation with the political sphere, and, according to Kurti (1996), the terminology is often borrowed from economics and political science. This preoccupation with socialist influence on actors as well as whether people were generally adhering to or resisting the system has resulted in numerous anthropological studies on underground society and underground economy (cf. Kenedi 1981, Mars and Altman 1983, Wedel 1986, Sampson 1987). Many of these, however, have been criticized for viewing socialism as an 'empty shell' (Sampson 1991) instead of discussing the strategies involved in moving in and between various economic and political contexts. Indeed, such 'dichotomy-thinking' is the second important feature of Eastern European anthropology. It has taken various forms. The region is presented by some researchers as generally less regulated and controlled than Western countries because of widespread oppositional 'private behaviour' (Wedel 1986, 1992), whereas others focus on the hegemony of socialist discourse in cultural production against the less hegemonic and less centralized cultural production in Western societies (Verdery 1991, 1996). In both cases, the presentation is closely interconnected with a politically defined, Western 'other'. This has also had consequences in studies of the transition, where for example the emerging markets in Eastern Europe are often perceived as being fundamentally different from markets in the West. For example, there is a tendency to focus on spectacular topics such as the Mafia, corruption, nepotism, and generally 'uncivilized' features of the Eastern markets. However, a focus of this kind might implicitly oppose such 'uncivilized practice' with an imagined smoothly functioning, non-nepotistic, non-monopolized Western market. An example could be the otherwise illuminating examination of 'the transition' in Russia by Gerner and Hedlund (1993), which, as a result of a very critical discussion of the Western neo-classicist economic discourse on 'transition', actually ends up presenting the emerging markets in Russia as wild bazaars and the wrong kind of markets.

The third, and perhaps for my purpose most important aspect of Eastern European anthropology and the focus on socialism, is a widespread *a priori* assumption that Eastern European countries are fairly similar because of their common socialist past. Comparisons between countries are often made in respect of their various socialist regimes (cf. Sampson 1993) rather than other cultural or historical features. It seems that this has moreover widened the gap between many Eastern European cultural specialists and their Western counterparts, since local researchers deliberately try to find national and regional traditions (often basing their research on ethnological rather than anthropological data). Although I agree with Humphrey (1995a) that anthropologists cannot be content with pure empiricism, the tendency to generalize the socialist experience is also problematic. This

---

[4] There are of course exceptions, for example Shlapentokh (1984).

applies specifically to studies on the Soviet Union, where it is often impossible to separate the various republics (let alone other regional, demographic, or social differences, cf. Shlapentokh, 1989). Boym (1994), although writing about and using data solely from Russia, has no difficulty in deciding that her conclusions may be generalized and apply to all countries that have been part of the Soviet Union. Furthermore, the former socialist countries are increasingly coming to diverge from each other as some have assumed 'highly authoritarian forms' while others have moved more in an 'unambiguously Western direction' (Humphrey 2002). Thus another aim of the present study is to go beyond the common term 'transition' by not only pointing to the specific characteristics concerning the processes of change, but also to the different forms of both 'socialism' and 'post-socialism'. Apart from obvious similarities, each country has experienced a unique set of changes, and we need to include such diversity when theorizing the 'transition' and 'post-socialism'. In Lithuania, socialist discourses must be viewed as shaped by other local or regional pre-war, or Polish, yet wholly different cultural traditions.

LITHUANIAN HISTORY AND SYSTEMIC CHANGES

Besides hospitality, the ethos of the Lithuanian people can be characterized by moral [continuity], expressed in lively ties with the people's past; strong attachment to the native country; love for the native tongue and great respect for the remains of ancestors. Remembering the past of the nation and reviving lost ties with the spirits of the ancestors is becoming like a national tempest. (Mikalkevičius and Šinkunas 1992: 53)

The above quotation shows clearly the rhetorical importance of 'the Lithuanian tradition', especially taking into account the fact that it formed the introduction to a report on alcohol problems in Lithuania!

In contrast to Estonia and Latvia, which did not become independent nations until the interwar period, the history of the Lithuanian nation dates back to the thirteenth century. However, the country's national traditions and history are closely linked to Poland, with which Lithuania was united from the fourteenth until the eighteenth century. The close connection with Poland resulted in a widespread Polonization of the Lithuanian upper classes, with the result that the Lithuanian language remained purely oral until well into the seventeenth century. It also resulted in the 'agrarianization' of Lithuanian culture, for native speakers of Lithuanian as a rule remained peasants until well into the twentieth century. This circumstance in turn influenced the demographic situation, with the result that until the last half of this century the urban population consisted mainly of Jews, Poles, and Russians. In connection with the present study it is also important to note that in the early Vilnius markets the traders were non-Lithuanians, mainly Jews, and that ethnic Lithuanians therefore had no trading tradition even before the Soviet occupation (cf. Buloff 1991). Under Polish influence, Lithuania remained Catholic, also after the Reformation, and the Church's strong position has had cultural and political consequences until the present day. The Catholic Church played a central part in organizing and conceptualizing opposition, first to the Russian and later to the Soviet occupiers.[5] After the various divisions of Poland, Lithuania, like the two other Baltic states, became part of the Russian empire, an occupation that continued until the end of the First World War in 1918, when Lithuania again became independent, although this time in a smaller version. In the present context it is important to note that Vilnius remained Polish during the inter-war period, and furthermore that this seriously hampered relationships between the two countries. In 1941, Lithuania was occupied first by the Germans and then in 1944 by the Soviet army. As a republic in the Soviet Union, Lithuania underwent rapid industrialization as well as collectivization of agriculture, but has not experienced the same degree of demographic Russification as Estonia and Latvia.

Lithuania was the first of the Baltic countries to renounce its membership of the Soviet Union. In 1989 the Lithuanian Communist Party broke its ties with the Soviet Communist Party and in March 1990 Lithuania declared independence. A difficult year followed, culminating in January 1991, where the Soviet army tried to reoccupy the country; thirteen people were killed. Not until August 1991, after the unsuccessful *coup d'état* in Moscow, did independence become a reality.

It is of course far beyond the scope of this study to list all the systemic changes that have taken place during the first years of Lithuania's independence. However, I shall introduce some important topics in order to contextualize the subsequent analysis of market trading. Perhaps the most important characteristic of the 'transition' was the general confusion within the legal system that resulted from new legislation, which often conflicted with other areas. Furthermore, during these early years, nobody really knew which set of laws were to be applied, since officially both the Soviet and Lithuanian legislative systems were in force. The result was a legal vacuum, which influenced, among other things, import/export patterns, border regulations, and economic criminality in general. As one of my informants expressed it: 'There were no borders at the time, and you could bring in anything!' This has resulted in a rather blurred boundary between legal and illegal activities. Another aspect of this confusion is the delay in introducing the national currency. The litas was not introduced until the summer of 1993 after more than a year with a temporary currency, the talonas, which was tied to the Russian rouble. The widespread use of American dollars, which has continued until recently, may be at least partially related to this unstable currency situation. Furthermore, knowledge of the new legislation, especially knowledge of taxes, is limited among the small (and even the larger) entrepreneurs. As these laws are moreover complex, inefficient, and sometimes contradictory, it is not only the substance of them that people react against, but their implementation as well. For example, a Lithuanian–American businesswoman told me:

---

[5] See Nørgaard *et al.* 1994, Misiunas and Taagepera 1993 (1983).

All these laws are stupid and bureaucratic. You have to have a licence for everything! And then they are inconsistent as well. If I go bankrupt I am personally responsible, but I can only deduct 20 litai a day ($5) for petrol for my cars. This is ridiculous for a delivery service!

The widespread tax evasion and grey economic activities must be understood partly in the light of this complex and inconsistent legal system. On top of all this, there is a feeling that the system might even work if it were applied as originally intended were it not for widespread discrepancies between the theory and practice of the regulations involved. What is of specific relevance to the following analysis is the fact that until recently this applied in particular to border regulations.

The emergence of such grey zones, ambiguous legislation, and questionable moral conduct must be seen as an almost inevitable result of the overall economic climate during these first few years of Lithuania's renewed independence. However, there is much more to it than that.

GARIŪNAI AS A 'STRATEGICALLY SITUATED SINGLE SITE'

It is the prolonged contact with people's experiences with the world, or what Sherry Ortner (1984) has termed 'the perspective of the folks on the shore', that gives anthropological fieldwork its distinctive character. When studying economic practices it therefore becomes important to find not only ways in which such practices may be observed, but also where experiences with them are being revealed and participation and social relations with participants are becoming possible.

Making the Gariūnai market the focus of my studies had several advantages. First, it provided me with a research site where I could observe and later participate in traders' activities as well gain broader knowledge about life in contemporary Lithuanian society. Although it took a while to 'break the ice' and make acquaintances in the market, in the end I not only took part in interesting discussions with traders about trading and business, but also through informal chat in the market became more familiar with everyday life in contemporary Lithuanian society. Trading in the market meant that there were always periods when business was slow and these pauses were usually spent with small-talk among traders.

Second, although being a distinct, physically bounded as well as culturally marked place, Gariūnai did in many ways reflect the cultural complexity of surrounding society. Although representations of it suggested some distinct and quite rigid cultural features (generally termed 'uncivilized'), activities in the market were highly differentiated in practice, and social relationships formed a loosely structured, highly hierarchic, and ever-shifting social structure. The market might be conceptualized as what Hylland-Eriksen (1995) has termed 'a cultural crossroad'. Traders in the market were a mixture of local Russians, local Poles, and local Lithuanians. Adding to the complexity was the fact that both women and men were trading, although often in rather different ways, as well as the fact that traders were of highly different professions and their motivations for being engaged in market trading also varied considerably. Generally, many traders had felt forced to begin trading, and the 'recent waves' of traders could be viewed as a result of increasing privatization and rationalization in Lithuanian State companies and the increased (although statistically largely hidden) unemployment figures that had followed. In this way the development of the market reflected the social problems of post-Communist society as a whole. Analytically, the choice of Gariūnai highlighted more general problems concerning the conceptualization of cultural complexity, as it is difficult to estimate the degree of cultural coherence among the various ethnic and social groups 'inhabiting' a cultural site of this kind. The study of the market place should therefore also be regarded as a study of the highly complex and dynamic social processes involved in the Lithuanian 'transition' and thus viewed as a contribution to the anthropology of cultural complexity, globalization, and social change.

Third, in addition to the physical existence of the market as a place, the symbolic meanings attached to it, or rather the symbolic production of the market, made it possible to study practised as well as imagined space within a multi-ethnic site. As Hastrup and Olwig (1997) have suggested, the growing gap between culture as imagined sites and culture as lived practice is one of the most distinct features of the contemporary globalization of culture. A growing number of people in practice live their lives in diasporic communities where global cultural flows seem deterritorialized and borderless (cf. Appadurai 1990), while simultaneously large groups of people attempt to strengthen the notion of a 'homeland' and the feeling of belonging to a local, firmly bordered, distinctive place. The popular notion of culture is thus becoming more essentialistic and fixed, while in practice culture is becoming detached from its imagined locality. The quest for anthropology increasingly becomes the ability to deal with culture both as imagined and as practised 'sites' (ibid.). But in order to be able to view practised culture one needs to 'site' culture, and in order to be able to analyse imagined sites, we need to follow, as Marcus (1995) has suggested, cultural processes that extend the 'site' itself.

The methodological advantage of studying Gariūnai can be related to this awareness of a growing gap between culture as practised and imagined community. But, as regards Gariūnai, we appear to encounter a somewhat different relationship between an imagined and a practised community. Whereas according to Olwig (1996) anthropological studies of images of culture often emphasize positive connotations of 'lost country', 'homeland', etc., the choice of Gariūnai points in a rather different direction, since the discourse about the market was both very vehement and very negative. I was reluctant in the beginning to choose the Gariūnai market as my main research site, because I thought it could only offer insight into a limited niche within the economic field. But precisely because the public discourse about the market is so vehement and negative, it reflects aspects of cultural production on a much more general level as well. Although the *site* being examined is the Gariūnai market, the *analytical* scope of the book is the social and cultural space between practised and imagined 'post-Communist society'. In a well-known article, Gupta and Ferguson (1992) suggest that ethnographers dealing with modern societies need to go beyond the assumed localized cultural differences and look at the conditions for, and production of, spatial hierarchy. By focusing on what they term the borderline not between 'us' and 'the other', but rather between 'ourselves as others' and 'others, as ourselves' we might understand more about the reterritorialization of space as well (ibid.). In relation to the present study, I suggest that in order to understand and conceptualize cultural differences within Lithuanian society as they are assumed or imagined, we need to investigate the conditions under which the borderlines between the market and 'society' are produced and reproduced as well as the flexibility and manipulation of this boundary. What kind of symbolic capital, for example, is necessary to cross the border between Gariūnai and the more prestigious business community in Vilnius itself? What can the spatial marginalization of Gariūnai tell us about the moral and symbolic construction of hierarchy and fragmentation, and how is the marginalization being conceived by the social agents involved?

Focusing on production of marginality includes a more global cultural level in terms of the production and reproduction of spatial hierarchy in society. At the same time, traders deal with their position at 'the edge of society' in various ways, which also becomes visible at the market place. The consequences of social stigmatization for processes of identity-making thus appear highly relevant as well. Finally, the study of the market also shows the seamy side of the recent political and economic changes in Lithuania and therefore the economic field as contested regarding both economic and symbolic capital. The choice to focus on a single ethnographic site in no way limited my possibility of doing fieldwork on the world system, nor did it prevent me from analysing the cultural complexity of modern city life. An ethnographic analysis focusing on Gariūnai, not as a site in itself but as a practised and imagined place, might be conceptualized as what Marcus has termed 'strategically situated single-site ethnography' (Marcus 1995):

This strategically situated [single-site] ethnography attempts to understand something broadly about the system in ethnographic terms as much as it does its local subjects: it is only local circumstantially, thus situating itself in a context or field quite differently than does other [conventional] single-site ethnography. (Marcus 1995: 110–11)

By looking at the position of the market within the general economic field as well as the processes, both symbolic and economic, which are producing this position, an ethnographical study of the market would include 'the system' as well as keep a local focus or perspective on it.

FIELDWORK IN GARIŪNAI

My information about the market has been assimilated from participant observation, qualitative interviews with traders, survey data based on questionnaires, and the presentation of the market in the Lithuanian media.[6] My material has been collected during two periods of fieldwork separated by an interval of one year in order to form an idea of the development of the market. At first, I was just observing the place, registering its physical shape, the way it kept changing throughout the week, the kinds of goods it offered, and engaging in casual conversation with market traders. Next, I conducted ethnographic interviews with traders in the market, and with most of them also at least one interview outside it after following their activities for several months. Furthermore, I wanted to submit questionnaires to traders about their ethnic, professional, and social background as well as age, gender, and type of activity, for example from which country or countries they obtained their merchandise. Because of the tense atmosphere in the market, and sensing that one was supposed to 'mind one's own business', I had been a bit worried about this part of the fieldwork. However, the survey turned out to be an immediate success. Although some refused to fill in the forms and many traders made jokes about the questionnaire such as 'If I fill this out—I will go to jail!' or 'Are you from Interpol?' most of them didn't mind answering the questions. In total, 137 questionnaires were answered. It should be mentioned, however, that questions about income and expenses etc. were sometimes left unanswered and sometimes obviously quite fictitious. The questionnaires provided me with interesting information about the age, gender, ethnicity, and professional background of traders, yet their main advantage was that they gave me an alibi to be in the market and just talk to people. In this way I slowly made new acquaintances and picked up a lot of stories about the market.

While conducting these interviews, I also met Irena, who agreed to let me trade with her in the market. She was trading alone, and as most traders formed partnerships of two, it seemed a good idea to join her in the market. Although she would only appear in the market three days a week, and on other days attended to her official work as the leader of a local kindergarten, this gave me an opportunity for a glimpse at the market from an insider's view.

Last but not least, I have included interviews with various traders outside the market as well as data concerning the Capitalists' Club, Russian and Polish organizations, and Women in Business. These interviews, although they were not specifically concerned with Gariūnai, do shed light on social and political processes in Lithuanian society at large, as well as more specifically on the development of the Vilnius business environment. In general, these interviews have helped me to use data from the market strategically and in this way make the conclusions transcend the market field itself.

I should mention that I have focused almost entirely on traders and not on

---

[6] I have analysed all articles about Gariūnai from the Lithuanian newspaper *Lietuvos Rytas* during the period from 1989 until the end of my fieldwork in November 1995. I have also included some articles from the yellow press paper *Respublika* as well as from a Lithuanian television programme, *Nesutinku*, about the Gariūnai market, broadcast in April 1995. The newspaper articles are listed in the Appendix.

customers. The moral stigmatization of Gariūnai seemed to be closely related to traders and not so much to customers. Thus a trader would find it embarrassing to meet acquaintances in the market (who were there as customers), but the acquaintances would not.

Apart from my first day, when my ignorance of the market must have been apparent, since my bag was slit open by pickpockets, I witnessed no criminal acts in Gariūnai. But I did hear a lot of stories and on several occasions I watched racketeers collecting money in the market. The racketeers presented a problem during my fieldwork in various ways. Many traders were afraid of talking to me, because they felt that racketeers might see this and then they would get into trouble. Interestingly, most traders would themselves begin to talk about racketeers, and although I seldom asked explicitly how much protection money they paid, the information was usually volunteered after some time.

Everybody had lots of stories about thieves. A few had actually experienced being robbed, a few had been threatened to keep silent about a robbery, and one trader I talked to had actually been beaten up by racketeers early one morning. Most of this, however, seemed to have taken place at least a year earlier, and most of my informants found that the atmosphere at the market had developed for the better and was now less 'tense' than it used to be. Still, in order to deal with the fear and influence of racketeers, I usually approached traders on the outskirts of the market. The market was hierarchically organized according to how much one was prepared to pay the racketeers. Thus the best places, near the main entrances (termed 'the centre' by traders), were usually occupied by the most successful traders. This was where racketeers earned most money, and where suspicion of outsiders was most apparent. I therefore conducted my survey in two different but rather marginal places in the market. I also managed to interview a few traders who occupied places in the centre of the market and thereby managed to get some 'success stories' as well, yet I only spent a little time in this 'centre'.

Generally, traders were reluctant to reveal too many details about trading when present in the market since the atmosphere was clearly dominated by an ethos of 'minding one's own business' (see Chapter 5). However, since knowledge of the market was closely linked to practice, for example wares, trading places, and so forth, it also proved difficult to conduct interviews outside the market context. One solution, which worked reasonably well, was to take a series of photos of various traders, trading stalls, and merchandise, and then to use these as a basis for the interviews conducted outside the market itself. In this way, traders could speak openly, yet at the same time topics could be closely related to market practices.

But the racketeers and other criminals were not only a problem for the traders. Although I knew that racketeers in Vilnius usually did not interfere with Western companies, I had no way of knowing how racketeers in the market would react to my asking questions about their activities there. The fact that one of the managers of the market had been shot a few months before I started my research made me somewhat uneasy. Consequently, I often told traders I was not interested in information about racketeers, at all events not in details or names. But as traders were often angry about the protection money that they had to pay, I was actually sometimes told more than I wanted to know. Most of my knowledge, however, amounts to what are 'public secrets' for anyone who has been in the market for some time.

The racketeers and the closed and 'tense' atmosphere in the market made research quite difficult. I wanted to present myself as a harmless but visible enquirer in the eyes of traders but preferred to remain invisible to racketeers. In retrospect, I would say that although some stories were true, much talk of racketeers can be linked to the social marginalization of the place and should not be taken at face value. The risk for me, as a Westerner, was probably small. Still, such concerns did form part of the overall atmosphere of my fieldwork and there were days when I would keep looking behind me as I left the market.

2

From 'Speculation' to Trading

The market may not only be regarded as 'a site' but can also be seen as a specifically morally invested 'practised place' as well as a specific phase in the process of change within the economic field. Although illegal trading practices have long formed an important factor within the Lithuanian economy, it was not until Gariūnai was established that such practices and the people engaged in them became publicly recognized. The establishment of the market therefore entails and indicates fundamental processes of reorganization within the economic field.

In addition, the market has changed considerably during the short period of its existence, and although the social stigmatization of it has been continuous, the basis for this as well as the market itself has changed drastically. The process of development from illegal, hidden, *ad hoc* exchange practices to more or less systematized and institutionalized trading therefore reveals more general processes of socio-economic change in the field of economics following upon the systemic changes from plan to market in post-Communist Lithuania.

A DAY IN THE LIFE OF THE GARIŪNAI MARKET

It is Tuesday at 4 o'clock in the morning in the Gariūnai market, and I am surrounded by activity and the noise of cars and voices, laughter and cursing. It is still dark, but here and there as traders get their cars and tents into position, small lights illuminate today's selection of goods, mainly clothes, but also tapes, toys, hi-fi equipment, and kitchen utensils neatly exhibited on the bonnets of cars or hung on the back doors of small vans. Within the next hour the market will fill up with cars, people, and tents, and the most successful traders may soon be getting ready to leave the market to fetch fresh supplies of merchandise.

The customers, mainly Lithuanian, Latvian, and Belorussian middle-aged women, are walking around the market with alert eyes and big carrier bags. They usually have only a few hours to find what they need and at the cheapest price before their bus leaves, and although they must be tired from travelling all night they show no sign of it. Everybody in the market is working hard. Walking along the rows of traders I hear quiet conversation and a bit of bargaining in Russian or Lithuanian. The weather is still mild now in September and traders are mostly standing together in front of their cars. When it gets colder in late autumn and winter, they will take turns in getting some warmth from sitting in the car. The market is reasonably quiet and most customers walk around undisturbed by the relatively passive traders. Only if a customer approaches a trader directly will he or she start giving prices and showing the variety of goods. Usually, however, customers can see the goods that are displayed for themselves.

Tuesday is always the busiest day of the week and the market is very crowded. Tuesday is also the day when regular customers come to the market, and greetings can be heard everywhere as they find their suppliers. These regulars are the most important customers, not only because they buy more (wholesale) but also because they may place orders for next week as well, thereby giving traders some information as to what goods they should buy in the future. Some of them, if well known and trusted by traders, may be given merchandise in commission. From a customer viewpoint it is also an advantage to achieve the status of a 'regular' who, in the event of damaged goods, will be allowed to return them to the trader (who in turn may be able to return them to a Turkish or Polish supplier).

The early morning market is also the time for selling domestic produce, and in one area there is always a group of women holding dresses, sweaters, or suits in their hands. They are standing in the market looking tired and bored, waiting for customers to come and ask a price.

The market is highly favoured by pickpockets and other thieves who steal goods and money from merchants and customers. Thieves have an easy time in the early morning darkness of Gariūnai, where they are seldom caught in the act, but afterwards people soon discover what they have lost. The darkness of the morning at Gariūnai is therefore tense as well as busy. Everybody is in a hurry and everybody is on the alert.

As the morning passes, the market becomes less crowded. The early morning trade is considered the best, because it is the time for large-scale wholesale buying. Already by 8 a.m. the rush hour will be over and many of the non-local customers will leave for Vilnius by bus or train. The market may still be busy later, but customers will now be 'locals' (from Vilnius), who seldom buy wholesale.

Every now and then one may catch sight of a couple of policemen in their characteristic blue-green uniforms. They may or may not decide to check the trading licences which all vendors must have. These can be bought for 700 litai and are valid for six months. Many traders are afraid of controls because they have failed to buy this licence. But the policemen may not check—they may just walk around. The problem is just that you never know . . .

At 8 a.m. Gariūnai Radio starts broadcasting commercials sponsored by travel agencies and local shops in Vilnius. Information is broadcast in Russian, Lithuanian, and Polish. The radio also plays loud music consisting of mainly American hip-hop or disco. People may ask the radio station to play special music, but it seems it is either the same people expressing their wishes or that there is only a limited choice, because the same songs are played over and over again. As music on the radio is always loud, and as there are additionally a number of traders spread around the market who are selling and therefore also advertising other kinds of music, the noise level in certain places can at times be quite intolerable. Some traders, for example those occupying places between a loudspeaker from the Gariūnai Radio broadcast and a 'local' trader, say in Russian disco music, consider noise to be their most serious problem in the market!

Breakfast time is between 7 and 9 a.m. All around one part of the market are small kiosks, where women sell microwave-heated, ready-made hot dishes. The kiosks are tiny (about 2 or 3 sq. m.) and two persons (usually, but not always, two women) often work together. Here, customers and vendors buy the national Lithuanian *cepelinai* or *kepsniai, karbonadai* or hot dogs with French fries and lots of gravy. This can be quite a mouthful at seven in the morning, but as most people have been awake for several hours and customers often all night there is obviously a demand for hot food and coffee by this time. Although kiosks have permission to sell food in the market, the problem of low hygiene levels is often a source of complaints from traders, who are generally unhappy about buying food from them. Most of them either bring food and coffee from home or buy from a kiosk where they know the owner. The main customers in the kiosks are therefore foreigners who have arrived with the buses. They need something solid before setting out on their journey home again.

Between 8 and 11 a.m. the market slowly develops a sleepier, quieter atmosphere. These are the worst hours for traders, who by now have little to do. Many customers have already bought whatever they needed and have either left or are having breakfast or are walking quietly around the market trying to spot new and interesting goods at cheap prices. Some of the luckier traders, who have managed to sell large quantities of merchandise, may use this quiet period to transport them, at the request of their customers, to the railway station or to their hotels. Although more local customers start arriving now, there are nowhere near as many as the early morning wholesale customers. A few women sell Lithuanian and Russian versions of the Lithuanian newspaper *Respublika*, and a few traders read quietly while customers are slowly drifting around. At 11 a.m. sales begin to escalate again. Now is the last chance to buy before the bus leaves—and it might even be possible to strike a bargain with a tired and unsuccessful trader. Although prices are generally fixed, there are many exceptions. Local customers in particular are believed to be very keen on negotiating prices, and may manage to bring down the price 50 cents or even a whole dollar. For this reason they are generally termed *kieks* (literally 'how muches'), and traders often prefer foreign customers to locals. By noon parts of the market will already be looking empty, although in the section called the New Market trading will continue for another two or three hours.

The above description may convey the idea that there is only one market, but when I returned to Gariūnai in 1995, the whole area had been divided into various sections. Although generally known as 'the Gariūnai Market', it was by then separated into three independently owned markets surrounded by four private parking lots and a filling station. In addition, the Gariūnai complex included several currency exchange offices, a visa administration office, and a local broadcasting station.

CARS AND YOUNG MEN

The car market had grown to be a huge and independent market of its own. Although no official figures were available I estimated that more than five thousand cars were on sale every weekend. Most cars had been 'imported' from Germany, Holland, or from elsewhere in Western Europe.[1] But not only Western cars were sold. Ladas seemed to be very popular among Russian customers, who came to Gariūnai from Russia to buy cars, because they were cheaper to import into Russia than Western cars. The car market was almost entirely run by young men.[2] They would go to Germany by bus, each would buy a car, and drive it back to Lithuania through Poland and sell it at the car market the following weekend. I was told that although the car market at Gariūnai was only held at weekends, the cars circulated all through Lithuania where one-day car markets were arranged in various towns during the week. If not sold, the same cars would turn up at Gariūnai the following weekend.

As I know nothing about cars (I was the laughing-stock of my neighbours with my 10-year-old rented Volkswagen) and the car market was only open during weekends, I decided to concentrate on the two other markets. However, I shall later return to the spatial separation of cars and clothes, because it reveals some important aspects of gendering in the market. The same applies to the private parking lots, which were rumoured to be operated by ex-criminals who had attempted to legalize their business activities in this way. Although I frequently used these private parking lots I made no attempt to get any interviews. Their number, however, illustrates the size of the market, for thousands of customers struggled to find a safe place to park their cars every day. The need for private car parks moreover emphasized the constant risk of theft and thus underlined the criminal aspects of the market.

I spent my time in what was also generally considered to be 'the Gariūnai market', where traders were mainly engaged in trading with Asian clothes and other cheap consumer goods. Yet even this market could be separated into subsections.

'THE OLD' AND 'THE NEW'

The market that was called *Senieji Gariūnai* or 'the Old Market' was (not surprisingly) the oldest part of the market, although it had changed and grown since it began in 1990. The Old Market was again divided into two sections: one where people sold their goods from tables, called *pastogė* (Lithuanian for 'under the

---

[1] I put 'imported' in quotes, because in reality many car owners have paid no import duty. The cars (like other products sold in the market) were therefore smuggled rather than imported into the country.

[2] I was told several times that the organizers of the car market were actually former racketeers who had 'gone straight' but I have not been able to verify this information.

roofs'), and another where traders would bring their cars, minibuses, or vans into the market, and sell goods directly from the back. This section had started as a wholesale market and at the time of my investigation in 1995 the most successful traders still mainly sold goods in large quantities. The *pastogė* area on the other hand was associated with retail sales and prices were somewhat higher. In general, however, there was no difference between the range of merchandise in the two markets. An estimate of the number of traders in the Old Market, based on an interview with the manager as well as on my own observations, suggests the presence of around 500–1,000 cars a day, thus (as there were generally two traders in each car) around 1,000–2,000 people were trading every day, depending on the weekday. In addition, an estimated 1,000 traders had tables in the *pastogė* area.

At the beginning of 1995 a market called *Naujieji Gariūnai* or 'the New Market' was started right next to the old one. This competitor, owned by a company named Jurgena, very quickly took the lead and by the autumn of 1995 many traders had moved from the Old Market into the new one. Those who had not done so were wondering if they should. The main reason for the success of the new market was that the bus-stop, which had previously been on the main road close to the Old Market, was removed and replaced right next to the entrance to the new one. Although the two markets were situated close together, customers generally had to carry heavy loads of goods, and the fact that buses could park nearby made the New Market an immediate success. Most traders (from both markets), as well as a few journalists on national newspapers, suspected that the New Market was run by a former high-ranking official of the Vilnius Police, in other words suggesting that the development of the New Market, especially the changing of the bus-stop and parking facilities, was not entirely a result of fair competition. In general, however, the New Market looked pretty much like the car section in the old one, except that it was larger, busier, and appeared somehow more 'orderly'. In the New Market, as in the old, people mainly traded from their cars, but had also erected tents in front of their cars to protect the goods and themselves in bad weather.

The New Market consisted of seventeen rows of traders—all trading from tents—but in addition had a small row of traders on the outskirts selling goods placed directly on the ground or laid out on small tables. This section of the market was referred to as 'the Belorussian market'. Most of the traders here were believed to be Belorussians who had come by train (usually) to sell various items that they had brought with them from Belarus, where prices were low in comparison with Lithuania. In the New Market, the daily number of people trading is estimated to be about 4,500.[3] Markets are open at weekends and all weekdays except Monday.

In order to understand the background for this development as well as general attitudes and the conduct of traders in the market, we must take a closer look at the Soviet-style economy, especially its 'dualist' nature of 'public plan' and 'private (underground) market'.

---

[3] This estimation is based on my own observations and counting of traders in the market.

THE SECOND ECONOMY IN SOVIET SOCIETY

Gariūnai came into being as a result of the political and economic changes in Eastern Europe and the Soviet Union during the latter half of the 1980s.

Underground economic practices, the so-called 'second economy', were widespread in all socialist systems in Eastern Europe and the Soviet Union, especially during the 1970s and 1980s. The most prevalent forms were: produce from farmers' private plots, a shadow economy within socialist enterprises, underground factories (especially in Soviet Georgia), and private and illegal trading and service networks in general (Sampson 1987: 120 ff.).

The general shortage of goods in the formal economy of course became even more severe as an increasing number were diverted towards the black market. This diversion took place at all levels: production, transportation, distribution to shops, and selling from the shops. Verdery calls this diversion and the resulting (private) redistributive potential of producers and managers the key feature of socialist society: 'Capitalist firms compete with each other for markets in which they will make a profit; socialist firms competed to maximize their bargaining power with suppliers higher up' (Verdery 1996: 22). Verdery suggests therefore that the crucial point in socialist economies was not demand but supply: 'Thus in socialism it was not the clerk—the provider or "seller"—who was friendly (they were usually grouchy) but the procurers, the customers, who sought to ingratiate themselves with smiles, bribes, or favours' (ibid.). In order to get supplies one needed to establish a personal connection with the supplier, either by bribery, mutual friendship, or through belonging to large networks based on kinship or friendship. This form of barter created social relationships based on the enduring obligation to repay a favour (Kenedi, in Sampson 1987).

There are several important points to make in connection with socialism's underground economy. First, it cannot be regarded as a suppressed capitalist market economy, mainly because it was parasitic to, and thus dependent on, the official economy, as supplier of goods to private networks. People involved in black economic activities were not interested in giving up their State job, and when private business became partially legal in 1986–8 only a small proportion of the people involved in these activities were actually registered (Verdery 1996, Shelley 1990). Second, the underground economy has had a political function as social mollifier (Cassel and Cichy, in Sampson 1987). Instead of political protest, people found individual solutions and in this way political criticism was transformed into black economic activities. Third, black economic activity, especially the cultivation of networks, could be characterized as obligatory and exclusive. The Lithuanian–German sociologist Bartusevičius emphasizes the coerciveness of the network system, in which it becomes necessary to cultivate certain relationships, where even unwanted gifts have to be repaid, and where the network undercuts any solidarity other than the one among 'us' as opposed to that of the 'others' (Bartusevičius 1993). As Sampson expresses it: 'Due to political, economic, and moral effects of the second economy, society degenerated into competing bands' (Sampson 1987: 135).

In Soviet Lithuania, most of these black economic activities—except perhaps underground factories—were widespread. However, such activities remained relatively hidden compared with Poland, Hungary, or Soviet Georgia. As a local (Russian) businessman in Vilnius explained:

> Black business was widespread in Vilnius during the Soviet period. For example in Vilnius there was this strong black company dealing in buttons and plastic jewellery. The 'godfather' of D. (known as the head of the local Mafia group, the Vilniaus Brigada) was in this business. It was not an unofficial production unit in the official company, but raw materials came from the official company. The most difficult thing was to get money from the official channels, because everything was still sold through these channels. The trick was therefore to have 'ghost workers' employed at the official factory and then their salary was taken. The black economy included everything sold in shops, such as clothes, sweaters, food (consumer goods). Sometimes it was possible to get the products straight from the shops, but then you had to have private contacts with the director of the shop . . . But black business was more hidden here than in, for example, Georgia. (local businessman, Vilnius 1994)

Yet for many of the recent entrepreneurs, participation in the former underground economy has provided a basis for their abilities to engage in private business after Lithuanian independence: 'Businessmen who operated in black economy (before) have an easier time now, of course, because they have initial capital' (local businessman, Vilnius).

Some activities were more acceptable than others. As Fisher-Ruge states in her book, *Survival in Russia: Chaos and Hope in Everyday Life* (1993), black marketeers in particular seem to have been socially and morally stigmatized. In Lithuania, the word *talkučkė* was often used to denote such 'black markets'. Furthermore, there seems to be a close connection between *talkučkė* and Gariūnai.

UNDERGROUND ECONOMY AND ILLEGAL TRADE—*TALKUČKĖ*

Although Gariūnai itself has always been an official and legal trading place, the connection between former illegal trading and Gariūnai was often expressed by traders:

> Gariūnai started very long ago, but then it had a form of *talkučkė*, a small place where 'speculation' takes place. It existed in Soviet society, because there was a shortage of goods. For example, if somebody was getting something from relatives in America, then they would trade in it. This trade was of course illegal. The term *talkučkė* then was used to cover (*ad hoc*) illegal market places forbidden in Soviet times. (Skirmantas 1.2)

By establishing the Gariūnai market, the 'floating' forms of *talkučkė* were localized and institutionalized within the boundaries of the market place, but those who traded there continued to be associated with black-market activities.

Black trade, or 'speculation' as it was called in Soviet times, became widespread during the latter half of the 1980s, when various forms of underground economic activities exploded all over the Soviet Union (cf. Shelley 1990). Lithuanian newspapers from 1989 and 1990 show pictures of empty shelves in the shops and carry stories of goods being sold by 'speculators' (black traders) outside the very same shops (*Komjaunimo Tiesa* (Komsomol Truth), 1989 and *Respublika*, 1990).[4] Although almost everybody had been taking part in what has been called the 'privatization of socialism' (Verdery 1991), a clear distinction was drawn between private supply and distribution networks and selling wares in the streets to strangers. As one informant explained:

I am not sure what to call it. But it would be like this. Supposing my mother would like to buy chocolate to bake a cake. She would call my aunt and ask where she could buy it and my aunt would say: 'I have my friend who works in a factory. She can get hold of some and sell it to you.' That's *not* 'speculation', which means people carrying bags of wares and offering to sell them to you. (Vytalij, market trader 14.1)

It seems that the early 'speculators' in Lithuania mainly got their wares in three different ways: underground production, pilfering from their workplace, and trading with Poland. Many traders who later started in the Gariūnai market had thus already some experience of the private economy during socialism. It is interesting to note some regional differences here. Underground production, mainly in the form of sewing and knitting (with many women producers), seems to have been very popular in the provinces, but not particularly widespread among the population of Vilnius itself. The town of Šiauliai is often mentioned in connection with the selling of home-made clothes. Several of the traders (present as well as former) that I met in Gariūnai came from Šiauliai.

On the other hand Vilnius seems to have managed to take advantage of its population of local Poles and its historically close links with Poland. Throughout the 1980s, local Poles as well as others with good connections would smuggle various cheap Lithuanian products into Poland and mainly bring back Western (or Asian) imported clothes or hi-fi equipment to Lithuania. After 1989, when Poland opened its borders to Germany, these trading relations were intensified. It also seems that the establishment of the Gariūnai market was highly influenced by Poles, who could quite easily enter Lithuania and thus obtain access to the entire Soviet market. It is important to note that at the time there was no restriction of movement between the Soviet Republics, and early trade at the Gariūnai market was based on 'recruitment' of customers from all over the Union. But the Polish influence on the market does not solely originate from the participation of Poles in the market, but perhaps even more from the fact that the Poles were 'faster'. Underground trade as well as a large amount of private legal business in Poland— closely connected with the period of political struggle during the late 1970s and 1980s—brought the Poles to the forefront of trading developments, especially in

[4] See Appendix (nos. 1, 30, and 31).

finding sources of supply. Many traders suggested to me that Poles started the trade with Turkey, China, and the United Arab Emirates, and that Lithuanian traders merely copied them (see also Hann 1992). Furthermore, it is the general opinion that the Poles have progressed into 'more civilized' forms of trade such as ordering goods by fax, selling from shops, or getting better-quality goods. But although Polish influence was becoming less apparent, many traders termed shuttle trading 'Polish-style trading'.

The market was established in late 1989, that is to say while Lithuania was still a Soviet republic. With the increase of underground production and 'privatization' of State goods in Lithuania in the late 1980s, the authorities were faced with a dilemma that is reflected in the way that they have attempted to deal with the phenomenon of *talkučkė*. In December 1989, according to the newspaper *Komjaunimo Tiesa* (later *Lietuvos Rytas*[5]), the chairman of the executive committee of Vilnius decided to move non-food traders (at that time they were called 'speculators') from the food market (Kalvarijos) to a place outside the town near the airport called Eišiškės. Yet in spring 1990 one could read in another newspaper, *Respublika*,[6] that the Supreme Council of the Soviet Socialist Republic of Lithuania had issued a decree to increase fines for 'speculation'. Thus, although both *talkučkė* and 'speculation' seem to have been officially recognized at the time, there was no agreement within the various sectors of the authorities about how to deal with it. Already in September 1990 the 'hard' party line was apparently defeated and the Gariūnai market was opened. The market was (and a part of it still is) jointly owned by a private company and the *seniūnija* (a local authority lower than the municipal authorities). The conflict within the various administrative sectors therefore seems partly to have been influenced by economic interests:

I know more or less how it started. The authorities and Posūkis got together and bought this place. The Kalvarijos market was too small. The *seniūnija* owned 31% of the market. It still does. (Kestas, former manager of the old Gariūnai market)

THE HISTORY OF THE MARKET

The Gariūnai market can be seen as the visible manifestation of the changes from command economy to market economy in the sense that all private non-food trading was forbidden in the Soviet Union. Under socialism, only markets for the private selling of food existed legally.[7] In Vilnius there were two of these, Kalvarijos and Halė, as well as several smaller regional ones on the outskirts. In these markets people would sell food products from private plots of land. The establishment of Gariūnai as the first 'trans-republic' non-food market therefore points to, if not an ideological shift on the part of the Soviet authorities, then at

---

[5] See Appendix (no. 1).   [6] See Appendix (no. 32).

[7] In 1986/87 private business activities, called co-operatives, were legalized within some areas (Humphrey 1995b).

least a pragmatic acceptance of the widespread practice of 'speculation'. In September 1990, the Gariūnai market opened at its present location. During the short period of its existence the market had been highly debated within Lithuanian society. Although the market itself was legal, this had not altered the conceptualization of it as uncivilized and morally problematic. Furthermore, although the market has only existed for a short time, it has changed considerably in terms of traders, customers, wares, trading practices, and sheer size.

The history of the market can be separated into four main epochs: illegal market practices or *talkučkė* (?–1989), the early market (1989–90), the 'golden years' (1991–3), and stagnation (1995–?).

The early market (1989–1990)

A few traders had been involved in the market in 1989. They all found that the early market differed from the way it looked at the end of 1995: 'Five years ago, the cars and clothes market, spare parts and food and vegetables were all sold in the same market. There was only one market and that was Kalvarijos' (Jonas 2.1). There seems to have been little difference in the products sold or in the number of traders involved when the market was in Kalvarijos and Eišiškės and during the first year in Gariūnai. During the early phase the market was small and traders were mainly selling their goods from the ground, or a few from their cars:

When I started, Gariūnai was a small place, because there was only one of these square places and there were only 50 cars where people were selling from and nothing else. The place which is now a car market used to be a parking lot and when the trade with cars escalated it was turned into a separate market place. (Jonas 2.1)

In 1990 it was still difficult for Lithuanians to travel abroad, and the goods offered in the market were therefore either brought by Poles or illegally produced in Lithuania. Furthermore, there was no separation of food products and non-food products in the early market, and the variety of products suggests that the early market offered mainly 'luxury' goods, difficult to get in the shops. According to the Soviet newspaper *Komjaunimo Tiesa* (Komsomol Truth, December 1989) and *Respublika* (March 1990),[8] the following products were on sale in the market: alcoholic beverages, caviar, smoked salami, velvet trousers (modern style), shoes, brassières, skirts, fur coats, and tape-recorders. Furthermore, it appears from interviews with the traders as well as from the newspaper article that several of the traders were from Poland:

Basically, Polish people were trading, people from Poland that is, and only a few local people were buying from Poles and reselling here. Gold was brought from Russia, from Siberia. It was in the form of jewellery. And Poles were buying this gold and bringing it to Poland. (Skirmantas 1.2)

[8] See Appendix (nos. 1, 30).

The Poles were selling jeans or other Western products in the market and they would buy gold in return. In fact several traders mentioned that gold was used as currency because of the lack of dollars. This trade in gold from Siberia to Lithuania and then to Poland seems to have been a popular way of earning money, although some traders apparently refused to participate in it on account of its semi-criminal aspects. People who got involved in the gold trade would often also be forced into more criminal activities because criminal groups were already controlling the business.

But apart from the Polish trade, Lithuanian underground production also played an important role when the Gariūnai market first started. Jonas, who did not start trading until the market was already established in Gariūnai, is an example:

The majority of goods were spare parts for cars, hi-fi equipment, and underground production from 'speculators' from Kaunas and Šiauliai. That was the biggest sector of the market then, but now this business has decreased. My own first business was . . . you know Šiauliai? It is the city of hand-knitting and sewing. Underground factories from Šiauliai were selling their production in the Gariūnai market for the Russian market. And we were bringing these goods from Šiauliai and selling them in Gariūnai. (Jonas 2.1)

During this first phase of establishing the market, most traders would not go there every day, for many of them would have a job outside the market as well. In addition, although some foreign goods were entering Lithuania via Poland, much of the early trade seems to have been based on goods taken from factories, presents from friends abroad, or Polish goods, either from Poland or imported from Turkey. During this first phase, trading was rather *ad hoc* and not in any way as systematic as later on. It flourished mainly because of the lack of goods in the shops and expanded as a result of the slow opening of borders via Poland. Although profits were high, the practical difficulties and relatively small volume of goods sold at a time limited the profits (at least for Lithuanians), although some traders mentioned that they had earned their initial capital from this early period. Finally, the Gariūnai market at the time was not yet a 'centre' for this kind of trading. Many traders would trade outside the market by buying cheap goods in Russia and then going to Yugoslavia or Hungary to sell, or take Lithuanian food products, cigarettes, and alcohol with them to sell at the market in Warsaw.

During this initial period of the market, between 1989 and 1990, reactions seem to have been dominated more by curiosity than by condemnation:

At the beginning it was interesting to try this kind of trading and people were happy, because there were a lot of new goods . . . There were no specific reactions in the beginning when I talked about Gariūnai . . . I think that people who are now angry about Gariūnai are simply jealous. . . . they also think that only criminals trade there . . . (Skirmantas 1.2)

'The Golden Years' (1990–1994)

Between 1991 and 1993, trading at Gariūnai market exploded. Traders often regard this 'golden' period with nostalgia. Customers would come from as far away as Kaukasus and Siberia, and local Lithuanian traders were making substantial profits. Gariūnai grew from a few rows of traders into a 20-acre, tremendously busy wholesale market and centre for private wholesale trade within the former Soviet Union. People would travel to Turkey, China, and Thailand and later also to the United Arab Emirates, Korea, and Syria to buy merchandise. But the risk was high and conditions were tough. As Algis E. so vividly describes it:

In the beginning our trips to China were horrible—Americans would be able to make a horror movie out of it. Nowadays it's easy by comparison. Today you can eat in restaurants, see the sights, etc. In the beginning it took twenty days . . . We would fly to Almata (Kazakhstan) for example and take the train from there to Urunzia (China). The hotels were terrible . . . we couldn't sleep, we were two in each room and the toilet never worked. We would buy during the day and then pack everything at night. In the beginning the Chinese provided no facilities and probably nobody would have wanted to pay for the packing of the goods anyway. It was disgusting in many ways. We had to bring food for a week. From the hotel we had to carry our bags back to the train and it was a long way and we walked along the rails. If a train came we had to get out of the way. My friend told me about a guy whose leg was cut off by the train. We had to go and look for the train, and wait for it and sometimes we were in the wrong place, or the train went somewhere else and we had to pick up all our goods and go and find the right train. Also there was always a fight for the compartments in the train. The journey lasted at least two weeks and you just managed to go home and take a bath and then you had to go to Gariūnai to sell your wares. And Gariūnai then was not like it is now. You had to go there in the evening, stay all night and guard the goods with a gun! If you were lucky you might sell everything within a week and then off to China again. Maybe fly to Vladivostok and then by train to the border and then pass the border and then another train . . . People's health suffered. Sometimes wives would help, but women could only be at the Gariūnai market together with their husbands. You can't imagine how hard this early trading phase was. I talked to doctors who said a new wave of patients had been generated by the market. They were in a constant state of stress because of the changes in sleeping times, the booze, jet lag, etc. The planes were terrible too. One exploded and burst into flames—my friend just managed to get out in time. Once the wheel exploded and another time the plane crashed. It was too heavy and couldn't take off properly and just crashed. I myself was on the one whose wheel exploded. A colleague saw the plane that crashed. We didn't tell our wives about these things until much later . . . (Algis E.)

Still, despite the difficulties involved in these early years of trading, many now well-established businessmen in Vilnius built up their initial capital during this early period.

Several changes which took place simultaneously caused trading to accelerate. After the collapse of the Soviet Union and Lithuanian independence in August 1991, borders were opened and access provided to countries like Turkey, China, and Thailand where supplies could be obtained cheaply. In addition, although officially an independent country, it has taken a while to make the Lithuanian border control work, and during these early years there was in reality no control of imports of goods into Lithuania. 'There were no Lithuanian borders, no import rules nor any control. Some people made a lot of money, because nothing was illegal at that time' (Vytalij 14.1).

This resulted in an outburst of black trading as nobody paid any import duties at all.[9] The demand for cheap goods was high especially at this time, when State-run shops provided nothing and new shops had either not yet been established or were so expensive that only very few people could afford to buy anything in them. Customers in the Gariūnai market were referred to as *čiukčia* (used in a sense of 'stupid people'), simply because they would buy everything available without trying to bargain or examine the goods more closely.[10] The result of the opening of borders with Asia, combined with the experience of shortage felt by large parts of the populations of the former Soviet Union at the time, resulted in a situation where almost anything could be sold and most commodities were in high demand.

Gradually, the increased number of traders going abroad resulted in a higher demand for travel services, and in the process this tended to institutionalize market trading even further. New travel agencies arose to arrange business trips to an even wider range of foreign countries so as to keep pace with the need to continuously explore new products and trading routes. As Skirmantas, a local market trader, explained:

More Lithuanians were going to Poland and then to Turkey and China. Some companies started to organize trips to these countries and the planes were refurbished for traders. The front and the back were empty—without chairs—so as to provide room for merchandise. But it was dangerous and scary to fly because the planes were always too heavy, for example flying from Minsk to Vladivostok was a long trip and with only two stops. (Skirmantas 1.2)

A last factor seems to have influenced the explosive growth of Gariūnai. Although Lithuanians could go abroad as from 1991, it took a while for many of the CIS countries to open their borders with Asia. In addition I was told that it was much more difficult to fly to Asia, at least from the CIS countries—even from the Asian ones—because of the lack of competition in the travel business. The result was that Russians, Ukrainians, and 'Caucasians' would travel to Lithuania, and specifically to Gariūnai, in order to buy Asian goods. During this short period Lithuania became 'the gate' of the former Soviet Union.

After this stupid perestroika, prices increased here and in Russia. That's why we became a kind of transit country for goods from Poland. The border between Lithuania and Poland was open, but for them (Russians) it was closed. We exploited this situation. We would bring stuff from Poland and they would come and buy it here. That's why two or three years ago this market was perfect because it was international. (Teresa and Jurij 16.1)

---

[9] Another result of this seem to have been the flourishing importation of drugs and weapons mentioned by Vytalij 14.1 and Vytenis 3.2.

[10] The word *čiukčia* literally means Asian or slant-eyed people, but although many customers were from Asian republics, the term was basically used metaphorically.

Stagnation (1995–?)

> Of course now the situation is different from what it was a few years ago. Then
> people would starve to be able to buy clothes, and you could sell anything—
> now they want guarantees and won't accept damaged goods. At present,
> people don't have any money. (Algis E. 11.1)

Between spring 1994 and autumn 1995, the market had changed in several ways.
First, visa restrictions between Lithuania and the CIS countries were introduced.
This seriously limited the number of customers from Russia and the Ukraine, who
'traditionally' had been the best and richest. Within a few months, profits started
to decrease and many traders tried to find new ways of making money. The growth
of the car market can be related to this development and the import of cars became
an important part of activities at Gariūnai—apparently profits are higher and the
workload is less compared with trading in clothes. But trading stagnation is manifested not only by the decreasing number of customers, but by different types of
customers. Back in 'the golden period', Russian customers, intent on buying
wholesale only, would come by train or in a lorry which they could then fill up with
goods. Nowadays customers, mainly Latvian and Lithuanian, arrive in buses with
a limited amount of space—and the capital they have at their disposal is also
limited. Whereas international wholesale trading dominated a few years ago, the
market is slowly turning into a regional market for cheap consumer products. This
development is most visible at weekends, when a growing number of locals (from
Vilnius) come to the market looking for cheap clothes or household products.
These customers visit the market, not because it offers special goods, but because
the goods offered are cheaper than the same products available in Vilnius. But it is
not only the market's customers that have changed. New types of traders have also
started operating.

   In the early period, traders were typically young men, although, as I shall return
to later, there have always been women traders as well. Furthermore, many of these
traders not only worked in the market, but also had another, State-sector occupation somewhere else. Many of the early traders were 'Polish Poles' or 'local Poles',
who could use their connections, for in Soviet times one needed relatives in order
to be able to travel to Poland. In recent years new social and ethnic groups have
entered the market, many of them forced by unemployment. Although the official
unemployment figures in Lithuania are very low, many people are on unpaid vacation[11] (see for example the *Baltic Observer* 1995: 14). Thus, at a time when the
fundamental conditions of the market are deteriorating, the numbers of customers
decreasing and travel expenses increasing, the market is attracting new groups of
traders. Many of these are intellectuals who were unable to survive on a State

---

[11] Unpaid vacation has been widely used in Lithuania, instead of dismissing people from their
former work, because, according to the law, the employer has to pay up to 6 months' extra wages in the
case of dismissal.

salary and many are women. Furthermore, it seems that an increasing number of 'ethnic Lithuanians' are among the most recent waves of traders. Although there are still some traders who are making a lot of money in the market, they are becoming fewer—and Gariūnai is no longer regarded as a place to build up initial capital.

Parallel to this development, the origins of goods have changed as well. In the beginning, almost all goods would be imported from either Turkey or from Asia. Nowadays Poland has re-emerged as a supply country as many traders cannot afford expensive trips to China or India any more. Moreover, a new category of traders emerged. They only import goods. Although they still travel themselves to Asia to find them, they employ people to sell for them in the market. This necessitates larger capital investments in order to yield good results. In this way an élite has been created in the market and a growing division is becoming apparent between those who import goods themselves, and those who only sell.

Another interesting development has been the renaissance of the Lithuanian home production of sewing and knitting—a kind of renewed underground production. Lithuanian-produced wares are contributing increasingly to the overall turnover in the market. Not only are single women standing in the market and selling their home-made dresses, but a growing number of smart businessmen now employ one group of women to sew and another to sell in the market.

Although profits have decreased and both traders and buyers have become poorer, it seems that Gariūnai today is by no means a negligible factor in the sale of consumer goods in Lithuania.

FROM 'SPECULATION' TO TRADING—THE EMERGENCE OF A NEW ECONOMIC FIELD

Changes have taken place at various levels during the phase of establishing the market as a legal trading-place, for example from the selling, during the early phase of the market, of luxury products that had somehow been diverted from their official distribution channels, to large-scale import of cheap consumer products from Asia. This has been accompanied by a process of institutionalization of trading activities evident in the emergence of travel agencies, fast-food sellers, and the establishment of semi-formal channels of information and advertising (for example the local market radio). In addition, the State has shown increasing interest in controlling and regulating the large market and the economic activities connected with it. So far, however, this has not been very successful. But the process of developing a market place, of legalizing and 'localizing' former *talkučkė*, and thus establishing a new framework of exchange, has also involved new forms of acting, thinking, and conceptualizing money, goods, and exchange as well. This signifies the development of a new economic field.

In an article in the *Lietuvos Rytas* in 1992, a journalist notes that the term 'speculation' was no longer used:

The word 'speculator' has slowly and unnoticeably disappeared from our vocabulary. But it doesn't matter what we call it, for most of us will never be attracted by this activity. Anyway, such is our life now. (*Lietuvos Rytas*, August 1992)[12]

Although many traders emphasized the close conceptual connection between 'speculation' and 'trade', and between *talkučkė* and 'market', traders no longer used the 'old' concepts. Outsiders, however, might do so, as a university lecturer reminded me, when she bluntly stated that they (traders at Gariūnai) were 'speculators' and that she would never dream of going to the market. Although there had definitely been a shift in vocabulary, the change was not unambiguous. Moreover, although the words had generally changed, their connotations had not, and terms like 'trade', 'trader', and 'market place' were still clearly linked to the socialistic conceptualization of private trading as illegal, illegitimate, and immoral:

The attitudes towards Gariūnai traders are the same as towards black-market traders before, during the Soviet period, that we are 'speculators'. I call it the Soviet virus—it is fixed in people's minds. In the USSR, everything private was illegal. Most trading too. Maybe it was OK for old women to do so, but when other people started trading they were called 'speculators'. I remember when I was small and women from the country used to come to Kaunas to sell socks and things illegally, they would knock on the doors of houses. People would then say 'Here come the "speculators" ', but without hostility because they were just happy that somebody had brought something. (Vytenis 3.1)

However, the change in terminology indicates a conceptual 'break' within the symbolic 'order'. Bourdieu, when discussing the development of 'the field of art' in Western Europe, has pointed out that an indicator was the linguistic shift from 'craftsman' to 'artist' (Bourdieu and Wacquant 1992: 107). Thus we may consider the change in terminology from 'speculator' to 'trader' and from *talkučkė* to 'market' as implying a radical change within the economic field, including new forms of capital, new economic practices, etc.

This does not mean, however, that connotations connected with the 'old' terminology have radically changed. What has happened is more a case of intensification of economic, social, and symbolic struggles in connection with the establishment of new cultural forms and social hierarchies. New forms of symbolic capital are becoming crucial as individual traders have attempted to build on their past economic and social experiences and extend their competencies in order to deal with the new possibilities. The individual development from 'speculator' to 'trader' has often been based on trial and error. As a whole, therefore, this development appears as much an unintended result of such practice as a planned development. This aspect is important as it emphasizes the fact that the road to the market economy is not so much an automatic and mechanical product of market forces as the sum of highly diverse and unregulated individual projects.

---

[12] See Appendix (no. 12).

3

Learning to Trade

In this chapter the emphasis will be on individual trading stories. Individual accounts of trial and error show which competencies were and are necessary to become a successful trader in post-Communist Lithuania as well as the changing conditions of trading. Many of the traders I met in the market had experience from illegal markets in Soviet society, and this has influenced early trading practices in Gariūnai.

Stories about early experiences of success or failure, of goods getting stolen, or damaged goods, not only reveal how people have attempted to deal with the activity of trading, but also how and what they learned from their mistakes. Their stories therefore demonstrate the slow process of routinization and institutionalization of certain practices.

The following four career stories are chosen first because they each contain an interesting and detailed personal history of 'how one becomes a trader', and secondly because, although some experiences are shared, the four trading histories are rather different and therefore shed light on different levels and aspects of the practices involved in market trading.

THE INVOLUNTARY TRADER

The career story of Stasė, a female trader, who I met in the market while doing survey interviews, would have been rather sad, had it not been for her sense of irony and humour when describing the absurdities of her career as a trader. She used to work in a theatre in Vilnius, but when I met her in the autumn of 1995 she was unemployed (maybe on unpaid vacation). She lived with her husband, their two children, and her parents-in-law in a two-room flat belonging to her parents-in-law. Stasė and her husband were unlucky because they had not managed to secure a flat before the Soviet system of housing allocation collapsed, and as real estate prices had exploded since then the family could not afford a flat of their own.[1] The main reason why Stasė was in the market was because she needed money to improve her family's housing situation. Stasė was not a rich trader. She sold goods on commission with a profit of one or two dollars per item. On a good day she might earn $60, but there were days when she would earn next to nothing.

[1] At the time, a one-room flat in Vilnius cost around $10,000–15,000.

Her story is in many ways an example of the growing group of 'involuntary' traders in Gariūnai that comprised intellectuals or former State-sector employees who could not live on their salaries, or were unemployed. (The interview with Stasė took place at her home, and was recorded.)

Stasė's story

Around 1989/1990 I had left my job at the theatre and I was just sewing at home because there were no other jobs to be had. Then my friend suggested that we should go to Poland to trade.

First, we tried to find out what to take to Poland and a friend of mine told us that tools, for example axes and hammers, were much in demand. We tried filling bags with tools of this kind but decided against taking them because they got too heavy. Fortunately my cousin works in Utenos Trikotažas (a clothing factory) and we bought some things from there and we also took some things from Gariūnai. Finally we set off without budgeting either what profits we might make or our expenses—we just packed our bags and got on the train without knowing where to go. All we knew was that there was a train from Vilnius to Šeštoke and then a connection to Suwałki.

We reached Suwałki at 10 o'clock in the evening. An hour later we were still standing at the railway station studying the map and trying to figure out where to go from there. And then a woman from Vilnius (a local Russian) came to our rescue and suggested that we go with her to Gdansk. There was a train at half-past eleven and we arrived in Gdansk early the next morning. She told us we could trade all day in Gdansk and take the train back in the evening. We followed her like chickens . . . It was wintertime and this woman was experienced. She was taking knitted berets . . . and by 8 or 9 o'clock she had sold everything she had. We just stood there for a long time, selling very little and we had to borrow money from her to go back. So we came back to Vilnius with all the goods we hadn't been able to sell, convinced that we should buy berets and then go back to Gdansk again. The whole week we went to Gariūnai at 4 o'clock in the morning to buy up a consignment of these berets. Finally we found some, one morning when it was still dark. We didn't notice that we had bought damaged goods! We used borrowed money the whole time, because we planned to make a 100 per cent profit. In the end we paid double the normal price for the tickets to Suwałki, because there was a shortage. Off we went to Gdansk again, and we came back again to Vilnius with all the berets . . .

Nobody had bought from us—there were too many in the market already—we were late. Later, every time I went to Poland, I would be bringing these berets with me—even in the summer time.

We kept going to Poland after that, but not to Gdansk, because it is too far to go and too expensive just for one day's trading. Then another friend told me about a firm that she was going with to Mwlava and Ilava in Poland.

She told me that in those markets people bought a lot, and she also told me that Hoovers were selling very well. So I went with the same firm and with Hoovers. I got them cheap, but they were heavy and it was terrible carrying them. I remember that I sold the last one for less than I had paid for it, because I just couldn't face having to take it back. I continued to go with the same firm for one year. We would stay in Poland for three days, two days in one town and one day in another.

Some smarter people would also take goods from here to Poland, sell them and bring back not dollars like we did but other goods to sell here such as jeans, shoes, and silk, mainly silk blouses. The trips were organized so that people could go through the Polish markets and buy something to take back to Lithuania. But at that time I was not trading in Gariūnai.

Each time I returned from Poland I would spend two days in bed because I was so tired. I started going to Poland that winter (1989/90), and after about a year I stopped, because business got slack. In the beginning I would come back with a profit of $20 or $30, which may not sound much, but at the time you could live on $30 for a whole month. But later it got worse and worse and in the end the $30 would last you only a couple of days. In Poland, the demand decreased and the supply increased and nobody wanted to buy anything. And then my husband got another job and was earning enough to keep our family. After that I started sewing again at home. Around autumn last year [1993] we needed money again, and so I started at Gariūnai . . .

To start trading at Gariūnai was a tragedy for me. I used to work in the theatre—I would never go and buy anything in Gariūnai. People in artistic circles still consider that Gariūnai represents something . . . I don't know, it immediately marks a person—only people of a certain kind would trade there. But my friend, who used to work in the theatre with me, was bolder. She started first. She was on maternity leave, and afterwards she didn't come back to the theatre, but went on selling things at Gariūnai. She suggested that I join her. The first day I had five sweaters in a bag and I kept one of them in my hand while walking around in Gariūnai. I kept looking around anxiously, afraid of bumping into someone I knew.

I sold three sweaters and I made a profit of $6. I was happy with that, and next time I went with ten sweaters . . .

In the beginning, my husband's friend supplied me with the sweaters. He wasn't trading himself, only buying goods wholesale, and he had a lot of money. He brought large amounts of sweaters, maybe two tons at a time, from China—and we were selling a lot, maybe 200 per day. In the beginning there was a huge demand. And the pattern in Gariūnai is that if goods sell well, then in a short time the market will be filled with the same article.

The friends I buy my goods from now, also go to China, so I still have Chinese articles. But they sometimes change country. At the moment I am trading with shoes that are brought from the Emirates, and I have sweaters from Turkey and also caps or hats from China—it is all from the same woman. She only imports, she doesn't sell in the market herself.

My husband's friend (the one that imported sweaters from China) is now trying to produce sportswear here in Lithuania, just like the ones that we now buy in Poland. It will be cheaper than the Polish sportswear and then there will be a demand for it. Then we won't need to go to look somewhere else for goods. He will be a producer and we will sell his products.

There are several interesting points in Stasė's story. First, when Stasė tells about her first trading experience in Poland, she enumerates (and is now laughing at) all the mistakes she and her friend made. They didn't try to estimate their expenses or mark-ups and so had no idea how much going all the way to Gdansk or having to buy train tickets at twice the normal price would influence their profits. In addition, they didn't know anything about which goods to bring, or rather, as they ignored the advice to bring tools, they didn't realize that one had to know what goods would be profitable to sell. When they finally discovered that they had brought the wrong goods, they were unaware of what Stasė later calls the inevitable pattern in the Gariūnai market, that if some goods are selling well, the market will immediately be flooded with them. The market had already changed. Thus, when they finally managed to buy the caps that had been sold so easily by the woman they met at the station, they were unable to sell them. In addition, they got cheated in Gariūnai and bought damaged caps, which of course made them even more difficult to sell in Poland.

Secondly, the story shows the importance of social networks. Stasė went with a friend to Poland, she borrowed money from friends, she obtained goods in Gariūnai through a friend and underwear from Utenos Trikotažas through her cousin, etc.

Finally, Stasė's story reveals an ethical distinction between trading at Gariūnai and other forms of trading. Despite the fact that Stasė had been trading for more than a year in Poland, and had been buying goods several times at Gariūnai, she still does not present it as an ethical problem. The tragedy does not arise until she starts selling in Gariūnai around 1993/1994, when the possibility of trading in the Polish markets no longer existed. Stasė's story therefore suggests that the stigmatization of market trading is not entirely connected with the conceptualization of trade as 'speculation', but rather with performing as a trader *in Gariūnai*. The stigmatization seems to be linked to the specific locality of the market.

For Stasė, trading was evidently a means of survival, not a career. She had no intention of continuing to trade in the long run, although she had got more used to being in the market and was not as embarrassed as she used to be.

FROM PROFESSIONAL TO TRADER

Algis E. sells computer equipment and software at Gariūnai together with four friends. I met him while conducting survey interviews in the market. Algis E. lives in a nice, newly-built house in town. Compared with housing conditions in Vilnius in general, his house is large and rather impressive. Algis E. has obviously made quite a lot of money from his business, although he is not a *nouveau riche*. During my talks with him, his wife was also present, and she made a few comments as well. I must also mention that Algis E. did not want me to use a tape recorder—'for political reasons' as he put it.

Algis E.'s story

We are five old and very good friends in our company and we have equal rights. One graduated in mathematics and does computer programming, another is a proper computer programmer, a third graduated in radio-electronics, a fourth (me) is specialized in the construction of radio-electronics (I graduated from Vilnius technical university), and finally the fifth graduated from Vilnius pedagogic university and has specialized in physics. He still teaches. We chose computer equipment because it is closer to our specialized field.

We trade in two types of computer games. But we also sell all sorts of other computer equipment apart from actual computers: joysticks, connections, spare parts, etc.

I didn't start my trading activities with computers, but with anything and everything. In 1990 I began this business in the Polish style. It is a pure Polish variant to take advantage of differences in price levels in various countries. The Poles would make prices equal in all the countries they went to. First, they went to Lithuania, then Lithuanians went to Poland. Between 1985 and 1989, Lithuanians were taking food products to Poland. Later, Belorussians and Ukrainians would come to Lithuania, they would bring two bags of food and Lithuanians would buy all of it, for example sugar or vodka, and they would sell it for a higher price in the Halė market.[2] So in that way, basically, the differences in prices were evened out.

I started with two friends who used to travel to Poland, to Yugoslavia, and to Turkey. I myself was very much against the market in the beginning—it was my wife who persuaded me to begin trading. I remember going to Yugoslavia. In the beginning it was very profitable, you would invest one dollar and get back three. Lithuanians would take canned fish, which cost 1 rouble in Lithuania, to Yugoslavia and sell it for one dollar. Other things that went to Yugoslavia were tools, for example hammers. The profit was quite high. With an investment of $50 the return would be $300. But we didn't have very much money to invest, so it was small amounts. Prices have increased a lot since then. For example I have just sold my car for $3,200. I bought it for $400 in Moscow five years ago.

---

[2] Halė market is one of the two large food markets in Vilnius—the other is Kalvarijos, which is often referred to as 'the 'beginning of Gariūnai'.

I think that the people who started earlier and who sold their flats to get a larger working capital—some of them were really clever . . . By 1990 it was too late—we'd missed the bus. Of the people who started early, for example in 1988, some of them now have shops or warehouses, or workshops—one of my friends is a good example of that. But some are also still in Gariūnai. Some wore themselves out, went bankrupt, or were ruined by thieves.

If I had been more inclined to make smart deals it would have been possible to sell the flat and build up even more capital—but the risk was too great. In this first wave of business a lot of people lost their flats.

I started to go to China sometime in 1991. Some of my friends were going, and I went with them, but everyone for himself—not together like now. The main problem then was the initial capital. I got a loan from friends, we borrowed $400 for the trip and $500 to buy goods with. In the beginning you could sell anything, it didn't matter what you bought. For example, I would have two bags, one with sports shoes, and another with jogging suits. The profit would be double—so I would invest $1,000 and I would get back $2,000–3,000.

About two years ago—1993—I started thinking that maybe it was time to do something else. Maybe rich people would buy computers. But we had to get rid of the clothes first—it took us half a year.

Now, one of us goes to China every ten days. It means that I go there every other month. We can call and order—we even have our contact person, a man from Uzbekistan who has a university degree in Chinese. We go to a city close to Beijing. We don't have a regular supplier—everything keeps changing. This year I went to China six times—last year it was fifteen times. We have changed the system. Last year two or three of us would go together, because it was too great a risk to take all the money alone. Now one person goes alone, but we still have to take all the money with us in cash.

The goods we buy come from Taiwan, Korea, and so on, but we buy them in China. They are produced without licence—of course they are cheaper. All goods of this kind are cheaper. In China all products are made this way and it has caused a lot of problems between China and the USA. We import them into Lithuania as semi-manufactures, and you can't say that it is illegal, because Lithuania hasn't signed the computer games convention. (Wife: Nobody checks when you give a bribe!)

It is a difficult area of course even for me. It is not possible to check whether the products I buy are made on licence or are copies. I don't consider this a criminal aspect, it is the way business is done. The Japanese also are making illegal spare parts for these computer games—not only us!

In the beginning we didn't need to pay taxes—everything was profit. Now the state demands 18 per cent of the turnover. We make a profit of 10–15 per cent on our turnover, so if we were to pay all the taxes we're supposed to we'd end up with a deficit of at least 3 per cent. We do pay some taxes, custom duties and licence fees. The State gets enough. If the State were to demand just a small payment, then everybody would pay. People should be allowed to earn something . . .

The work we do is really *juodos darbas* (hard work). You suffer from jetlag, you have to make all the agreements, you have to look after the goods and make sure they are secure. It's really not very healthy work, and you get black rims around your eyes.

Most of the money is made because acquaintances in Kaliningrad, Estonia, and Latvia distribute further. But they come to Gariūnai to see other products as well, competitors' products. Often they just order from the office in advance and send a driver to pick up everything. If they buy large quantities they get a discount. Our company has three places in Gariūnai, but we also have people selling for us on commission. Some of them, the ones we know, are given credit. Others buy wholesale from us.

My opinion is that Gariūnai is not a bad place for business. Of course it is a different situation now from what it was a few years ago. Then people would starve in order to buy clothes. You could sell anything. Now they want guarantees and no damaged goods. Now people don't have any money.

The Gariūnai market's reputation has improved. Maybe Gariūnai itself is becoming more civilized. However, opinions differ. People who are living on a State-sector salary haven't changed their opinion. Private business people are more positive . . .

Algis E.'s story is rather different from Stasė's, particularly because he regards himself as a professional and has been able to use his educational background in private business. I suggest moreover that this has been important for his own acceptance of Gariūnai. Although Algis E. also remembered his own reluctance to start at Gariūnai, he no longer seemed embarrassed about his trading activities. He not only firmly stated that what he was doing was just 'business', but also found that Gariūnai was not such a bad place in which to do it.

The business story of Algis E. and his friends suggests that Gariūnai-style trading cannot just be dismissed as 'petty'. Although I have no exact figures, Algis E.'s income must be quite high for him to be able to build his own house (especially taking into account that his wife does not have a job). But although he may be operating at a different level of business, there are also similarities between his and Stasė's strategies. In both cases Gariūnai was by no means their first experience of trading and in both cases friends proved important, not only in order to be able to borrow capital, but also as a way of getting information about where to go and what to bring. Algis E., however, seem to have had more competent friends (and perhaps listened more to what they had to say). At any rate he seems to have gone through his first few years of trading without losing too much money and in this way established a basis for his present business. Success during the first 'golden years' of trading seems to have been of considerable importance. Algis E.'s story moreover emphasizes the development of the market from these 'golden years' to the present period of 'stagnation'. Earlier profits were 100 per cent, whereas now they are down to 10 or 15 per cent. Earlier, anything could be sold, but now it has become necessary to specialize. Another important point in Algis E.'s story is the continuous importance of the Gariūnai market as a place to sell goods, even for a company like that run by Algis E. and his friends. So although in terms of turnover, organization, and so on, Algis E. may be viewed as having developed his business beyond Gariūnai, he still finds it necessary to stay in the market.

Finally, an important aspect of Algis E.'s trading is the kind of products he sells. These are mainly pirate copies of Western computer programs and equipment.

TURNING 'TRADING' INTO 'BUSINESS'

I met Rasa through her mother (Irena), who was trading in the market. Rasa was in many ways an example of a successful market trader, especially because she was no longer working in the market. When I met her she owned a shop selling women's clothes and a café, and was considering expanding her activities even further.

Rasa's story
I started my business long ago. Around 1984 I used to knit garments at home and then sell them. The government called it 'speculation', ordinary people didn't call it that. When I got pregnant, I started to sew. There were a lot of fashionable things from Poland at that time, so I would put 'Made in Poland' labels in the clothes I made. Later on, when the government decided to permit individual production, I got a licence for producing and selling. I started to sell my things in the Kalvarijos market. The first time it was terrible. I remember finding a very small chair to sit on, so that it was hard to see me behind the table, because it was so embarrassing. At that time a woman in the market was called *turgaus boba* (market bitch). We were not regarded as respectable. I would go to the market every morning at 7 o'clock except on Mondays. I would get materials for making clothes from Moscow and then sell from the tables at Kalvarijos. It was terrible and not very pleasant at the market in those days. But we needed the money. Later when I discovered there were doctors and teachers in the market too, I found it much easier.

In 1989–90 I was trading in Kalvarijos and in Eišiškės, mostly dresses and skirts for women. In 1990–92 I was sewing and trading at Gariūnai. I can't remember exactly, but I don't think there were any cars in the beginning. Besides we didn't have a car, so in those days my mother would drive me to the market with my big bags.

After some time I wanted to try to find an easier way of making money. It was too hard, I was trading during the day, sleeping a little after I came back, and then in the evening and at night I would sew for the next day. I thought that going to Turkey and bringing goods would be an easier way. I remember the first time I tried to get to Turkey very clearly. I had bought a ticket from a woman who was supposed to organize everything. The plan was that we should go by bus to Poland and then by train and then again by bus. But this woman was to anxious to make money and didn't do her job very well, and we never got to Poland at all. We waited at the Polish/Lithuanian border for 24 hours and ended up returning to Vilnius again. All thirty-two of us, can you imagine! After two days I managed to get a plane ticket on a direct flight from Vilnius to Istanbul, and then it was OK. I was very nervous the first time but I made friends on the plane. There were both women and men on the plane. Of course I didn't know exactly what to buy, but I knew what was fashionable and aimed for the right things: clothes for women. I went to Turkey regularly for about two years. I would go about once a month, or every three weeks. I also tried to go to China, but I didn't like it so much. You had to bring a lot of money with you as well as many goods. When I came to Kaunas everything had to be transported by bus to Vilnius. Our flat was filled with goods from floor to ceiling and in the end we had to move out. My husband said it was impossible to live there. So I stopped going to China.

After trading with Turkey for about six months, towards the end of 1992, I started buying leather jackets only. Almost all leather jackets in Gariūnai are from Turkey, even if people say that they are from Germany or from Italy. Leather jackets sold very well.

I then started to trade in the *mugė* (indoor market).[3] That was in 1993. For a period, I was trading both in the *mugė* and in Gariūnai. In the morning I would be in Gariūnai and in the afternoon I would be in the *mugė*. The reason to start in the *mugė* was that I wanted something better than the market. It is more prestigious, not so cold, more comfortable and so on. But the trading is not so good in the *mugė*. People don't buy so much. They go and look, just to pass the time—it was more popular in the beginning. The spring of 1995 was my last *mugė*.

Last year in July a woman offered me a place where I could open a shop. Before that I hadn't even thought of getting a shop, but when she suggested it, I immediately accepted. Usually it is difficult to find a place, and it is expensive. This building used to be a shoe factory. Then a supermarket opened downstairs last year in the spring. And so I started.

I get goods for the shop from many different places. The articles are different from the kind you get at Gariūnai, because in Gariūnai trading is mainly wholesale, and things are usually cheap—not the best quality. I still get goods from my mother, from Poland, or friends bring things for me if

[3] A *mugė* is an indoor market, which were very popular during the first years after independence. It consists of numerous small stalls where imported goods are sold. Goods here resemble the articles sold in Gariūnai, but these markets are more prestigious. In Vilnius (1995) there was a permanent *mugė* in a large hall next to a cinema, and during the summer the stadium was also turned into a *mugė*.

they are going somewhere. I order by telephone and give them money to bring back goods for me. There are also firms that import from Germany or England into Lithuania. I go there and see the samples and then I choose.

I have ideas about starting a sewing workshop. I don't know yet how to do it, because I have been away from sewing for so long, but it is an idea and I may be able to realize it.

Rasa, like Algis E., started trading during the early phase. She earned most of her capital during the 'golden years' at Gariūnai and had already left the market when profits started to decline in 1994. Before that she too had tried various goods and ways of trading, and although her first trip to Poland with the bus was unsuccessful, she, like Algis E., had tried various methods without losing too much money. One reason for this seems to be that she had a knowledge of clothes and fashion when she started trading and therefore knew what to buy.

Although Rasa has always been trading alone, she has had assistance from her mother, Irena, who is still trading at Gariūnai. For years Rasa's mother would drive her daughter to the market before going to work herself. Apart from the help from her mother, Rasa also received help from friends. It is interesting to note that the friend who offered Rasa premises to open a shop was also a woman, and that having influential friends—especially women friends—seems to have contributed to her success. Such business contacts among women are rare and this contributes to the unfavourable position of women in the new economy.

Interestingly, Rasa's decision to open a shop was taken only after she had been offered the premises. This suggests not only that shop premises are very hard to find, but also that Rasa's activities were unplanned. She seized the opportunity when it appeared, but it was not something she had anticipated or aimed at. Her career as a businesswoman in this respect is not so different from women's business activities elsewhere.[4]

Finally Rasa, like Algis E. and Stasė, was terribly embarrassed when she started trading at Gariūnai, and she too remembers clearly the shame she felt in the beginning, even though, like Stasė, she had been engaged in illegal economic practices before she started as a trader in Kalvarijos. The uneasiness Rasa felt about her activities therefore seems to be connected not so much with the illegality of making clothes and selling underground but more directly with the activity of selling the wares in the market. Thus Rasa's story not only confirms the difference in 'moral standing' between trading in the market and being involved in underground economic practices in general, but also suggests that the moral stigmatization is not solely linked with Gariūnai, since Rasa felt the same way in the Kalvarijos market. Her observations about her knitting and sewing at home to the effect that the government called it speculation, but ordinary people did not, furthermore

---

[4] See, for example, Aalten (1989), who writes about female entrepreneurs in Holland. She finds that Dutch businesswomen seldom planned to go into business. They told their stories as if business had 'happened to them', rather than being something they had aimed for.

suggests that attitudes towards underground economic practices in general were not very negative during the last years of the Soviet republic. According to the official discourse of socialism they were, of course, problematic, but what Rasa's and Stasė's stories suggest is something different. What made their activities shameful for them was trading in the market, and not trading as such.

Rasa makes an additional symbolic and perhaps moral distinction between Gariūnai and Kalvarijos on the one hand, and the *mugė* (indoor market) on the other. It is definitely more prestigious to trade in the *mugė*, although there is less money to be made and goods are often exactly the same. What is interesting to note here is not only the difference in status between indoor and outdoor markets, but the clear distinction between economic and social capital. One could apparently get rich at Gariūnai, but for this to have any effect on one's social position one needed to get engaged in some other more socially acceptable activity. The difference between Rasa and Algis E. is worth noting here. While Algis E. had used his education, Rasa had utilized her underground experiences, which had never been part of her public social life. The fact that Rasa aims at getting out of the market and prefers to work in the less profitable but more prestigious *mugė* may be seen as her way of narrowing the gap between what we could term social and economic status systems. Algis E. managed to make use of the market as something which could illuminate his professional standing, something which Rasa apparently felt she could not do.

FROM STUDENT TO GARIŪNAI TRADER

Vytalij, a young man in his early twenties, has a fairly advanced education, but has been unable to find a job which could fit his ambitions and give him a secure income. Although he speaks Lithuanian, Russian, and Polish fluently, and has a good knowledge of English, he had not managed to find a use for these competencies elsewhere in society.

Vytalij traded in the market together with his father and mother. Usually he or his mother went to Poland to buy merchandise, mainly children's jogging suits, which they sold in Gariūnai.

Vytalij's story
The reason why we started trading at Gariūnai was that we had no money to pay for my school. For three years I have been studying in a private school, the Vilnius College of Management and Foreign Languages. I have now graduated. We learned English, marketing, and management, but on a very general level. I had to go to a private school—it is very difficult to get admitted to a university here because our society is terribly corrupt. I would have had to pay a lot of money to get to university. So my family decided to send me to a private college instead. At Vilnius University they told me that all vacancies had already been allocated in advance for the next three years.

The school I went to was good and very popular. Words like 'management' and 'marketing' are unfamiliar to most people and now they are very popular. I thought that after finishing this school I would become a manager. I thought I would easily get a job, but the situation has changed, and it is more difficult now.

I went to this private school, and I had to pay. Not much, but around 6,000 roubles for five months. But after the first five months my parents had no more money, so we asked our friends, who were trading in Gariūnai, to help us and they accompanied us and helped us to start trading there. They helped us to start this business. The main problem was capital, for we had no money to start with. We borrowed $1,000 from our friends.

In 1992 my father started to go to Poland with friends and later he helped the same friends to sell goods they had brought from China. Then my father tried to do business on his own without any friends. He went to Poland several times. It was very successful. Then he went to Syria. It was terribly unsuccessful! He was robbed in the hotel. He had no experience and he put the money somewhere in his hotel room and when he came back it was all gone.

He came back full of remorse with no money and no goods, but a lot of debts. So we had to do something. We saw an advertisement about going to India so my father and I went along. We borrowed some more money and we mortgaged our flat for $6,000. The first time was very successful—the most successful. We bought cheap and good merchandise and made quite a good profit. We paid all our debts and we had some money to start our own business. Later, I went alone to India, because I speak English. I had made some friends in India from our first trip, so it was easy for me. I went to India eight times. The first, as I said, was very successful, the following were reasonably good, though not as good as the first, but the last time was terrible! In the beginning Indian goods, Indian sweaters, cardigans, pullovers were unknown in Lithuania. It was something new. Now it isn't any more. The last time I went to India it was in January and in Lithuania January, February, and March are bad for business. After New Year nobody buys. I didn't know that—I thought it was winter and I thought people would buy. I tried to sell my goods for four months, but made no profit because I had to sell at a very low price. Then we started to go to Poland again. Not too bad, not too good, but better than the last time in India. After some time we decided to go to India again. This time before Christmas when trading was good. But then we heard about a whole plane that had been arrested in Šiauliai. They came back from India but there was some mistake. The goods were confiscated and I don't know if they got them back at all . . . and after that I decided not to go to India any more. I continued my business in Poland. It is not so good as India, the investment is smaller and the profit is less, but the risk is also less.

The larger the investment the larger the profit and the larger the risk of course. Trading is very risky, even for me. I take goods from Poland and if business is not good I may sell them at a very low price. I may even lose money, but I will get some money back too. And then I may go again and try with different articles. Of course it is risky, but it is not too risky. But for people who invest a large amount of capital of course it is very risky.

I go to Łódź in Poland. We always go with the same company, even with the same bus. So we go, mother or me. Ours is a family company. It is good because it is not so risky. If you form a company with strangers it is risky, because people are so different. I am sure that my mother will not cheat me.

Now my business is clothes for children from five up to fifteen years. For a long time I kept changing commodities, but now I have decided to specialize in one kind of business. I had success with this in the summer. All children go to school on 1 September and parents buy different articles for them. In July I tried to sell these suits for children and it was quite successful. People came to me all the time and bought ten or twenty suits and they know now that if they want to buy sports clothes they can get them from me. So when business got slack we decided not to change this line but to wait until the end of this period. My customers said 'Well, it's not good now, but we'll come back in December and buy for Christmas.' Even today some customers came, because they knew I was selling sportswear.

The Polish markets are practically the same as Gariūnai, but more civilized. On a higher level. People are more cultured. They don't talk as rudely as in Gariūnai. If you understand Russian you'll hear an awful lot of bad language in Gariūnai, because the people in the market come from different backgrounds: teachers, technicians, workers. We have to stand in our market even when it's raining and snowing. Our government is not interested. They only remember Gariūnai when it is time to collect taxes, whereas in Poland the government encourages trading, which is legal, whereas I am an illegal trader. In order to be legal I would have to hand over all my profits to the government. We sell goods in the market, so we have to pay an entrance fee and taxes, but the tax system is very stupid. I and my friend, who goes to China, have to pay the same amount of money for a licence. If the situation were normal I would pay all those taxes. It would be better for me. I wouldn't have to be afraid of the economic police the way I am now. Some days if they say 'Watch out, the police are coming to check', a lot of people pack up their goods and leave the market. Some months, especially in summer, I may earn 1,000 litai a month, but this month, October, I shall probably earn 300 litai, and yet they want me to pay this to the government. So what will I eat?

The Polish prices are always given without VAT. So when we go through customs they say: 'You must pay VAT.' But I don't know the laws and I don't know my rights. One customs official may want 20 per cent, another 28 per cent, and they decide what the merchandise is worth!

So money is collected from all the traders in the bus to bribe the customs officials in order to avoid problems. But if I was sure that I could pay the same or less by going by the rules, of course I would rather pay the government, but I don't know. I have nowhere to phone and ask about the rules, and tell them about the corruption that takes place at the borders. I think that the corruption even penetrates our Seimas (Parliament) and some of the money that is collected at the borders finds its way upwards through the system. I don't believe our government wants to change anything.

Then there are my parents, my brother and me, and we have a dog, and my very old grandmother, who has her own flat, but can't afford the rent, because she only has a very small pension. We help her to buy the necessities of life and we pay for her flat. We need about 1,000 litai per month for our own living expenses—not extravagances, just living expenses.

If taxes were reasonable I would pay them. If I sell $1,000 worth of goods, and if I know that after paying tax I will still have a profit, I will pay, but the situation now is either tax or profit. You can't afford to pay tax.

In some ways Vytalij's story is similar to the other three. First, you need good friends to start trading, you need to find some way of obtaining working capital, and you have to watch the market closely to read the trends, observe the seasons and which goods sell well, the ways of importing merchandise, and so on. But Vytalij's story reveals a feature of market trading that may have influenced the other three as well. Vytalij demonstrates that he does not have the social network necessary to succeed outside the market. First, he was unable to enter Vilnius University, because he had no contacts. Second, after finishing his education he was unable to get a job in a private company. To get a job, qualifications are not so important, but connections are vital. Vytalij was fairly open in stating that he and his family had no contacts. His story reveals that the social networks dominating Soviet society have not changed fundamentally in recent years, although nowadays membership of them may be based on different grounds. I suggest that this is therefore not only a feature of Vytalij's story, but an important reason why many people start and continue trading in the Gariūnai market (see also Chapter 8). As stated by one of the participants in a television programme about Gariūnai: 'Gariūnai traders are people without uncles and aunts in important positions.'

Vytalij, like Stasė, started late in the market, and therefore has not been able to take advantage of the most prosperous years. Moreover, the story of failures in the case of Vytalij's family emphasizes the narrow borderline between success and failure in this kind of business. They were unlucky and lost all their money twice during their 'training period' as traders. Not surprisingly, Vytalij's story therefore centres around risk, risk-taking, and risk-reduction. Vytalij sees risk as inevitable in market trading but also closely connected with the authorities and the legal system. He not only finds taxes too high but specifically points to the uncertainty connected with the various authorities he has to deal with. Doubts about legal rights, laws, and taxes mean that he cannot calculate the risks he takes—business becomes too insecure.

It is therefore not only the 'unreasonableness' of the tax system that matters for Vytalij, but the fact that the legal system is so inefficiently implemented. Vytalij's main point of criticism is the lack of regulation and the lack of rights. Bribing the customs secures the substitution of one constantly changing and furthermore largely unknown (official) legal system for another set of rules—a private agreement, whose conditions may be negotiated. In this way bribery has become an integral part of trade, where bribes are given collectively in advance. But it does not always work, and getting goods through customs is a continuous problem for traders. The risk involved in dealing with customs is not only the amount of money needed for bribes, but in addition that customs officials may hold back goods to be checked further for a considerable period. The seasonal character of trading makes this a serious matter. On the whole, bribes are not only paid to cover up illegal aspects of trading, but also, and perhaps more importantly, in order not to be checked at all.

Vytalij emphasizes another point, namely the difference between the Polish markets and Gariūnai. According to Vytalij there is a cultural difference, in the way people talk to each other, in the fact that most of the Gariūnai market is outdoors, and finally because trading activities in Poland are legal. What Vytalij means when he states that his trading is illegal is that he, like Stasė, has not bought a licence to trade at Gariūnai. In several ways, Vytalij's activities appear similar to Stasė's, especially since they both aim to get a job and make a career for themselves elsewhere.

A RAPIDLY CHANGING MARKET

Although the four traders have different backgrounds, an examination of the individual stories given above reveals some similar trends. It is also important to note that the individual careers and their changing strategies and orientation both reflect and constitute the structural changes of trade during the past ten years.

First, all four traders had been involved in other forms of trading before they started at Gariūnai: Stasė went to Poland to sell—like Vytalij's father—Rasa was engaged in underground production, and Algis E. sold canned fish in Yugoslavia. The stories therefore sustain the idea that Gariūnai and Gariūnai trading are closely linked to earlier (Soviet) forms of trading. Second, all four traders have experimented with various forms of trading such as selling goods from various countries and trading with several different articles. This means that after some time in the market, there is a clear tendency towards specialization. This is also reflected in an increasing division of labour. A growing number of entrepreneurs have specialized in the import of goods and employ traders, like Stasė, to sell their wares in the market. Third, certain general trends can also be observed in the development of various trading forms. Traders are travelling further and further away in order to buy cheaper products and new products. Until around 1991, when the Soviet Union still existed (more or less), traders generally made a profit by selling cheap Soviet products in Polish or Yugoslavian markets. Later, in the 'golden years' of Gariūnai, traders would either sell Lithuanian underground products or simply import goods from Poland. But gradually traders started extending their trade-routes to Turkey and later also to China and the United Arab Emirates. Finally, India became a source of supplies. Recently, an increase in Lithuanian small-scale production of clothes has been taking place, and these goods are popular among commission traders in the market as the profit margin is higher than in the case of imported products. Thus one can observe a gradual institutionalization of imports and selling practices, including the development of travel agencies and new ways of transporting merchandise. At first individual traders would fly to Turkey and fly back with their goods in the same plane. Later, a separate cargo plane would be chartered to bring back goods, and recently some importers have begun to order goods, and have them sent, without having to travel and bring them back them-selves. However, there are several obstacles to this continuous process of institu-tionalization. It is still risky to send merchandise back to Lithuania unaccompanied as there is no guarantee that it will ever arrive unless kept under close surveillance. The problems involved in getting through customs have to be handled by some-body at the border. Finally, since transferring money through banks is not favoured in this kind of trading, the only practical solution is to go and hand over the cash in person.

Since these changes have taken place within the past ten years, traders' career stories suggest not only rapidly changing conditions in connection with fashion or the variety of goods that can be sold in the market, but also more structural changes such as increased specialization and division of labour and a development towards more sophisticated forms of importing goods.

FEELING SHAME

As the cases of Stasė, Rasa, and to some extent Algis E. suggest, many traders feel terribly ashamed about being in the market. Over the span of a trading career, this feeling of shame can be specifically connected to the point in time when traders began their activities in Gariūnai. The shame and lack of social prestige is connected with the market, and cannot be found to the same extent when traders recall their early selling activities in Poland or elsewhere. This suggests that although there is clearly some connection between the illegality of private trade, unequal prices and so on in Soviet society on the one hand and Gariūnai on the other, there is also a clear distinction between them. In general, therefore, when focusing on trading practices there is a close connection between Gariūnai and other forms of trade. When it comes to morality and social prestige, however, there seem to be considerable differences. According to traders, underground activities and even the selling of goods in Soviet society were not a serious moral problem for those involved, although this view was of course not shared by the Soviet authorities. This makes it difficult to treat the social stigmatization of market traders and the shame connected with the market as purely a matter of 'remnants of socialism', because the symbolic marginalization has actually increased after independence. The moral stigmatization of Gariūnai traders therefore seems to be connected with the development of the market and market trading and not with trading as an activity *per se*. In addition it is considerably more shameful to sell than it is to buy in the market. Thus it is more embarrassing for a trader to meet a customer whom she knows from outside the market than it is for the customer whom she meets. Traders would try to hide if they spotted acquaintances in the market.

In general, the four case stories, although revealing similarities, also point towards a diversity of trading patterns as well as to varying degrees of success. Furthermore, the borderline between success and failure is often narrow and it definitely seems that a certain amount of luck is necessary too. But one needs to learn, or to 'become experienced', in order to benefit fully from the possibilities offered by the market.

4

How to 'Read the Market'

> The search for information one lacks and the protection of information one
> has is the name of the game. (Geertz 1979: 125)

When analysing the Gariūnai market one is in many ways tempted to think of it in
terms of what anthropologists as well as economists generally have termed 'bazaar
economy'. Alexander (1992), who has criticized the traditional dichotomy of
bazaar economy versus the Western market economy, characterized the (image of)
the bazaar-type economy or peasant market as follows:

In peasant markets[1] commodities are seldom standardised or pre-packaged and are often
subject to marked fluctuations in supply and demand. Production or overhead costs are not
calculated and most traders do not keep written records after a transaction is completed.
Vendors of particular commodities cluster together in one section of the market-place,
rather than distribute themselves throughout it, and do not overtly compete to make a sale.
Advertising, other than sales patter, is almost unknown and although many transactions are
between persons previously unknown to one another, the market as a whole is structured by
enduring trading partnerships, which channels credit and supplies. As prices are seldom
marked on goods or on the stall, except when required by the state, bargaining is the usual
means of setting prices. (Alexander 1992: 80)

In a now classical study of the Moroccan bazaar, *Suq*, Clifford Geertz has
suggested that searching for reliable information forms the key to understanding
the bazaar as an institution (Geertz 1979). Knowledge about things and people is
difficult to obtain, and both the institutional structure and the market culture are
double-edged, since they simultaneously facilitate the search for information and
make the distribution of knowledge highly discontinuous. The reliability of any
piece of information is therefore hard to evaluate (Appadurai 1986: 43 ff.).
Although the rigid typological division between bazaar economies and modern
market economy is questionable,[2] such an 'information search' seems to be crucial

---

[1] Alexander 1992 and Geertz 1963 use the concepts of peasant market and bazaar synonymously.

[2] As already mentioned, Alexander 1992 criticizes the traditional opposition between bazaar and
market economy among other things by suggesting that studies of the 'two kinds of economy' have
usually been based on different methodologies. Whereas anthropological studies of the bazaar usually
build on empirical studies, there has been a tendency to model analyses of Western market economy on
its neo-classicist theoretical assumptions. Alexander is supported in this by Gudeman, who points out
that such analyses 'continually reproduce and rediscover their own assumptions in the exotic materials'
(Gudeman, cited in Alexander 1992). Alexander gives various empirical examples of 'bazaar features'

in exchange settings characterized by a lack of standardization and weak institutionalization:

> bazaar-style information searches are likely to characterize any exchange setting where the quality and the appropriate valuation of goods are not standardized, though the reasons for the lack of standardization, for the volatility of prices, and for the unreliable quality of specific things of a certain type may vary enormously. (Appadurai 1986: 43)

The Gariūnai market is both a legal and a publicly recognized market place. At the same time it is characterized by a lack of standardization and by rapid changes in prices, legal and actual trading conditions and thus generally by rather unstable trading practices. Although there are official managers, owners, and trading places, the actual social structures in the market are much more complicated and it is essential for traders to have access to information from the largely informal and hidden power structures in order to know the 'rules of the game'. A knowledge of trading conditions, trading hierarchies, and informal social rules of conduct is therefore essential for traders in the market. This knowledge is furthermore unevenly distributed among traders and the central factor is therefore the existence of many layers of such knowledge as well as its shifting and contextual character. Although from the outside trading at the Gariūnai market appeared to be something anyone could do and the market could well be viewed as easily 'accessible', a closer examination revealed a rigid separation between 'insider' and 'outsider'. It was by no means easy to start trading in the market. One needed knowledge about commodities and trade routes as well as continuous access to information, since trading conditions as well as the actual social structure in the market were constantly changing. These continual changes, which may be seen as a product of the routinization of individual trading practices and of competition within the field of trading, epitomize the overall 'in-the-making' feature not only of the market place but of the economic field in general.

HIDDEN PATTERNS

Apart from a few distinct areas in the Old Market and the Belorussian market in the New Market, there was no clear spatial organization in Gariūnai. Interestingly, before the New Market appeared, there were some clear, although rather informal, spatial divisions in the Old Market. Traders would refer to areas such as *centras* (the centre), *uzantis* (a place that is nice and warm), *karakumai* (desert), and *petačiokas* (small coin, or Piglet from *Winnie-the-Pooh*). A place outside the Old Market, where Poles used to sell cloth, was referred to as 'Chocolate Hill'. After the drastic changes in the Old Market in 1994, when the market had shrunk considerably after a mass exodus of traders following an attempt by the manager to reorganize the market, the 'old' names had ceased to

of Western markets, mainly imperfect information concerning prices and imperfect information about the quality of goods.

have any meaning, and new ones had not yet appeared. The lack of spatial organization may therefore be viewed not only as a structural but also as a processional phenomenon.

Although traders usually stated that there was no spatial order in the market, they would often reveal a subtler pattern, either by their conduct or sometimes in interviews. Generally, however, such patterns remained unarticulated and must be viewed as belonging to what Gudeman (1992) has termed 'local practice knowledge'. Inherent in such knowledge are 'practice models' of the market. As these are often implicit it may be necessary to follow trading activities and market conduct closely in order to discover them.

In 1995, the organization of the Old Market had recently changed and its spatial patterns were therefore even more subtle than they used to be, yet sections of the market were actually dominated by certain goods and often referred to as 'islands'. The largest of these was where trading in spare parts for cars took place, because such spare parts were only sold at this specific place in the market (this was moreover a highly masculine area of the market: see Chapter 7). In addition I discovered an 'island' of nylons, another of perfumes, and one of amber. The existence of more criminal places in the market was also brought to my notice:

There are a few criminal places in Gariūnai. In one place you can buy precious metals (gold, silver, platinum) and 'coloured' metals (copper, iron, etc.). The other place is where trading in firearms is carried on. They mainly sell gas guns. You can also buy other types of weapons but then you have to go somewhere outside the market to make the deal. They have to be cautious because it is illegal. (Vytenis 3.1)

These two places were furthermore well guarded, and after learning of their existence I made no further enquiries. Apart from such 'islands', including the one for spare parts for cars, which were dominated by men, specific areas of the market were dominated by women. At the entrances, a group of elderly women, often pensioners, would sell carrier bags for customers. At other places, groups of younger women would gather to sell their home-produced clothing.

Notably, for such a multi-ethnic market, there were no ethnic divisions. Trading places, although not entirely accidental, were not chosen according to ethnicity nor, apart from the few 'islands' mentioned above, on the basis of specialization in certain commodities. Yet in other ways commodities played a key role in determining traders' social position in the market. Before turning to these, however, it will be necessary to clarify the various forms of trading and social stratification.

THE SOCIAL HIERARCHY OF TRADERS

The market was characterized by a high degree of social stratification among traders. There were people who made thousands of dollars a month, although it was not as profitable to sell in the market as it had been a few years earlier. It was of course not easy to check incomes, but some traders were definitely well off.[3] At the other end of the spectrum there were people who would make only a few dollars a day, all of which were spent on daily necessities so that such traders never managed to save up the initial capital necessary to expand their business further. I am convinced that most traders earned more than the 200–300 litai representing the monthly wage in a range of State-sector jobs. (Irena, who traded only a few times a week and who ranged among the least prosperous traders, was making an additional 400 litai a month from the market.)

In general there was only a narrow dividing line between success and bankruptcy. For example, Andrei and his wife, who occupied a central place in the New Market and had quite a successful business dealing in Turkish goods, nearly lost a lot of money at the time in 1995 when I visited the market. Because of the tighter control at the Lithuanian customs at the airport, they had decided to send their goods home in trucks instead of by plane. When I met them, they were greatly distressed, because they had only received four of the six large bags of goods that they had sent with the trucks from Turkey. Furthermore, because the two missing bags contained articles for schoolchildren, they were afraid that, even if they did get them back, they would suffer a heavy loss, because it would then be too late to sell them. In the end the bags were found, not too late after all, so they managed to sell their contents at a reasonable profit. The example indicates, however, that even if one is an 'experienced' trader, there are no guarantees against losing one's savings later on.

Certain distinctions in the market were generally recognized. There was a clear dividing line between traders who sold goods on commission and those who brought goods from abroad into the country themselves, the latter being the most prosperous. Finally, there was a third group of suppliers who only imported goods, but employed others to sell them, often referred to and acknowledged to be the most prosperous group of traders. Most traders knew, just by casting a glance at another trader's goods, to which category he or she belonged. It should be mentioned, however, that they did not always reach the same conclusion.[4]

Traders who held goods in their hands while standing or walking in the market and traders who spread out their goods on camp beds were called 'commission traders' (Category 1). Such traders were mostly women, often retired, who were unable to live on their pensions. Some traders with small passenger cars would also take goods on commission. They usually had regular suppliers of goods, but instead of occupying a regular place in the market they would look for a vacant

---

[3] One indication of this is the fact that several of the most prosperous traders were either building houses for themselves or had bought large apartments. As real estate prices were skyrocketing in the Lithuanian capital in the first years after independence, this was a safe indication of these traders' financial success.

[4] This became apparent during some interviews in which I used photographs of various traders in the market. When I compared them later on it appeared that there were divergent opinions about the various traders in the pictures, especially when it came to distinguishing between 'independent importers' and 'commission traders'.

TABLE 4.1 *Types of traders in Gariūnai market*

1. Selling goods on commision	2. Traders (importers and sellers)	3. Suppliers (importers)
Mobile	*Regular trading place*	*Not present in the market*
Selling goods held in their hands or spread on the ground	Selling from a car	
Selling from beds or tables	Selling from a car with a tent	
Selling from a car (with a parasol)	Selling from a mini-bus	
	Selling from a van	

place each day. Sellers on commission were therefore also more nomadic than regular traders. Although some of the more successful commission traders sold their goods from cars, 'traders with cars' generally also imported merchandise themselves. Those who sold on commission could also be spotted by their lack of a partner. Almost all traders had one, or in some cases several partners in the market. This was considered necessary as one would otherwise lose customers and income during periods spent abroad buying merchandise. People generally traded together with a family member or close friend. Many married couples traded in the market and many young (male) friends likewise had formed partnerships. Another advantage of being two was that one could be selling while the other went around studying the market. When I started trading with Irena in the market, she was unhappy about not being able to do this, since she traded alone, so when I was with her she asked me to 'do a bit of spying' on the prices of 'her' articles elsewhere in the market.

The majority of traders in the market therefore traded in partnerships of two and would do both the importing and the selling of the merchandise themselves (Category 2 in Table 4.1). This group was fairly heterogeneous and further distinctions could be made between trading from a car with a parasol, a car with a tent in front, or trading from a minibus or van. The vehicle was in itself an indication of a trader's wealth, since getting a minibus or van was, as one trader expressed it, 'an indication that the trader could afford better conditions for himself'. The group of traders all had a regular place in the market and their spatial position would further confirm their social and financial abilities, since trading near the main entrances was considered much more profitable than somewhere in the 'outskirts'. Thus areas around the main entrances were occupied by the most successful traders.

In addition, a trader's financial position could be estimated by looking at the origin of the goods, since obviously more capital was required to go to China than to Poland or Turkey. Going far would often be an indication of having a large income. Going to China required an investment of around $15,000, while going to Turkey required only $5,000 and Poland much less. When I went with Irena to Łódź she bought merchandise for $1,500. Some of the other Poland traders would invest less, some more. Traders at the market included all layers. As Vytalij explained:

Of course if you have a lot of capital you can go to China. There your profits will be higher. The amount invested is larger and so are the profits. People may invest $10,000 or $20,000 or even more. In Poland I can't invest so much and I would have difficulty getting through customs in a bus with so many goods. People with medium-size capital go to Turkey. People with only a small capital go to Poland or Hungary. People with very little capital to invest go to Kaunas, or to Klaipeda and they distribute all their goods all around Lithuania. They buy maybe 10 or 15 items and then go to Kaunas and sell. They make maybe 50 or 100 litai—I don't know. Their profit is very small but then their investments are also small. The larger the investment the higher the profit—and the larger the risk, of course.

Yet such distinctions were not clear-cut. Although most of the traders going to Poland made only small profits and often brought back only a small amount of goods each time, some of the most successful 'Poland traders' would transport Polish goods to Vilnius in their own cars several times a week and run a thriving business.[5] Social borderlines were further blurred by the fact that some traders would pool money in order to obtain goods, especially from China or India, the most expensive supply countries. Therefore although the country of supply was some indication of one's position in the market, other factors had to be considered as well.

One such indicator of social position was the goods themselves. Special goods would denote prosperity. Expensive goods like leather jackets or fur coats would immediately signal a trader's wealth. Similarly a certain amount of specialization in combination with a large turnover and a minibus also served as indications of having a 'good business'. Actually such multiple distinctions might do even more, since they would sum up the general distinction between 'business' and 'survival'. Only the most successful among the importers were considered to be building 'a business for the future'. The rest were just 'surviving' or engaged in what they themselves termed 'one-day trading'.[6]

The lack of a stable social hierarchy made it difficult for traders to estimate and explain social distinctions. One could only know such things by using one's knowledge of the whole process of procuring and selling goods. Thus traders rely on a

---

[5] There were several problems with this form of transporting goods in one's own car from Poland. First, there were a lot of bandits and much organized robbery from private cars on the highway between Warsaw and Lasdijai (on the border). Organized trips with buses would usually have armed guards in the bus, to minimize the risk of goods getting stolen. Secondly, the drivers of the buses attempted to make deals with the customs, thus ensuring that traders would get their goods through customs without paying too much. This meant that only traders with good contacts at the border and a fair amount of courage would attempt the trip to the Polish markets on their own.

[6] The distinction almost replicates that of seller on commission versus trader, but some traders would also be considered as survivors because of their limited incomes.

number of different indicators in order to deduce social information about each other. The broader one's experience of merchandise and countries the better one's chance of evaluating other traders and thus general trading conditions in the market. The way merchandise was organized and sold could convey information about a particular trader and the relative prosperity of his or her trade and then be used to develop knowledge of the market and the possibilities of developing various forms of trading. Since the market was changing rapidly, one needed constantly to re-evaluate conditions within each line of business so as to compare it with one's own and act accordingly. In order to do so, knowledge of many different kinds of merchandise played a crucial role.

THE PHENOMENOLOGY OF MERCHANDISE

Apart from the hot food in the kiosks, only non-food consumer goods were allowed in the market. These were mostly clothes (especially women's wear), but also a range of other items such as hi-fi equipment, kitchen utensils, toys, perfume, music cassettes, etc. As I have indicated above, most wares came from Poland, Turkey, the United Arab Emirates, and China. But India, Korea, Thailand, and Syria also appeared as countries of supply. In addition, a growing amount of locally produced clothes was entering the market and new countries of supply were constantly emerging. Notably, expensive items such as fur coats and wedding gowns were sold in the market. There appeared to be no particular limits to what could be sold, although the choice and presentation of goods was not entirely fortuitous.

Merchandise is always in the forefront in the market rather than people. A particularly surprising pattern was the rather passive and uninterested position taken up by traders and hence the central position occupied by the goods. Everything was done in order to make commodities visible and to present them as attractively as possible. The traders, on the other hand, would either sit in their cars or stand close by, talking to each other, and in this light appeared almost as a sort of appendix to the often 'sparkling' goods laid out on cars and tables or hung in tents. On sunny days, only the framework of the tent would be put up, and goods were hung in the open air, so as to be as visible as possible. Although traders would of course approach customers who showed a particular interest in their merchandise, the general attitude was that the seller could do nothing to stimulate sales. Goods were principally believed to be 'selling themselves'.

Traders who imported merchandise into Lithuania themselves generally sold only goods from one single country, although they might sell various kinds. As examples of 'country-specific goods', umbrellas were usually from the United Arab Emirates, fake Levis, leather jackets, and a certain style of women's clothes came from Turkey, and most winter clothes, including coats and sweaters, from China, where most of the (likewise unlicensed) computer games and equipment, music tapes, compact discs, and videos were acquired as well. Cheap perfume came either from the United Arab Emirates or from Poland, and Poland also provided hair spray, toothpaste (unlicensed Colgate), face cream (unlicensed Nivea), and most of the leather shoes. Traders who knew the market well were usually able to point out exactly from which country a trader had obtained his goods. However, the 'country of origin' was no simple matter, since many of these goods might have been resold in various countries before they turned up in Lithuania. This was especially the case with 'Polish goods', which had often been imported to Poland from China, Turkey, or the United Arab Emirates. In addition, goods from the Emirates often turned out to have been produced in Indonesia. Thus there appeared to be some confusion about the concept of 'country of origin'. It is important to note, however, that in spite of the obvious difficulty in knowing where the goods came from, traders always attempted to categorize goods in terms of 'country of origin'. Since traders booked their trips abroad through travel agents, they usually all ended up in the same cities and even at the same markets. To go to the United Arab Emirates, China, and Turkey therefore in reality meant to go to certain market places in Dubai, Beijing, and Istanbul. With regard to Poland the picture was a little more complicated, and the choice of market depended on the choice of goods. There were three main places of interest for traders wishing to acquire goods in Poland: Warsaw, Łódź or Bialystok. I was told by Vytalij that Łódź and Bialystok were famous for their home production of clothes and shoes (Łódź for clothes and Bialystok for shoes) while the Warsaw market was more complex but in particular provided traders with many imported Asian goods. For traders selling at Gariūnai it was considered more risky to buy such goods, since the same kind might turn up in Gariūnai as 'direct import' and thus cheaper. It seemed, however, that Polish traders would sometimes manage to monopolize the export of certain kinds of goods, and these would be very profitable to sell at Gariūnai, as they would be in short supply.

If one then further takes into account the fact that goods had to be cheap and moreover not weigh too much or take up too much space, there were not that many choices left. The result was that traders who went to the same countries often ended up with a limited range of goods. This tendency towards 'homogenization' of merchandise was strengthened because traders would be quick to copy each other if someone had discovered a line that was selling well. In the market, traders were constantly watching each other, estimating each other's turnover and profits. Trading in the market was coloured by the tension between finding the best merchandise and keeping on good terms with one another by not yielding completely to free market principles and 'stealing' another trader's goods. If asked, traders would always deny that they ever copied anybody, yet despite this restrictive normative codex the practice of copying was widespread. One way of restricting one's goods in the market was by monopolizing. As Czesław, a successful, middle-aged local Pole stated quite bluntly:

I deal with umbrellas from Poland. I have monopolized the trade with one make and there my profit is 125 per cent. I also aim at controlling the market with another make, but at the moment we have a competitor. But I can easily push him out of the market. I buy 200 at a time, he buys maybe 30. At the moment he sells his for $10, but I sell mine for $7. It doesn't give me any profit, but I want to make sure that he never buys them again! (Czesław 20.1)

In order to be able to control the flow of a certain commodity in the market, traders would also attempt to find a specific supplier and make a deal with him not to sell to anybody else. In general it seemed difficult for traders to pull off such deals and the instability of the market in terms of the flow of goods was a constant source of complaint. Sometimes the potential conflict occurring from selling the same goods was solved by attempting to disperse such products over a larger area in the market. If two neighbours in the market both went to Istanbul, they would try not to buy goods of the same kind. If they ended up with similar items, one would attempt to sell them through a friend elsewhere in the market. This was considered a proper way to resolve matters.

SEASONAL CHANGES

The seasonal character of market trading also added to the complexity of the 'commodity situation' in the market. One's country of supply typically offered a certain pattern of seasonal changes of goods and also shifting incomes, since no countries could provide 'success goods' for all seasons. Thus the United Arab Emirates had specifically good wares for the summer (school goods, photographic equipment, sports shoes, and bathing suits), while most Chinese goods, as mentioned above, were more popular in the winter. (Chinese summer goods were considered to be of poor quality.) It seemed, however, that most of the traders who imported merchandise themselves did not switch country according to season, although they might obtain additional goods in commission during the weak period of 'their countries'.

There were two definite 'peaks' of market trading, one late in November and December just before New Year, and one in the summer, before 1 September, when the school season began—in between, turnover was small. This seasonal character of trading influenced traders' dispositions in several ways. In the summertime the market was not only flooded with bathing suits and cheap cameras for the holidays, but also with school goods such as school satchels, notebooks, pens and pencils, etc. Beginners in business often failed because they were unaware of these peaks. They would watch the good sales, in December or August, hurry off to buy a lot of goods, but fail to realize that by the time their goods arrived the good trading period would be over. Vytalij (see Chapter 3), who got stuck with all his winter goods in January, is an example of such a beginner's mistake.

Experienced traders would plan their trading and stock up before the busy season in summer, but they too were often left with goods they were unable to sell. This was one of the reasons why traders were so afraid of tax inspections and customs. In the case of such check-ups, not only could traders end up paying huge fines, but the holding back of goods for even a few weeks could seriously affect their incomes for a long time.

More unexpected changes might occur as well. Commodities might become 'old' in a few weeks, new customs officials might be employed who declined to take bribes, or new and cheaper trade-routes might give other traders huge benefits. Traders needed constantly to know and evaluate the changing conditions of the market. The important point here is that there was no single way of obtaining knowledge about such factors—it had to be elicited from various sources. Many traders found it difficult to talk about commodities and how to evaluate them because the subject was too complex. Instead, they would 'read the market' by means of close daily contact, watching neighbours, and a process of trial and error. As one trader told me: 'If I have been away from the market for three weeks, I don't know it any more.' By following the market closely, successful traders could develop an intuitive feeling for its mechanisms, which enabled them to judge what to buy as well as how and when to go abroad. An important way of 'reading the market' was, not surprisingly, by watching other people's goods. Goods provided strong indications of traders' social situation and position in the market, but also signalled a certain style. This in turn formed an important indicator for customers in terms of reliability and level of 'professionalism'.

COMBINING COMMODITIES

Most traders had given a great deal of thought to the kind of goods they wanted to sell. Although it might not be immediately apparent to an outsider, there were no accidental combinations of goods in the market. Wares were evaluated in terms of saleability, but also with regard to one's total combination and style of goods, including appearance on the car, in the tent, or on the table. Irena, who allowed me to trade with her for a few weeks, sold selected goods from Poland (Łódź). She had sportswear for children, sweaters for men, woollen trousers for women, and a few suits (skirt and blouse) for overweight women. But a woman's blouse, which she had intended for her daughter but later decided to sell, was hung at a neighbour's place because, as Irena said: 'She sells blouses and I sell sportswear.' Similarly, her other neighbour, who in late autumn would switch from sweaters to winter coats, would start leaving the 'Puma' training trousers behind when she went to the market, because she found they no longer went with her personal style of goods. It was regarded as unsuitable to combine what were regarded as different styles of goods. Apart from 'styles' such as 'sportswear' or more 'fashionable styled clothes', some traders would specialize in other ways, for example in children's clothing, toys, perfumes, or make-up. These forms of specialization were more visible, although considerable variations were still possible.[7] Finally, some of the more

---

[7] For example, I noticed that one trader, who was selling perfumes and hair spray, also had a product for cleaning ovens. The basis for specialization here seemed to be that all these products were in spray-cans.

experienced traders had built up a circle of customers who would buy from them regularly. This made a certain degree of specialization and continuity necessary, because it takes time to build up relationships with customers. As traders grew more experienced they would often tend to singularize their imports and specialize in one item only. Buying large amounts would make the purchase price per item cheaper, which in turn would make it easier to build up a clientele to whom one could offer lower prices. Older traders (an experienced trader would often be referred to as *liutas*, a lion) would almost always trade in one product only, such as computer games, music tapes, videos, bags, small backpacks, ties, amber, umbrellas, jeans, leather jackets, or knickers for women. Generally, but not always, turnover and profits of the single-item traders were higher than for multiple-item traders.

Apart from all this, the 'style' of trading was characterized by a widespread tendency to trade in unlicensed or fake Western goods. This did not seem to worry traders to any great extent. However, it conveyed important information about 'the local practice trading model'.

ASIAN GOODS WITH AN AMERICAN ACCENT

Unlicensed goods or fake 'Westernized' goods were a widespread phenomenon in the market. It included falsification of brand names such as 'Levis', 'Adidas', and 'Colgate', and also the import and sale of unlicensed copies of computer games and music tapes. Finally, many of the imported clothes as well as the local production had 'Made in Italy' or 'Made in Germany' labels sewn in them. Since most of these goods were produced abroad, such falsification cannot be understood as an entirely local phenomenon. However, as local producers also used Western labels in their clothing, there was apparently a local demand for Western-style products in Lithuania. It was even possible to buy a wide range of 'Western' labels at a stand in Gariūnai market, even though the labels themselves were imported from Istanbul.

Most traders at the market would sell at least some 'duplicates' or 'Western copies', yet I found almost no indication that traders were embarrassed about such unlicensed sales. Only Algis E., whose story I told in Chapter 3, seemed a bit embarrassed about the unlicensed computer equipment he was selling. He stated firmly, however, that what he was doing was not criminal, because Lithuania had not signed the 'Convention of Computer Games'. When I was doing participant observation in the market, I also attempted to buy Western labels to sew in the clothes. As it became evident that I was a foreigner, the man flatly refused to sell me the roll of 'Made in Italy' labels I asked for. To get rid of me he threw some samples at me and told me to leave. Although he may just have been tired of foreigners using his commodities as souvenirs, I suggest that his action also indicated a certain uneasiness about the whole business. Generally, when I asked traders whom I did not know personally, they would omit to reveal the Asian origin of the Western-style goods.[8] Such knowledge may be termed a 'public secret' in the market, yet by asking I gave myself away as an outsider and thus as somebody not entitled to know. Later, I found out that none of the customers were fooled by the labels and that such labels were generally considered unimportant by both customers and traders. This was indicated by the following statement:

If someone wants to buy real Reebok or Adidas shoes, he won't go to the Gariūnai market. People who buy Reebok shoes in the Gariūnai market know that they are not Reebok, and for them it doesn't matter whether it says Reebok or Raabok or Ruubok. It makes no difference to the seller nor to the buyer. They don't think about these things. For them it is not a reason . . . If somebody finds a new article and it is labelled 'Reebok', and he thinks it will be a good article to sell, he will buy a batch and sell them, but not because of the name. It doesn't mean anything. I don't know why factories in Poland and in China copy these names, because everybody knows that they are not true. I really don't know why those manufactures have these names sewn in. Of course it's not a good thing, it's a bad thing, but . . . (Vytalij 14.1)

The falsifications as well as attitudes towards them therefore convey no simple message. Nevertheless, some interesting information concerning traders' attitudes towards free-market features such as copyright and property rights were clearly revealed.

Traders often suggested that there was no real distinction between their copied product and the 'Western equivalent', or that their product was of an even better quality. Several traders also legitimized the copies in other ways:

First it is necessary to ask what you mean by the term original. For example Adidas shoes are produced in Korea and sold in America, so are they original or not? All these companies like Nike and Puma manufacture goods in Korea and other Far Eastern countries because labour is cheaper there. Sometimes when I buy something that says 'Made in Japan', I think I'm buying the original article, but there are a lot of pirates, producing very similar products. Sometimes they are very difficult to distinguish from the originals. Even the Japanese don't always distinguish between them. (Mikhail 5.1)

In this case Mikhail is clearly connotating 'original' with 'Western'. What is at stake is not so much the protection of a brand name but the fact that this product (in his view) is supposed to be produced in America, because its originality derives from its Western place of origin. Thus, in Mikhail's view, the manufacturer of Adidas products is already violating his own copyright by producing them somewhere else. The prestige of a given product derives not so much from its specific brand name as from its 'Westernness'. The high status enjoyed by Western clothes was apparently already prevalent in Soviet times. According to the Soviet dissident and sociologist Vladimir Shlapentokh, the West and Western items were not only very popular in the Soviet Union during the 1980s but were also copied by Soviet factories and sold as imported goods:

---

[8] Later, when I got to know some of the traders better, they would laugh at my stupidity if I was fooled by the 'French' origin of a perfume or the 'German' origin of dresses.

The devotion to Western attire is so great that Soviet factories have begun to produce shirts, blouses and sweaters bearing various Western commercial logos printed in England, such as Marlboro, Mercedes Benz, or Levi-Strauss. The manufacturers attempt to pass them off as Western products. Given the ideological climate in the country in the 1980s this action by factory directors is truly remarkable. (Shlapentokh 1989: 151)

Although this is the only source I know of that mentions the fact that Soviet factories produced Western-style clothes, I have heard traders who were involved in the underground production of clothes talk about sewing in 'fake labels of origin'. Rasa, whose story I discussed in Chapter 3, is an example. I suggest that the quality of such goods was evaluated not on a basis of their specific brand names or 'functional quality', but more in terms of their ability to communicate a certain Western style. Seen in this light the discussion of originality versus falsification turns out to be simply unimportant. Another trader in the Gariūnai, Oleg, who was in fact himself producing clothes, went even further towards a 'deconstruction' of the term 'original':

I make skirts and I sell them in the market. It's a form of industrial espionage. I go and see the foreign [Western] goods and then I buy the labels and make the same articles. It is a good business. A skirt from Germany costs $50, and I can sell the same for around $15 and still make a profit. I have given it some thought and I don't think our goods are fake, because even in the case of what are usually called 'original articles', it is only the first one that is really original—all the rest are just copies too. (Oleg 6.1)

Thus for Oleg the whole idea of a 'copy' versus an 'original' made little sense, and although there were others who worried more about copies and fakes, this was not considered an important problem either inside or outside the market. Traders would never bring up the theme themselves, not because of any sense of taboo, I believe, but rather because the subject was regarded as trivial. It should be noted, however, that most traders were well aware that this practice was considered illegal in the West and this created some uneasiness when discussing the matter with me.

By far the most common defence of such falsifications was '. . . but everybody knows!'—the inference being that nobody was cheated by the labels, since it was common knowledge that if you bought something in the market it was obviously not a 'real' Western product. Thus by using the expression, 'but everybody knows', traders not only in a sense defended unlicensed copies, but also conveyed what they considered the potential trouble involved. The parameter of evaluation was not along the lines of any possible violation of international copyright laws, but rather a matter of cheating or misinforming buyers. Thus, instead of discussing the legality of the act of falsification the dilemma was transferred into the sphere of morality. Furthermore, there was no indication that the Western falsifications contributed to a trader's position in any way, negatively or positively: socially, they were absolutely neutral. Finally, it is interesting to note that of all the criticism I heard about the market in terms of its being criminal, black, and generally uncivilized, no mention was ever made of unlicensed merchandise. Not only was

Westernization of products considered a normal strategy, but the distinction between 'duplicate' and 'fake' was not an issue worth much concern.

On the other hand the widespread use of US dollars most certainly was. Usually prices were shown as well as calculated in dollars, and several traders said that dollars represented 'the currency of Gariūnai'. However, as the litas was tied to the dollar at the time (1 dollar = 4 litai), there was no problem in using first the one currency then the other, both being accepted. Often, though not always, if one asked for the price in Lithuanian, one was told the price in litai, and if one asked in Russian, one would be given the price in dollars, the reason for this obviously being that foreign customers usually carried dollars. On the other hand, except for cars, where the price was given only in dollars, there was no special preference for dollars, although in the early phase of the market, before the litas was tied to the dollar, dollars prevailed. Although dollars were still regarded as 'Gariūnai currency', it was generally acknowledged that this was one of the things that distinguished the market from surrounding society, and the association of Gariūnai with dollars was one of the factors contributing to the market's stigmatization. The use of dollars in the market signals a 'wrong' form of Westernization, as it tends to be connected with Sovietism and underground economy rather than with a modern Western national state.

PRACTICAL KNOWLEDGE AND PUBLIC RULES

As I have demonstrated, several interesting features have appeared that contribute to a practice model of market trading. Although the market was conceptualized as spatially disorganized, there was actually a more subtle logic in the way traders were distributed throughout the market as well as in how commodities were combined and presented.

Regarding social stratification, there were clearly and widely shared principles of separation and differentiation among traders that were based on country of supply, vehicle, position in the market, and kinds as well as amounts of merchandise. Traders constantly evaluated each other socially and economically in order to glean information about various changes in the market. As such practices remained hidden from the outsider, such knowledge was for insiders only. But even among insiders, some were more inside than others. A central part of the constant struggle in the market therefore centred around access to various layers of information that might benefit one's position.

Konstantinov, in a study of trader tourism in Bulgaria (1996), terms this style of trade 'theatrical', because traders constantly assume different roles (especially alternating between tourist and trader, when they were crossing the borders). Such a 'theatrical quality' seemed to be part of Gariūnai trading as well, not only because Lithuanian traders would also cross the border as tourists, but also because traders in the market had to manoeuvre constantly between various versions of reality. I suggest, however, contrary to Konstantinov, that such theatrical qualities cannot be understood as 'fake' or untrue. This seems rather to be a continuous strategy dating back to Soviet society, when ritualized performances were a part of 'being' in a strongly ideologized society. The apparent conflict between 'front stage' and 'back stage' performances here is therefore only apparent, since it indicates different contextualizations of the same thing. This became specifically obvious when discussing the prevalence of counterfeit goods and the general tendency to Westernize goods. What I would have termed falsification of Western brand names was conceived here as unimportant. Nobody knew why it was done, yet there appeared to be no other way to style this type of goods. As mentioned above, this is not only a Lithuanian phenomenon, as these articles are produced for the international market, yet the way that such labelling had become linked to various consumer goods suggests that such styling is being built on 'traditions' from the underground economy in Soviet society. The main reason for this Westernization was therefore, I suggest, the fact that prestige and good quality were still largely associated with the West. In other words, traders as well as buyers operated with a different set of oppositions from the Western idea of 'original' versus 'copy' and licenced versus unlicensed products. A genuine article was understood here more in terms of its quality and this was apparently emphasized by its Western style. Opposed to genuine articles, I suggest, were the bad quality products of Soviet or Chinese origin. Although most traders were well aware of the illegal aspects of their trade in this respect, the general attitude towards Westernization was coloured by local interpretations of such market concepts.

Because Gariūnai in many ways can be understood as a market-in-the-making, the specific character of 'bazaar-style information search' forms a key to an understanding of the market as an institution as well as of market culture, although in a different manner from that mentioned at the beginning of this chapter. In many ways Gariūnai differs from the typical bazaar as it has been described by Geertz (1963, 1979) and Alexander (1992). The main difference seems to be that although the Gariūnai market is not formally standardized and trading is not formally co-ordinated or institutionalized, it appears rather more structured and less *ad hoc* than is the case with the ideal bazaar. But this does not mean that the bazaar as an analytical framework may not be useful. Geertz (1963) suggested that one of the most important differences between the bazaar economy and what he called firm-type economy is the fact that in the former case the locus of competition is between seller and buyer, whereas in the firm-type or Western consumer market it is between sellers. In the bazaar, traders appear to have a somewhat fatalistic attitude towards the market, where one is not considered to have any influence on where a certain buyer decides to buy. The difference means, according to Geertz, that in the bazaar traders do not attempt to attract more traders, but merely see their sale as a matter of chance (ibid. 35). This passive attitude was prevalent in the Gariūnai market as well. But in contrast to Geertz's Indonesian bazaar, buyers in Gariūnai were by no means ignorant of prices and quality in the market, and even though bargaining did take place it was mainly as a sort of ritual, getting a reduction of one or two litai, because in practice most prices were fixed. Although there were of course buyers who were cheated, it was difficult, especially at the time of 'stagnation' in 1995, for traders to raise prices much, because of fierce competition. Since buyers could generally choose where they bought—for several traders sold similar goods—lack of information and prices was not a large problem for customers. It was the seller who, by acquiring additional knowledge about countries, commodities, and transportation, might be more successful in the market by introducing new goods, or by lowering the expenses of 'import'. The notion of an 'information gap', suggested by Geertz and Appadurai, may be understood here more as a problem for sellers, who needed constantly to be up to date about rapidly changing goods, countries of supply, and trade routes. The discontinuous flow of information therefore first and foremost resulted in an increasing social differentiation among sellers. Pushing this argument a bit further one may argue that there was in fact very fierce competition between traders, but it took place in the realm of knowledge and information and thus remained hidden rather than appearing in the form of visible competition on prices and quality.

Another area where a bazaar-style framework is illuminating is by looking at morality and trust. When legal and standardized procedures are lacking, the argument runs, traders tend to get involved in long-lasting relationships based on mutual trust in order to minimize risks (cf. Alexander 1992). Gariūnai traders did not, as a rule, give credit to customers. When credit was given it was for small amounts and only for a short period at a time, thus the accumulative credits or debits that Geertz mentions were by no means prevalent in Gariūnai. However, invoking a strong moral codex took place in other ways. I found that there was a tendency to transfer legal dilemmas into the sphere of morality, as mentioned above in connection with the 'falsification' of commodities and in dealing with the widespread copying of other people's techniques and commodities. The situation characterized by the lack of formal rules and sometimes by breaking the law was being coped with and controlled by evaluating action according to moral terms. However, here too a certain theatrical quality seemed to be important as there were wide discrepancies between the explicit demand for moral conduct and actual practices in the market.

Finally, I want to emphasize that perhaps the most important feature of the market was the status of being rapidly changing and thus 'in the making'. In several ways, trading practices as well as the market place itself were becoming more standardized and thus one would imagine the market becoming less and less like a bazaar. However, it seems that although new social structures were definitely in the process of formation, the market did not seem to be developing into an officially controlled and publicly regulated market place. This was mainly because of the continuous 'underground' power structures in the market, chiefly (but not only) the racketeers. Furthermore, such emerging structures were by no means stable, since the market was characterized by quite a violent struggle for control of market territory by the competing actors, mainly bands of racketeers.

5

New Forms of Discipline

The uneven flow of information and knowledge cannot be understood without including an analysis of the power structures in the market. Especially because the formal leadership was weak, an opening had arisen for an alternative form of order, and the market was in reality being controlled by various 'informal' agents, mainly bands of racketeers. These partly hidden agents of power and their internal competition may be viewed as influencing the flow of knowledge and information in two ways. First, since their activities often had consequences for the development of the market, knowing about their plans, decisions, and general conduct there was important in order to predict what was going to happen and then act accordingly. Second, they had influenced the market by their way of disciplining (or scaring) traders into a certain pattern of conduct and thus, as we shall see, induced a certain communicative style. In this way the 'field of power' had important consequences for the general atmosphere in the market, and for what I shall call the 'market culture' (although most informants would deny the existence of any 'culture' at all).

Generally the development of the market can be viewed as a process of reterritorialization—a struggle for control over new social and economic fields. The establishment and development of Gariūnai as a new place and institution may therefore be seen to reflect, and to be an integrated part of, the reorganization of the social hierarchy in society. In this way Gariūnai itself may be regarded as a very visible example of the reorganization of space involved in 'the transition'.

But it is no easy task to write about the power struggle and competition of the various 'rulers' of the market. Such activities are always partly hidden, and although racketeers did appear in the market I obtained most of my information about them from stories told by traders. The criminal and semi-legal groups involved were often referred to as 'the Mafia'. Since the discourse on 'the Mafia', both in Lithuania and elsewhere in Eastern Europe, is complex and ambivalent, it is generally difficult to know precisely what people actually mean. I discovered that the term was used in three different senses. First, to denote the existence of racketeers as a social phenomenon of some importance both inside and outside the market; second, to cover the (not necessarily illegal) personal groups based on private networks that were generally believed to influence important areas of the economy outside the market; and lastly, the term was often used by traders and outsiders alike to connote a sort of 'conspiracy' behind all the technicalities and partially hidden mechanisms of market economy (see also Verdery 1996: 219). It is thus important to emphasize that in Lithuania the meaning of the term 'Mafia' oscillates continuously between factual social forms and a rather vague metaphor for 'hidden forces of violence and control', and that it never unambiguously refers to one specific phenomenon.

POWER CONTESTATION AND CHANGING FORMS OF CONTROL

As already mentioned, the formal leadership of the market was weak, and moreover divided between two competing companies: Posūkis, who owned the Old Market, and Jurgena, who had opened the New Market in 1995 (*Respublika* 1995).[1] The difference between the two markets was often 'metaphorized' by traders calling the Old Market 'the State market' and the New Market 'the private market'. There was some truth in this, as Seniūnija (the Vilnius local authorities) owned a part of Posūkis. I attempted to interview the managers of the two markets, but these interviews shed little light even on the parties involved in the formal leadership of the two markets. Although the manager of the Old Market explained that the Seniunija owned 31 per cent of the shares in Posūkis, he avoided revealing who the other owners were.[2]

If ownership on the surface seemed unclear, in practice the power structure was even more complex, variable, and violently contested,[3] because the official management exercised little control over the organization of the market. The allocation of trading places in the market is significant since the various ways of 'getting a place' not only reveal the various groups controlling the market, but also reflect the growing institutionalization of market practice, the consolidation of a certain power structure, and changing strategies of discipline and control. In order to get a place, it was necessary to deal with racketeers.

The experienced market trader Vytenis, whom I met first in 1994 and then again in 1995, described the illegal power structure in Gariūnai as follows:

The situation at Gariūnai is tense but not just because of the relationships between traders. Thieves are the reason. They steal from cars and from customers' bags. Even if you see something happening you can't warn anybody, because the thieves are so well organized you will find yourself in trouble—they may well follow you to your home and steal from your house. At Gariūnai there are legal thieves and legal racketeers. (Vytenis 3.0)

---

[1] See Appendix (no. 34).

[2] In a television programme (*Nesutinku*) shown on Lithuanian TV in April 1995 a team of journalists tried to investigate the management behind Posūkis, but they too had to give up trying to find out who they were. Three journalists from *Respublika* tried to do the same with Jurgena in 1995, and although to them the name suggested a combination of the names of the late manager of the Old Market, Jurgaitiene, and Genas, a former head of a section of the Vilnius police (Gariūnai!) they had no way of proving the truth of their analysis (see Appendix, no. 34)

[3] As mentioned in Chapter 1, the previous manager of the Old Market was murdered outside her house in the spring of 1995. The murderer was never found.

During a later interview Vytenis explained to me that to his knowledge thieves and racketeers were connected under the same Mafia groups, and he elaborated in further detail about the various racketeering groups:

There are different groups of racketeers, and they demand a lot of money. I know 'the Boas', 'the Sportsmen', 'the Blacks', 'the Grey-haired', 'the Greens', and 'the Elephants'. (I pay 'the Blacks'.) These are not all the groups, but as many as I know. It is a hierarchy. In Gariūnai there are only the lowest levels, but the bosses get their share. They have a system: those who get caught by the police are bought out later. If somebody gets jailed, the bosses pay for their families. When they come out of jail they are given a holiday in the United Arab Emirates. We just know, but we can't tell anyone. (Vytenis 3.1)

During the first few years, trading places in the market were (officially) free. Traders would pay an entrance fee (5–15 litai per day—depending on the form of trade), but it was not possible to buy a particular place, for example in the centre.[4] In reality, various groups of bandits had divided the market between themselves, for the lack of formal control had resulted in a vacuum in which various groups would compete for influence and shares of the profits. Stasė (whose trading history is discussed in Chapter 3) gave me an example of her own start as trader in the market:

They would say, 'Who are you paying?' and I would say, 'Nobody.' And they said: 'The system in Gariūnai is like this, everybody is supposed to pay $3 per day and $10 per week.' They explained the whole system and said: 'Everybody is supposed to pay and you too.' And I said: 'I don't know whether I will come the whole week.' Then they said: 'Then you must pay [three dollars] for today, and remember that you pay Marquivars and next time, if some-body asks you, then you say that you pay Marquivars.' Another day they would come again and ask: 'Who are you paying?' and later they would recognize me. Also other groups, like the Sportininkai, would come and ask me, and I would say that I paid the Marquivars.

All the names are Russian, because all these racketeer groups are Russian. There are Sportsmenai, Marquivare, Sedyje (they are the only ones left now). It means 'the men with grey hair', but it is a Russian name . . . Malishi, Čiornai (Blacks), Udavai (Boa Constrictors). (Stasė 13.1)

Using various names seemed to be the method by which the racketeers made themselves visible to the traders as distinct groups, but it also shows that at that time the territory of the market was not clearly divided between them. Stasė would pay the Marquivars, but the vendor next to her might pay another group. Many traders told me that the racketeers were mainly Russians.[5] I have not been able to verify this, nor do I have any good explanation why that should be the case. It should be noted, however, that 'Russians' in this context may sometimes also include, for example, Ukrainians and other post-Soviet nationalities. (For a more

---

[4] A good place is usually one in the centre of the market. Places near the main entrances are highly valued because so many people pass through them.

[5] I was told that most of them were locals, thus not Russian Russians. There may be foreign groups involved as well.

thorough discussion of the meaning of ethnic and national terms, see Chapter 6.) In general such 'Russian' gangs were regarded as having 'colonized' much of the Soviet and Eastern European territory and during my trip to Poland with the bus my Lithuanian informant told me that many of the bandits in Poland, like in Gariūnai, were Ukrainians and Russians.[6]

When I came back in 1995 the whole system of allocation of places had changed, partly it seems as a result of the emergence of the New Market and partly (according to an article in the newspaper *Lietuvos Rytas*, 1995)[7] because one of the gangs had managed to gain control of the whole of the Old Market. Vytalij, who was still trading in the outskirts of the Old Market in 1995, gave the following account of events:

We entered the market and found a vacant place (1992). And we stayed in this place and it became our place. Then some 'crazy boys' came and asked: 'Is it your place?', and we said: 'Yes.' 'Then you have to pay money for this place.' We paid some. Then the new Gariūnai market was opened and a lot of empty places appeared in the Old Market and we moved to this place, which is now our place. First we stayed in *Karakumai* (literally 'desert', because traders stand on the sand). Later the administration reorganized the market and made numbered rows, and they had to give us a *žetonas* (card with name and place number). The administration were supposed to give them to us, without our having to pay. But instead they gave them to these 'crazy boys' and now they are offering to buy this card for about 1,000 litai. Some people bought one and they now have places in the first and second rows. Not many people in the third row bought this *žetonas* and we of course didn't buy one. They might come and tell us to get out, because the place is sold. (Vytalij 14.1)

In this way the system changed. Traders still paid nothing to the official owners of the market (except $5 each day at the entrance) but actually paid protection money to the same racketeers. Yet the introduction of the 'card' suggests a shift towards a legalization of payment to the racketeers and a growing institutionalization of practices of control. The money was no longer paid for 'protection' but for 'the place'. Still, since the same groups were demanding the payments, traders saw no improvement. Many in fact felt the shift was a distinctly backward step as they could no longer count on any sort of protection and help in the market against criminals.

It appears that the introduction of the cards failed to make the power structure in the market any clearer either:

---

[6] One trader even mentioned that Russian bandits were going to China in order to 'racket' the traders there. Stories about Russian bandits were numerous in the market. This does not mean, however, that Lithuanians were not involved in organized crime. Although I made no attempt to verify statements about 'the Mafia', I was often told that different towns had their own different Mafia groups. In Vilnius they were called 'Vilniaus Brigada' (the leader everybody knew about, and whose son was executed in 1995 for the murder of a journalist, was a Georgian). In Kaunas I was told that various families had split the town between them and were engaged in a sort of territorial warfare, while Šiauliai was dominated by former 'underground producers'. In addition there were speculations that 'the Russian Mafia' was gaining control all over Lithuania and would in time conquer the 'local groups'.

[7] See Appendix (no. 29).

We knew beforehand that there would be these new rows, and we went to the manager and asked him to reserve two places for us, but the manager said: 'I am not the boss here. The racketeers handle everything.' Then, after the racketeers were pressuring us very much we went back to the manager for the cards. He said he had the numbers in the row which was next to us, but that row was completely empty. It would make no sense to take this, and he had two more places in *Užantis* (a former section of the market), where perfumes are sold. The system with these cards was that the manager of the market owned a share, and then the policemen owned a share in them too, and then the racketeers had the largest share. It so happened that my place's card was in the hands of policemen. And I think that is why racketeers didn't come to me again, because they didn't have my card. But one day another man came and said: 'I have a card for this place and I am going to stay here.' And it was a former policeman—a friend of these policemen—who had my card, and as I didn't have a card, I had to leave the place. (Stasė 13.1)

As is clear from the above statement, the formal manager of the market has no real influence in distributing the cards in the market. Although on the surface he could take part in the distribution of places—for he did have some cards—in reality his cards were useless, as he only controlled the trading places situated on the outskirts of the market, and they were not attractive for traders to buy. Since the Old Market was already decreasing at the time (late 1995), only the very central places in the market, the first and second rows, were of any interest to traders. I suggest, however, that in order to understand how the system works it is significant that he actually did have some cards, as he could then be used as a puppet so that more powerful groups could hide behind him.

Although many traders suggested that the number of different groups of bandits in the Old Market decreased after the New Market was established, the traders were convinced that part of the reason for this was that a group of policemen had entered the scene as a new powerful agent. Although there had been talks before about policemen being bought and bribed to disregard racketeering activities in the market, the emergence of the New Market was explained by the traders as a result of a specific privatization that had taken place within a certain section of the police. Formerly, individual policemen were believed to be accepting bribes to supplement their (meagre) income, whereas later traders suspected that a group of them were actually 'changing sides' completely.

The stories about police influence in the market not only signalled traders' discontent with the police and in general their criticism of State control in the market, but also suggested to me that it was not only the agents of power that were changing, but also the forms of control. Although the cards had in a sense changed the racket into a 'legal' payment (because on the surface traders were simply paying to obtain a certain place), the actual payments became more difficult to trace. In the beginning the places in the New Market would cost $200 to $400, but later, when the market became more popular, prices increased. In the autumn of 1995, traders estimated that a good place in the New Market cost around $2,000! But it was no longer clear who was selling:

The good places cost $2,000. These prices are not fixed by the owners (of the market), because all the places have already been bought. If you want to buy one now you have to go directly to the people and buy from the people who have bought the right to a place. Nobody announces publicly that he or she wants to sell the place, but you have to ask people, and somehow the word will spread. And it is like a Russian saying: 'Tongue-wagging will lead you to the key.' (Mikhail 5.1)

Nobody knew who was selling the places. People could only speculate as to which powerful groups might be controlling the New Market. Furthermore, even though part of the former system of protection rackets had been transformed into a payment for the places, many traders were in reality still pressured into paying for protection as well. The amount of protection money varied according to the position of the place, but all stable traders in the New Market and in the centre of the Old Market paid at least $75 a month (in 1995):

The New Market is organized in this way. Everybody says you only have to pay an entrance fee, but here we also have to pay for the place. $400, $500, $800, up to $1000 to get the place and $75 per month to the racketeers. Now we have to pay two months in advance and even though I know I shall not be trading in October I still have to pay. It was better with racketeers in the Old Market. They would offer some protection and at least you knew who you were dealing with . . . and they would help to find thieves. (Andrei 17.1)

What Andrei complained about is that the power structure had become invisible. Instead of the racketeers, another trader would collect the payment, and, as in the case of buying a place, the traders would no longer know to whom they were paying. This not only changed the atmosphere in the market—I shall return to this—but it also broadened 'the information gap', and promoted speculation as to the identity of the rulers of the New Market. Since at least one former person connected with the police was involved in the New Market (I actually met him in the office of the manager of the New Market), and, furthermore, the traffic in front of the whole of Gariūnai had been completely changed in favour of the New Market, traders were quick to conclude that the police had more than a coincidental interest in the New Market (cf. Chapter 2).

THE DOUBLE AGENT—THE POLICE

I can tell you straight that the police at Gariūnai can be bought. But on the other hand these policemen only get paid 300–400 litai a month, and all these racketeers and thieves have their pockets filled with money. If they are caught they are sent to court or to the prosecutor, and both are very weak here. They too can be bought, added to which the policemen are rather afraid of racketeers—also because they might catch one, but others are at large and they might well take their revenge on him. (Vytenis 3.2)

One day, at the very beginning of my period of observation in the market (participation came much later), I watched three policemen who were moving slowly along the lines of traders in the New Market, apparently asking to be shown some sort of permit. At the time I had no idea what they were doing—only later was I informed that they were checking traders' licences. In 1995 these were obligatory for all traders.[8] The policemen started their control at about 9 o'clock in the morning and as they were only three of them they progressed slowly along the lines, giving traders plenty of time to react. As a result, traders simply started packing up their wares and around 9.30 more than two-thirds of them had gone, leaving the market looking rather empty with the rest of the traders scattered around in small groups (most likely the ones who were left were those who had actually bought a licence).

The way this check was carried out by the policemen seemed odd and raised several important questions. First, what did the three policemen hope to gain by walking slowly along the lines, checking less than ten traders in about one hour, and letting two-thirds of the traders get away? It was obviously not their intention to catch as many traders without licences as possible. The slow almost 'ritual act of control' performed by the three policemen seemed more than anything to work as a kind of warning to the majority of traders, although of course a small number of them were actually fined. Their approach seemed at most to have some preventive effect, yet all traders were back at their places again the next morning (and I think very few of them will have hurried into Vilnius to buy a licence). The second odd thing about the control process was the uniqueness of the event. Why, if the police were indeed trying to make traders buy licences, did it only happen on this one occasion during my almost four whole months in the market?[9] The third curious thing in this connection is that there were always policemen on patrol in the market. What did they do, since they were obviously not checking traders on any regular basis? I have no straight answers to these questions, and I have not inter-viewed any policemen, mostly because I was afraid traders would regard me as a spy if I did, for most traders were very hostile towards them. Still, I have some suggestions that might shed more light on policemen's roles and activities in the market as well as on how they were perceived.

A group of seven policemen were permanently based at a small local police station in the market (*Respublika*, 1995).[10] So there were always police somewhere in the market. They would walk around in small groups, sometimes greet traders, and occasionally argue with one of them, but they usually appeared not to interfere with the activities in the market. This group of 'market police' was generally

---

[8] There were several ways to trade legally in the market. The most common was to buy a trading licence for 700 litai for half a year. Many traders were discontented with the system, either because they wanted to buy a licence for a brief period only, or because they found that the price was unfair as all traders, regardless of their incomes, had to pay the same. I have no statistical information about this, but it was my impression that less than half of the traders had actually bought a licence. Especially among the poorer traders, it was uncommon and considered a 'waste of money' to buy a licence.

[9] I must mention, however, that I did see policemen check traders more often, but these were singular instances apparently triggered by some conflict or discrepancy connected with normal routines. Only on this one occasion did I observe systematic police control of a large part of the market.

[10] See Appendix (no. 34).

considered as having been 'bought' by traders. This does not mean that they were on their side, but simply that they were under the influence of some of the dominant groups or persons. This point of view was supported by the above-mentioned article in the newspaper *Respublika*. According to journalists, not all policemen could get a job in Gariūnai and the policemen operating in the market were close friends or family. There was a rumour that one had to know one of the founders of the New Market, a former, high-ranking police officer. This supported the view that there was a lot of black money to earn by working in the market. The policemen who were on patrol in the market every day furthermore seemed to be quite passive, and I was not the only one to wonder what they were really doing there:

Do you know that our toilets have become more expensive now? When you are standing in the cold sometimes you have to go very often and then people don't want to pay 1 litas, so they just go to the bushes somewhere outside. Now the police have started looking for people who go into the bushes, and if they find them they are made to pay a fine of 100 litai. The joke nowadays is that this is why this market needs police. They don't catch the racketeers, they don't catch the thieves and they don't control the business operations. All they do is extract money from people who go to pee somewhere outside the market! (Teresa 16.1)

Traders were never sure how to deal with these local policemen, because they could always shift between two different roles: their 'public role' as the executive power and their 'private role', in which they could disregard formal rules and, for example, accept bribes. Both roles were problematic for traders, yet they conflicted with traders' interests in different ways, and they required different actions. The 'public' set of rules demands that traders pay taxes, buy licences, etc., while the 'private' rules are less demanding, yet unpredictable. When policemen were acting according to the 'private' set of rules they would usually be more passive, for example by not catching racketeers, not seeing a robbery, and not controlling traders. Since traders had to adapt their strategies according to the shifting set of rules applied by the policemen in the market, they had to develop skills in 'reading' the 'staging' of policemen's shifting roles. What I suggest is that usually traders could ignore policemen, since they would not seriously attempt to impede trade, but on special occasions they might be forced to react 'as policemen' and 'go by the rules' and then all 'illegal' traders had to leave the scene. What is interesting about the above example, however, is the double-act it entails. The policemen are really checking traders, thus 'going public', yet they perform in such a way that they simultaneously signal to traders what they are going to do. They only 'stage' their public role, but in doing so they actually emphasize their dissociation from it.

In addition to the 'local market-police', groups of policemen would arrive from Vilnius in order to check the market. These policemen, I was told, would usually arrive in larger groups. Their activities differed. They could be looking for thieves or racketeers, or controlling licences, but they would be more likely to 'go by the book', although the ambivalence between 'public' and 'private' social roles was always a part of any encounter with official persons and many traders told me that all policemen could be bribed. In the opinion of many traders the 'town-police' never caught any of the main criminals in the market either, because they would always be warned in advance when the police were planning a razzia. I did not witness any police raids during the four months I spent in the market.

DISCIPLINING THE COMMUNITY—'LEARNING WHAT TO SEE'

The market was characterized by a remarkable lack of any visible social structure. Formal or even semi-formal forms of social organization were completely absent, and although social networks constituted an important asset in gaining access to resources such as information, gate-keeping, or simply money, such personal networks were highly atomized, and actually often quite small. Neighbours generally formed an important source of gossip and therefore provided some form of information, but the only reliable and long-lasting relations were the close friendships created outside the market. Social groupings in the market were formed on an *ad hoc* basis and were of a totally different nature.

The lack of structure and solidarity among traders must be understood in relation to the (changing) power structure in the market, although the competition no doubt also formed a part of the 'not too friendly' atmosphere. Furthermore, the boundary between 'insiders' and 'outsiders' in the market was emphasized surprisingly forcefully considering the lack of mutual solidarity among traders.

Despite the lack of formal rules, relations and communication in the market were characterized by a range of normative rules of behaviour. From these, I suggest that two general interrelated principles of conduct may be deduced. First, one was never supposed to ask direct questions in the market and second, one had to learn what to see, but not to notice. Let me take the second point first:

The saddest thing was that you could see somebody was being robbed, but you're not supposed to see. My neighbour saw that somebody was stealing from me, but he couldn't tell me. Because earlier he (the neighbour) was trading in the centre and somebody was stealing the stuff from his car. And his neighbour shouted to him: 'Watch out, somebody is stealing your stuff!' and then these thieves ran up to her and slashed her eyes and said to her: 'You won't be able to see anything any more.' And everybody was afraid because there were a lot of stories like that about thieves slashing car tyres and things like that, only because you were warning somebody about theft. (Stasé 13.1)

The above statement suggests how fear was instilled in a very crude way to teach traders 'not to notice what they saw'. Especially when the market first started, many traders complained about the lack of solidarity and the loneliness, because traders would never try to help each other in the event of robbery or theft. The story about the woman who had her eyes damaged by a racketeer and the lesson she was taught about 'learning not to notice' may or may not be a true story. (I was told several similar stories, though none as cruel and as clear as this one.) True or not, as a narrative, the story emphasizes the importance of pretending not to notice, thus knowing when to notice and see and when just to see. When racketeers came along the lines in the market collecting payments, all other traders would look away. The same principle of non-observation seemed to dominate traders' mutual relations and nobody would openly stare at somebody else in the market, though they would engage in small-talk and inspect each others' wares. Although the market had already become 'more civilized' when I arrived in 1994 and methods of control had become more sophisticated, the message was still the same. Traders would openly watch goods, customers, and cars, but generally refrain from seeing racketeers, policemen, and, in some ways, each other.[11] 'Teaching people what to see' had not only become an effective strategy of control—it had also become an integrated part of the cultural knowledge one needed to trade or in fact be accepted in the market.

As mentioned earlier, this 'market behaviour' made research difficult, as observation and asking questions were, no matter what the subject, a breach of rules of social behaviour. Asking questions or 'staring' marked a person as an outsider, and thus provoked a hostile reaction from traders. Traders were suspicious of outsiders especially because they were very aware of the social stigmatization of Gariūnai. Seeing that market conduct was to a large degree based on illegal or semi-legal activities, and a knowledge of these as 'public secrets' was shared inside the market, an outsider was simply not entitled to any knowledge at all about the market. Only another trader could be trusted in the sense of accepting 'the rules of the game'. Furthermore, the insider/outsider boundary became accentuated in various ways, generally every time somebody's 'lack of knowledge' was revealed. All knowledge in the market was in this sense 'insider's knowledge' (insiders being mainly traders, but also regular customers). Being an insider and being knowledgeable came to be the same thing. But practical knowledge, for example knowledge about goods and countries, taxes, police, and racketeers, was, as described in the previous chapter, unevenly distributed among traders and in no way shared. What was shared, however, could be termed a certain 'meta-knowledge'. Here we may invoke the first 'general rule of conduct', that of not asking direct questions. What was shared among 'insiders' was how to deal with knowledge and how to acquire additional knowledge without breaking the rules of not asking direct questions. In this way the boundary between insiders and outsiders was signalled, not only by the level of 'practical ignorance', but even more by one's 'knowledge management'.[12]

---

[11] For example, I was often surprised how openly traders counted their money in the market. I believe this was one of the numerous situations where staring would be considered 'out of place'.

[12] It followed from this that traders in general knew very little about each other. Only close friends, people whose relations originated outside the market, would know about each other's families, living conditions, etc. Neighbours could be standing next to each other for years without even knowing the other's (former) profession!

COMMUNICATING IN HALF–WORDS

Although traders are not supposed to ask questions and not supposed to see, the rapidly changing market, its lack of formal rules and open decision-making bodies paradoxically help in creating a 'quest for information and knowledge'. Traders not only need knowledge about goods, taxes, and new routes of business but also information about changes in the market. This became especially clear when the New Market was established. Traders who had access to reliable information about the removal of the bus station and the particularly 'good connections' of the ownership of the New Market managed to make the decision to move to the New Market at an early stage, when trading places were still relatively cheap. Those who did not and who believed in rumours about another bus station being built next to the Old Market, missed the opportunity of moving while there was still time, and ended up stuck in the Old Market. It was therefore not surprising that traders often stressed the importance of 'being able to communicate' in order to be a successful trader in the market. To be able to communicate was not only important between traders, but also so as to make customers feel comfortable. But because of the fragmented social structure and the above-mentioned 'rules of conduct', communication in the market was not easily accessible and traders needed special talents to obtain the necessary information. One definitely needs to know not only what to say, but also about what—and when—to keep quiet. Communication at Gariūnai can be characterized as what Boym (1994) has called communicating in 'half-words': 'What is shared is silence, tone of voice, nuance of intonation.' She adds: 'This peculiar form of communication with "half-words" is a mark of belonging to an imagined community that exists on the margin of the official public sphere' (Boym 1994: 1).

Boym uses the expression to cover the form of communication that took place between intellectuals in Russia during Sovietism, and the context here is of course rather different. Yet I suggest that both the 'silence' and the 'halfness' that it connotes adequately capture the 'style' of communication in the market. This form of communication may not have been very different from other contexts in Lithuania both in Soviet times and later—it was definitely essential when trading in Gariūnai and perhaps may even be seen as the most distinct feature of 'Sovietism' in the market.

But although the Gariūnai market appeared to be a community controlled and structured by certain hegemonic discourses as well as by certain very real and very powerful agents, the forms of control were, as mentioned above, changing. However, as a part of this process of contestation and change, traders played a role too, and were not only passively 'getting disciplined'.

CHALLENGING THE HEGEMONY: TRADERS' TACTICS

Many traders would begin their descriptions of the market by telling me about the racketeers. They would complain about the situation and about the lack of State control and justice in the market. It was therefore a surprise for me that several traders would often, during the second or third interview outside the market, casually tell me that actually they were not paying racketeers 'at the moment' (though most of them had been doing so earlier). I suggest that the reason why traders always introduced the market and their own situation as being dominated by racketeers was that paying racketeers had become part of the discourse about the market. 'We all pay racketeers' had become a self-evident truth, although there were areas in the outskirts of the market where traders in increasing numbers had refused to pay. Still, in traders' minds they were still paying, although 'at the moment' they were not.

Interestingly, I only heard stories about refusal to pay from women traders and (perhaps not so surprisingly) from the poorer ones, who had little to lose but much to gain by refusing to pay. But dealing with racketeers was still regarded as a dangerous game to be handled delicately:

Six tall guys came up to me and sat on my car (they even sat on top of the bras) and asked: 'Have you paid for your place?' I said: 'No'. They asked me: 'Why not?' I went to the manager and asked for my card but he didn't give me one. He didn't have any cards. Then one of them took a card from his pocket, showed it to me and said I had to buy it. And I said: 'No, I don't want to buy it because I am already paying $5 entrance fee—hundred per month and I won't pay anything to you.' Then they said: 'You won't trade here any more. You have to stay out of the market.' But it was just a threat. I am not very brave but I just got angry and I pushed them away and said: 'Now I have to drink my tea.' I put down my Thermos and started to drink in front of them and they just waited a little while and then went away. (Teresa 16.1)

As I have already mentioned, when racketeers came along, all traders would normally look away, except the person whom the racketeers had started talking to. In this way racketeers control traders' conduct by establishing rules about when and where to look. It is therefore worth noting that when Teresa attempts to challenge their power, she not only states that she does not want to pay, but moreover, by starting another act—drinking tea—refuses to accept the rules of conduct. The act of drinking tea not only ends the conversation, emphasizing that she will not make a deal with them, but Teresa also breaks the rules of conduct by applying 'the rule of not noticing' and ignoring their presence. Furthermore, the act of drinking tea in itself is disarming, since it is so trivial. It would have been difficult for the racketeers to react violently while she was drinking her tea. In this way she limits their possible reaction. I suggest that Teresa's act can be interpreted as a 'tactic' as described by de Certeau in his book *The Practice of Everyday Life* (1988), where he attempts to illuminate and specify the processes of manipulation with dominant discourses through various kinds of 'practice'. His distinction between 'strategy' and 'tactic' is useful, since 'strategy' is a rational act with a specific purpose, and therefore—as I understand him—in reality closely related to the discourse that it attempts to modify. 'Tactic' on the other hand is more subtle, less structured, always individual and often inherent as a synthesis or specific combination of various elements of action. Thus the tactical character of a given act will often, as de Certeau expresses it, indicate 'the act and manner in which the opportunity is seized' (de Certeau 1988: p. xix). What I am suggesting in this case is that the way Teresa refuses to pay is just as important as the actual refusal. The act of drinking tea simultaneously questions the power structure and rules of discipline in the market while at the same time disarming the whole situation by its triviality. I would also suggest that social practices in the market are often tactical in character, and that this has several important consequences for the role of market traders as a transformational force both in and outside the market.

CONCLUSION: MAKING POWER ANONYMOUS

The various forms of behaviour in the market can only be understood if they are related to the changing power structure in the market, so I have also discussed the changing practices, not only among 'the powerful' but also among 'the powerless'. These changing forms of discipline and practices in the market suggested a shift from physical and visible action to more anonymous forms of control—a development from a 'scared community' to a 'disciplined community'—because traders were becoming less scared, yet the rules of conduct were still generally being adhered to. The changing technologies of control can be visualized by the difference between the Old Market and the New Market. The State market has become poor, feminine, 'Lithuanian', and dying, the private is rich, masculine, 'Russian', and thriving. In the Old Market, where I was doing most of my participant observation, racketeers would still walk around and collect protection money. In the New Market, power had become invisible and thus more difficult to challenge. In the Old Market the manager agreed to be interviewed even though I had omitted to use a 'gate-keeper', whereas in the New Market, the manager refused, although I had been introduced to him by one of his employees. In the Old Market, the manager told me his name and gave me his telephone number. In the New Market there was no identification of the power or its source.

6

Ethnic Relations and Trans-Ethnic Discourses

> Gariūnai? I haven't ever been there and I don't want to go there, because it is *bardakas*! (Quoted from *Nesutinku*, Lithuanian television programme, April 1995)

Although criminals in the form of racketeers and thieves formed an important axis around which the negative images of the market were formed, this does not explain the social stigmatization of the market. Not only crime but the whole Gariūnai market was presented as dirty, uncivilized, and 'out of order' and the market in general was considered a chaotic place associated with immoral or anti-social behaviour. Therefore, although association of the market with crime and violence obviously did influence opinions, the feelings of moral ambiguity that were so dominant in public discourse on Gariūnai may also be related to much less spectacular social domains, where they even, viewed in a longer time perspective, may have more transformational potential, not only socially but also on the symbolic 'order'. The concept of *bardakas* was frequently used to describe 'the problem' about the Gariūnai market both by people inside it, and in public discourses as in the above example from Lithuanian television.[1] The term *bardakas* means 'completely without order'. In addition it connotes normative 'disorder', and thus may refer to a *particularly morally contaminated place.*

This local image of Gariūnai as a place outside the normal cultural order can be illuminated by looking at three social domains dominated by normative confusion and moral ambiguity. An analysis of such forms of ambiguity and the ways that people attempt to deal with them may shed important light on processes of cultural reproduction and thus contribute to a more precise picture of the cultural processes involved in 'the transition'. An analysis of the marginalization of the market therefore not only involves a synchronic analysis of structural relations between the market and various social fields in society but will in addition point towards what I term a transformational potential of the normative and symbolic 'order'.

---

[1] Although the social stigmatization was most apparent outside the market, for example in the media or in political discussions, an image of anomie or 'normative disorder' was also prevalent among traders in the market and most of them were quite negative when they spoke about the market.

These three domains are ethnicity, gender, and work. I have selected these three domains because each of them enlightens different aspects of 'the normative disorder'. The domain of ethnicity and specifically ethnic minorities is closely related to the political discourse of the emerging Lithuanian nation, and ethnic minorities is a theme highly debated in public discourse as well as in Western (especially anthropological) discourses on the transition. Within the national Lithuanian discourse, Gariūnai was often referred to as 'the ethnic market', thus positioning it as a non-Lithuanian social space. The prevalence of the Russian language in the market as well as the association of the market with Polish traders was often used to emphasize the point. However, an analysis of the various ways ethnicity is conceptualized in the market (and especially of inter-ethnic relations) suggests a more complicated set of practices—some of them specific to the market, others shedding light on inter-ethnic practices in society at large.

Women's activities in the market and their roles as traders form another area of moral ambiguity, although this was less of a public issue than 'ethnicity'. On the one hand, increased mobility of women as traders highlighted their economic capabilities, but on the other the femininization of the market and the association of women with the 'roughness' of market trading was considered highly problematic and contributed to the image of women traders and market practice in general as being 'uncivilized'. As Verdery (1996) has convincingly argued, since gender and nationality were closely linked in socialist societies, changes in gender-specific practice as well as changing contexts, for example changes in women's economic activities from private to public spheres, may eventually transform cognitive categories of 'gender' as well as more general ideas of 'family' and 'nation'.

Finally, the development of 'trading' as a more formal and more 'public' activity can be viewed as a breach of existing categories of 'work'. This not only leads to a stigmatization of individual traders as well as unemployed persons (or both categories), but may also in the long run contribute to the creation of new cognitive categories, especially of 'work', and also have consequences for other categories, for example 'solidarity' and 'community'. By viewing the Gariūnai market as an example of a new economic institution we may follow such a social pressure on the cognitive categories and on the idea of cultural order.

LITHUANIAN, ETHNIC, AND TRANS-ETHNIC IDENTITIES

Vilnius has been a cosmopolitan city for centuries. Until the second half of the twentieth century, Lithuanians[2] formed only a small minority in the largely Jewish, Polish, and Russian city (Milosz 1975: 351–2). There are several reasons for the relatively small proportion of the titular population in Vilnius, all of them related to Lithuanian history and especially to the history of Vilnius. There are also significant occupational differences between the various ethnic groups, because, in

---

[2] In the sense of people who speak Lithuanian.

contrast to the Polish and Jewish city dwellers, Lithuanians have mainly been peasants until the last half of the twentieth century. After the Second World War, the German occupation, the Holocaust, and the subsequent Soviet occupation of Vilnius altered the composition of the population dramatically (ibid., see also Lieven 1993: 139–58 and Misiunas and Taagepera 1993). Although the 'ethnic agglomerate' of Vilnius became increasingly complex during the Soviet period as a result of well-educated immigrants from Russia, inter-ethnic relationships in Vilnius are still to a large extent marked by the historically close relationship between Poland and Lithuania. This has been noted by Czesław Milosz (1975), who contends that the changing relationship between the two groups in this century and the fierce competition between local Lithuanians and local Poles has made the two groups each other's most significant 'other'.[3] In 1989, Lithuanians formed 51 per cent of the population of Vilnius followed by Russians (20 per cent) and Poles (18 per cent).[4] Compared with other large cities in Lithuania such as Kaunas and Klaipeda, Vilnius still has the lowest proportion of ethnic Lithuanians. A recent investigation indicates that in 1993 the proportion of ethnic Lithuanians in Vilnius had increased by 10 per cent, which would indicate a fairly rapid 'Lithuanization' of the capital after independence (Kasparaviciene 1996).

In order to understand inter-ethnic relations both in Lithuania and in the Gariūnai market, it should be borne in mind that the educational standard reached by the Polish community in Vilnius is considerably lower than that of both Lithuanians and Russians (Kobeckaite *et al.* 1992: 23). Recent Russian immigrants (those who immigrated after the Second World War) have generally settled in cities and have a higher education level than both the Lithuanians and especially the Poles. However, since these Russians were mainly working in the large industries or in administrative posts during the Soviet period (and few learned to speak Lithuanian) Lithuanian independence has resulted in a high level of unemployment in this group of Russian immigrants. For the Poles, Lithuanian independence (especially the present predominance of Lithuanian over Russian) has had similar consequences, as many Poles went to Russian rather than Lithuanian schools and thus also find it difficult to make themselves understood in Lithuanian.

CONCEPTUALIZING ETHNICITY

Present-day inter-ethnic relations in the area have been influenced by Vilnius's multi-ethnic history, especially its relationship with Poland and also, of course, by Soviet ideas of nationality. Before reverting to Gariūnai, I shall give a brief

---

[3] Ethnic relationships in the Vilnius region as well as more generally in Lithuania are still greatly influenced by Poland and therefore differ considerably from conditions in other Baltic countries with large Russian minorities.

[4] In 1989 'other' ethnic groups, mainly Belorussians, Ukrainians, and Jews accounted for an additional 11 per cent of the population (Kobeckaite *et al.* 1992).

summary of what I regard as the most important 'local traditions' of 'ethnicity' or 'nationality'.[5]

Czesław Milosz (1975), in the above-mentioned article 'Vilnius, Lithuania: An Ethnic Agglomerate', shows how multi-ethnicity, locality, and the relationship between the Lithuanian peasantry and the Polish or Polonized upper classes led to a specific conceptualization of national difference, especially in Vilnius, based on a strong sense of locality. The statement 'I am a Lithuanian' would mean 'I am from here' and thus if made by an 'ethnic Pole' would not contradict his Polish ethnicity, but be meant in contrast to 'being from there' (Poland). As we shall see later, this locality-linked understanding of ethnicity is also one of the ways of conceptualizing ethnic differences in Gariūnai.[6]

The Soviet official policy was known as 'national in form and socialist in content' (cf. Fedoseyev *et al.* 1977: 13 ff.). Nationality was an important social and administrative marker, and in spite of the ideology of socialism and internationalism within Marxist-Leninist ideology, it never lost its classificatory power. Soviet passports included an (obligatory) classification according to nationality. But nationality was not only of administrative and official importance. The recognition of national boundaries was significant in many social interactions ranging from intimate relationships such as marriages and friendships to more remote interactions in the workplace and in public places (Karklins 1986). Officially, the question of a citizen's nationality in the Soviet Union was fixed according to the parents' nationality, and was furthermore unchangeable. The result was that the official classification would serve to uphold rigid ethnic boundaries for generations, even though in practice the basis of national and ethnic distinction was much more flexible and mixed marriages were common (Zaslavsky 1982: 91–129). This not only means that 'national' categories were not as rigid as they may have appeared officially, but also that individuals in practice could (and did) negotiate nationality in several ways. First, for the children of mixed marriages in the Soviet Union (around 15 per cent! See Karklins 1986) nationality was always a personal choice between the nationalities of their parents. Second, changes in nationality were not

---

[5] In Soviet society 'nationality' was generally used instead of 'ethnicity' or 'ethnic minority', and the term 'ethnic groups' was reserved for 'primitive tribes' with no national homeland (Fedoseyev *et al.* 1977: 44 ff.). I shall use the terms 'national' and 'ethnic' about the various groups contributing to the multi-ethnicity of both Vilnius and the market. The term 'national' is used in the Soviet sense of the word, indicating the official classification of all Soviet citizens, as it is still used in some contexts. I use the term 'ethnicity' to cover the flexible and strategically negotiated aspect of cultural identity as well as the recent formations of ethnic minorities in Lithuania.

[6] Lieven (1993) gives a generalized version of this locality principle from the interwar period by quoting an exchange between a German frontier guard and a Baltic (German-speaking) woman refugee on the quay at Rostock in 1919 as being emblematic of the experience of all the Baltic peoples:

'What nationality please?'
'I'm a Balt.'
'Now look, gnädige Frau, you can't be a Balt. There is no such nationality. You have to be either German or Russian.'
'But I'm a Balt! A Balt!' (Lieven 1993: 137)

rare in practice (Belorussians and Ukrainians, in particular, might 'change' over to Russian nationality, although it seldom happened the other way round). Third, cultural classifications would often cross-cut the official categories, since more general classifications of 'Balts', 'Slavs', 'Europeans', or 'Asians' would be common and in addition some 'nationalities' would connote more than one—for example, 'Russians' would often include Belorussians and Ukrainians if living outside their native republics (Karklins 1986: 22–47).[7]

Although officially Soviet citizens could only have one nationality, in practice the basis of ethnic difference was ambiguous and situational. The importance as well as the acknowledgement of 'ethnic signifiers' differed interrepublically, though there were also some consistent features. In some places it may have been impolite to ask questions about nationality (for example, Moscow, Leningrad, and other big cities) and yet the categorization of others in terms of nationality was generally a significant basis of social orientation in Soviet everyday life (ibid. 29). On the basis of a complicated, but to me convincing analysis of Soviet and American survey data, Karklins suggests that *language* formed the single most important classificatory principle when people had to estimate each other's nationality. Interestingly, she contends that the classification of others by language is 'cited most frequently for the Baltic Republics' (ibid. 27). She suggests three subcategories of 'language': speaking Russian, speaking Russian with an accent, and not speaking Russian. The latter includes two subdivisions, since there is a difference between not knowing Russian and making a political point out of not speaking Russian.[8]

All in all, 'nationality', both as an official category and as negotiated practice, was an important form of social classification in Soviet society. In particular, the use (or non-use) of Russian seem to have carried important political messages. Although the official and administrative practice was based on a single, unchangeable nationality, the same as one's parents, in practice these 'national' boundaries could be crossed. Yet the official national classification policy maintained formal national boundaries. This seems to have hampered the integration of 'minorities' in various republics, and worked against the idea of Sovietism as the supreme national identity. These 'segregative' consequences of the Soviet national policy seem to have had particularly important consequences in all three Baltic states.

---

[7] According to the manager of the Russian Cultural Centre it was difficult to estimate the number of Russians in Vilnius because of the number of Ukrainians and Belorussians (who would have Ukrainian or Belorussian passports) but who would 'feel themselves as Russian'. He furthermore suggested that the local Russians could be divided into eight different groups according to various migratory waves. Only the latest group would feel more Soviet than Russian (Russian Cultural Centre, Vilnius, 1994).

[8] Karklins mentions Estonia as an example of a republic where people would often refuse to speak Russian.

ETHNIC COMPOSITION OF TRADERS IN GARIŪNAI

There are no statistical figures available about traders in the market, but since I included a question on native language[9] in the small survey of 137 traders that I myself made in 1995, I shall use this as an indication of ethnic diversity in the market. I want to emphasize, however, that since the survey is not representative of the market (for reasons discussed in Chapter 1), it may only give an idea of the ethnic heterogeneity.

There are several interesting characteristics when examining the ethnic 'geography' of Gariūnai. First, it suggests that ethnic Lithuanians form a much smaller proportion of traders in the market than in Vilnius as a whole. This tendency seems to be particularly strong in the New Market, which is generally associated with higher incomes than the Old Market. Since it was also more difficult and expensive to get a place in the New Market, it seems that many Lithuanians have not acquired the necessary capital to move from the Old Market to the New Market. According to one informant, the reason for this is that Lithuanians started to trade later than most local Russians and local Poles:[10]

This kind of trade started in Poland, and local Poles had contacts there, so when the market started, there were more Poles. Also, the fact that Lithuanians are better educated meant that they were usually occupying high positions in society whereas there were more workers among Poles (and Russians). Also during the Soviet period, speculators tended to be local non-Lithuanians, and Lithuanians were slower in accepting that trade is not speculation. (Vytenis 3.3)

TABLE 6.1 *Ethnic differences in Gariūnai based on native language*

	Lithuanian	Polish	Russian	Mixed*	Other	Total**
New Market	15	13	31	1	2	62
Old Market	27	17	21	4	1	70
Total	42	30	52	5	3	132

Notes
* For example: Ukrainian and Russian, Russian and Polish and Lithuanian, or Polish and Russian.
** 5 of the 137 traders did not answer the question.

[9] There were several reasons why the question was formulated in this way. Most importantly, if I had asked about nationality, a majority would have said 'Lithuanian', since most 'minority-group members' in Lithuania hold Lithuanian passports. A direct question about an informant's ethnic identity would, I felt, be regarded as provocative under the circumstances, since people deliberately downplay ethnic distinctions in the market. To ask about mother tongue would both be neutral and would give an indication of ethnic diversity. I am aware, however, that because of this, the group of 'Russians' may be larger than if I had simply asked about ethnic background, since many local Poles regard Russian as their mother tongue. Furthermore, since my questionnaires were only administered in Lithuanian and Russian, some traders with a Polish background may have been further prompted to opt for Russian rather than Polish.
[10] Henceforth, when referring to Poles and Russians living in Lithuania, I shall use the term 'local Poles' or 'local Russians'.

Here Vytenis is making a clear distinction between Lithuanians and local Russians and Poles. In his view, ethnicity makes a difference for structural reasons (contacts with Poland and level of education), as well as historical reasons (trading experiences in Soviet society). He also distinguishes on a more normative level by suggesting that differences exist in attitudes towards trading and speculation. The early influence of Polish traders is confirmed by most informants, and so is the explanation that Lithuanians started later than Poles and that they do not as yet have 'trading in their blood'. The difference between Russians and Lithuanians is less frequently commented on and appears to be more difficult to explain, although many of the local Russians I talked to indicated that they had been fired from Soviet military factories or had previously worked in administration or education. The large number of local Russians in the market is surprising, since the market is generally associated with Poles (from Lithuania as well as from Poland). It should be noted, however, that the high number of Russians may, as mentioned, be connected with the way the question was phrased in the survey. The number of local Russians may include people of Polish origin as well as some Belorussian and Ukrainian traders who may have got used to classifying themselves as Russians. Finally, I find it significant to emphasize the group of traders who could not point to one specific native language. Although in the survey this was only a small number (5), the question in several cases aroused some frustration, since many traders were bi- or trilingual. This, I suggest, may be related to a more general feature of what I term 'trans-ethnicity' in the market. By 'trans-ethnicity' I want to emphasize patterns of boundary-crossing and the practice of transcending the somewhat rigid and static concepts of 'nationality' and 'ethnicity' that originate from the Soviet classification of its citizens. Such trans-ethnic practice may be viewed as both individual strategies of combining multi-ethnic resources and as a social feature, since the distinction between the various national or ethnic groups became blurred in the market. Since the market, through its creation, had in a sense transferred private practice to a public space, such boundary-remaking or boundary-crossing became especially visible there. Furthermore, this 'trans-ethnicity' or creolization (Hannerz 1987) seems to have triggered much of the stigmatization and atmosphere of *bardakas* or disorder reflected in prevailing images of the market. An image of 'the ethnic market' may therefore not only be understood literally as referring to the many non-Lithuanians in the market but in addition as connotating national and ethnic 'trespassing' and, as we shall see later, a partial collapse of the very principles of 'constructing national differences'. Yet it would be an over-simplification to suggest that all distinctions were blurred in the market, or that trans-ethnicity could simply be understood as a process of creolization (cf. Hannerz 1987). I suggest instead that several ethnic discourses were present in the market, and furthermore that national trespassing was not only a transitional phenomenon but can be related to past discourses of local identities as well as more global processes, disrupting national boundaries (cf. Appadurai 1991). Below, I shall use 'multiple discourses', much in the same way as Barth, as coexisting, positioned, contextual, and as having different social origins (Barth 1989).

ETHNIC DISCOURSES IN THE MARKET

Ethnic boundaries were a delicate matter in the market. First, as with other personal matters, people did not ask about each other's national background, although traders usually knew about other traders' nationalities (or at least thought they did). But the fact that people did not talk too loudly about national differences does not mean that such distinctions were not significant, for nationality and ethnicity established the basis of distinction in various ways. I found four different though more or less coherent ethnic discourses in the market, as shown in Figure 6.1. These four fundamentally different ways of conceptualizing ethnic differences were used in a complementary way by individual traders in the market. I shall give some examples of their use below.

1. Locality: recognizing territoriality

One of the first things that struck me about the market was its lack of spatial organization along ethnic lines. I suggest that this disregard of ethnic boundaries was not only strategic but also could be found in the way traders talked about differences in the market where they would often use a terminology of 'territorial belonging'. In such contexts, ethnicity was not an important basis for social distinction.

Within this discourse of 'locality', I suggest two different ways of speaking about 'the people living inside the Lithuanian nation'. First, some traders (mainly local Poles and local Russians) would simply not use the term 'Lithuanians' but would call themselves 'locals'. Second, the term 'Lithuanian', when used, especially by ethnic Lithuanians, would refer to 'those living inside the Lithuanian territory' and thus disregard the internal diversity and emphasize common territoriality instead. In both cases, several different ethnic groups were included in the category of 'locals'. The following excerpt from an interview with Teresa, a local Russian, may illustrate how 'locality' was used in this way (my italics):

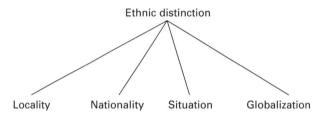

FIGURE 6.1. Principles of ethnic distinction in the market

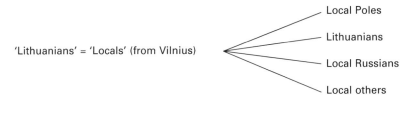

'Lithuanians' = 'Locals' (from Vilnius)
- Local Poles
- Lithuanians
- Local Russians
- Local others

FIGURE 6.2. A semantic model of 'locality'

P. Do you think that *pastogė* (part of the Old Market) has more *Lithuanian* customers?
T. *Local people*, usually.
P. Is it right that *Lithuanian* customers are more choosy and that they always look for the cheapest goods in the market?
T. *Local people* who would look for cheap things are usually traders themselves . . .

Throughout the interview, Teresa never used the word 'Lithuanian', but always 'local people'. For her, the meaning is the same, and although she probably finds her own expression more precise, she was not, I think, very conscious of my continual use of the term 'Lithuanian'. Ethnic Lithuanians used the word 'locals' too, although, I believe, not as often as Russians and Poles. Instead they would sometimes use the word Lithuanian in the same 'localized' sense. In the following excerpt from an interview, I attempted to ask Jonas, a young ethnic Lithuanian, about possible ethnic 'niches' in the market, but because I used the wrong terminology, I failed to make myself understood:

P. At the place outside the market where they sell fabrics, is it only Poles who trade there?
A. Poles are only in the textiles and jeans business.
P. So Poles do have their own businesses in the market?
A. Yes.
P. Have Russians also specialized in certain products?
A. I don't understand . . .

Although the whole interview had been conducted in English, with my Lithuanian interpreter silently present, the informant asked for a translation of the question about Russians, and then the interpreter asked me: 'Are you talking about local Russians?'

P. Yes, I am speaking about local Russians.
A. We have citizens of Lithuania . . . not Russians . . . no problem?
P. When you talked about Polish people before you meant . . .
A. From Poland, not Lithuanian Poles!

What I had in mind when asking the question was whether any division of labour occurred between the local ethnic groups. Such a question, however, failed to make any sense to Jonas, because I used the wrong terms. When I asked about Poles and Russians in the market, I meant to refer to them as ethnic minorities in Lithuania.

This was, however, not what Jonas understood by my question. For him a Pole was someone from Poland, and a Russian, someone living in Russia. The reason why the misunderstanding was cleared up at all was because of my question (totally incomprehensible to my informant) about the possible specialization of Russians in the Gariūnai market. As Russians from Russia never appeared as sellers, but only as customers, the idea of a possible Russian niche in the market made no sense to him. However, since a small number of Poles still crossed the border from Poland in order to trade in the market, Jonas was thinking of them when discussing 'Polish business' in the market.

This way of 'thinking about ethnicity' in the market not only emphasizes the close relation between 'ethnicity' and 'locality', but at the same time makes the notion of 'nationality' inclusive rather than exclusive, for the statement 'being a Lithuanian' simply means 'anyone from here' (much in the sense pointed out by Milosz (1975) above.)[11] But although this points towards a sort of 'neutralization' of 'national' distinctions, the discourse of locality was not the only 'ethnic discourse' in the market.

2. Nationality

I found that 'nationality' was used in two distinct—although interconnected—senses in the market. First, as being from another country, as used by Jonas above, and therefore used about Poles from Poland and Russians from Russia. Second, it also covered 'Lithuanian' Poles and Russians, but only in certain contexts. For example, later in the same interview Jonas was shown a picture from the market of some middle-aged women selling sunflower seeds, and I asked him to explain what he knew about their business.

They are selling seeds. It is a business you know. Different people live in Lithuania—Poles, Russians, and Lithuanians—and Polish and Russian people like to chew these sunflower seeds. We chew chewing-gum like the Americans, Russian people chew these seeds. (Jonas 2.1)

Jonas thus distinguished between the various national groups (although such distinctions were usually not very important to him in the market). Another example of the use of the 'national' discourse was in the above-mentioned explanation of normative differences between Lithuanian and other traders: 'Lithuanians do not have trading in their blood' (Vytenis, above). Although definitely recognizing such differences, and often using them as explanations of differences, traders would usually disregard them if directly asked about them, as Jonas did in the earlier interview ('We are citizens of Lithuania . . . not Russians . . . no problem!').

---

[11] Since most traders were from the Vilnius area, the notion of locality may be most prevalent within this region. According to Milosz, however, this conceptualization of national difference as being based on locality can be connected to the historical close connection with Poland and Poles. The specific conceptualization of ethnic differences presented here may therefore be found in other Lithuanian regions as well.

Of course the refusal to talk directly about ethnic differences might suggest that relations are strained in the market, but this was hardly the case. I did not witness any arguments in the market based on national differences. The only point where ethnicity was seen as a problem was when talking about racketeers, because racketeers were always called 'Russians'. Even though this could have influenced opinions about Russians in general, traders made a clear distinction between 'Russian racketeers' and other Russians, and although, as I have discussed in Chapter 5, racketeers were considered a serious problem in the market, the ethnicity of racketeers was not singled out as a matter for concern.

I suggest, therefore, that ethnicity in the sense of former Soviet 'nationality' did indeed function as a structuring principle in the market, and as an explanation of behaviour, but that national differences were unimportant. People would acknowledge national differences (and refer to them), but they did not form an important basis for social organization, although the atomized social structure and the small fragmented networks were mainly restricted (though definitely not always) to people of the same 'nationality'. National difference were of some importance, however—for example, the most important social relationships, those that had their origin outside the market, often consisted of people with the same ethnic background. But there were also friendships between people with different ethnic backgrounds, especially between local Poles and local Russians.

3. Situation

A more important way to distinguish between social and ethnic groups in the market seemed to be by following a group's position and activities. As in the example I discussed above in the section on 'locality', activities may intersect the 'national categories'. Such differences were further closely connected to people's position in the market, i.e. Russian Russians were buyers and local Russians were vendors. Much along the same lines, I found that the term 'Russians', when used in the market, would also include Ukrainians as well as other customers from CIS countries. Following this situational ethnic discourse, Jonas's confusion above, when asked about Russians as traders and about their position in the market, is easier to understand, as traders used the term 'Russians' to indicate a certain category of (rich) customers. Mikhail, a local Pole trading in the market, shared this definition of 'Russians', as the following excerpt from an interview shows:

P. I have heard here that Lithuanians [the more correct expression 'local people' had still not dawned on me at this point] sometimes refer to Russians, Ukrainians, and Belorussians as Russians?

M. Oh no. In Gariūnai there is a big difference between them. The best buyers, the ones who would buy big amounts and wholesale, they were from Russia. We would never group Belorussians together with Russians.

P. What about Ukrainians?

M. Well, they used to be good customers too . . .

Ukrainians—but not Belorussians—could belong to the category of 'Russians' in the market. Although, as mentioned above, Belorussians might be termed 'Russians' in other contexts, Belorussians did not belong to the category of rich wholesale buyers, and were mostly known in the market as small traders. What I suggest therefore is that, in the market, distinctions were also structured along the lines of trading activities in the market, and that the designation 'Russians' was different when used inside the market compared with outside it.

Finally, the conceptualizations of 'ethnicity' in the market were confronted with other national discourses on 'Sovietism'.

4. *Globalization*

In general, traders were often travelling outside the national borders and when doing so they also took part in and were part of other people's cultural constructions of 'Lithuanian', 'Russian', and 'Soviet'. The physical crossing of national borders has several implications. First, concerning traders' relationships with the national administration, since they were in fact smuggling and thus violating the national borders. Second, because the travelling itself confronted traders with new ways of classifying ethnicity. Several traders, non-Lithuanian as well as ethnic Lithuanians, emphasized that one of nicest things about going abroad was, 'in the plane we are all Lithuanians', indicating that this was not always so elsewhere. In addition, when traders left the plane in Istanbul or Dubai, they would all be categorized as 'Russians'. Ethnic Lithuanians thus suddenly also belonged to the category of 'Russians'.

Regarding the first point, the internal solidarity, it seems that the feeling of togetherness, of belonging to the same group of Lithuanians, was even more important in the early years of Gariūnai trading. As Algis E. emphasized when he talked about the first trips (by train) to China in 1990/1991:[12]

the only nice thing was that we were together—the Lithuanian group—we all stuck together. There were no national conflicts. From time to time the racketeers (from Ukraine and Russia) would appear. When the racketeers came everybody would speak Lithuanian and pretend to be Lithuanian. Also, we would feel together . . . like a group . . . not alone. So if one was attacked by the racketeers then a hundred people would get out of the train to defend him. (Algis E. 11.1)

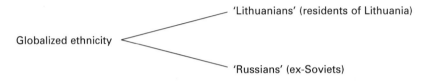

FIGURE 6.3. Ascribed ethnicity abroad

[12] The rest of the story is told in Chapter 3.

What is striking about the above statement is not only the praise of solidarity, which was completely lacking at the market place back in Lithuania, but that the fact of pretending to be Lithuanians suggests that this was really not the case elsewhere. It was only by leaving Lithuania that the category of 'Lithuanians' was firmly established as inclusive of all ethnic groups.[13] Furthermore, the Lithuanian language was used as a tactic to deal with racketeers who did not speak Lithuanian and who could therefore be verbally 'disarmed' by traders' collective use of Lithuanian. Outside Lithuania, all traders in this group constituted themselves as Lithuanians. But when they finally reached Istanbul or Dubai they would check into hotels that were for 'Russians' only, thus being confronted with yet another conceptualization of their inter-ethnic differences—that they belonged to the same group.

There are special hotels for *Russians*—especially for Soviet people. In our hotel there are living only people from the Soviet Union: Russia, Ukraine, Uzbekistan, Lithuania . . . (Jonas 2.1)

The same forms of categorization take place in Poland:

In Poland they usually don't use names . . . but Polish people would usually say, 'Let's go and buy from the *Russians*', because everybody, Lithuanians, Russians . . . everybody from the Soviet Union would be called Russians. (Mikhail 5.1)

Within the global world order, 'Soviet people' still exist as a social and 'national' category after the actual collapse of the Soviet Union. Thus, viewing the constitutionalizing of national and ethnic categories from a global point of view makes inter-ethnic boundaries even more ambiguous, since both a Russian and a Lithuanian citizen in Dubai are categorized as 'Russian', while they see themselves as Lithuanians. The process of travelling from the market, crossing the Lithuanian border, and being placed in Dubai is therefore also a journey or a change of ascribed ethnic and national identity. As Oleg, a local Russian expressed it, 'in the plane to Istanbul, we are all Lithuanians' (Oleg 6.1), while one may add that as soon as they arrive they are all 'Russians'. It may be noted here that the local Russian may find that the only places where he still belongs to the category of 'Russians' may be in Dubai or in Istanbul.

Finally, I would like to emphasize that globalization had interesting consequences for linguistic competence among traders. Not only was Russian an important resource in the market, since one needed to communicate with Russian-speaking buyers, but I also found that the Lithuanian woman that I was accompanying to Łódź in Poland had had to improve her Polish in order to communicate successfully with Polish traders. Similarly, the traders going to Turkey

---

[13] I am not suggesting here that people did not recognize ethnic differences within the group. When I joined a group of traders on a bus trip to Łódź in Poland, most traders were local Poles and the drivers gave most of the information about the trip in Polish. But although the local Poles were in the majority, Lithuanians were in no way isolated or made to feel uncomfortable, and towards the end of the trip they would all help each other filling out forms for customs, etc.

insisted that the only means of communicating with the Turks was in Polish, because the Poles (from Poland) had been there first and thus Turkish traders had learned some Polish.[14] Since both local Russians and Lithuanians from Vilnius had at least some knowledge of Polish, linguistic competence was further developed in this way and added to the atmosphere of trans-ethnicity by further transcending any remaining ethnic or national boundaries.

CONCLUSION: TRANS-ETHNICITY AND SHARED EXPERIENCES IN THE MARKET

In the market as well as more generally in the social space that market traders have created, definitions of 'ethnicity' are ambiguous, open-ended, and changing. Boundary-making takes place at various levels according to the different social contexts and a trader's own position within the social space. Furthermore, the market as an emerging trans-national institution and the international contacts that it entails tends to promote new kinds of ethnic boundaries—although the process of boundary-making is also heavily influenced by Soviet ideas of nationality as well as Lithuanian discourses on locality.

The conceptualization of Gariūnai as 'the ethnic market' therefore signifies a complex set of ethnic discourses, practices, and meanings which are appropriated rather differently by 'outsiders' and 'insiders' in the market. Both, I suggest, are based on a concept of 'trans-ethnicity' which may be found in social practice in the market, but may have been further promoted by what can be termed a collapse of the basic principles of national classification. To term the market 'the ethnic market' thus not only reflects an indication of a non-Lithuanian social space but also—and perhaps more importantly—conveys a feeling of a 'lack of ethnic (and national) boundaries'. This may then be interpreted as a disregard of national differences as opposed to the political discourse of Lithuanian nation-building.

The main feature of this kind of 'creolization' is the use of Russian in the market. The privileged status of Russian can of course in some ways be related to a large proportion of native Russian speakers as well as to the fact that many customers were from Russian-speaking countries, especially since it became clear during the survey that many of the non-Lithuanian traders neither spoke nor understood much Lithuanian.[15] But I suggest that the use of Russian also served as a way of coping with 'ethnic diversity' and confusion by deliberately emphasizing an atmosphere of internal 'togetherness' towards (mainly Lithuanian) outsiders. The Russian language was used as a 'marker' of market boundaries, as for example when traders insisted on translating their Russian conversation into

---

[14] These Polish trade routes to Turkey are also mentioned by Hann 1992.

[15] Out of a total of 137 people, 72 asked for a questionnaire in Russian. Since I always started interviews in Lithuanian, these 72 all had some difficulty in understanding Lithuanian.

Lithuanian to outsiders, even those known to be able to speak Russian.[16] In this way Russian may be used politically by traders in their everyday social exchanges, not only with customers but also with each other. The use of Russian was also one of the main complaints of people outside the market, since it not only contradicts the idea of Lithuanian cultural homogeneity inherent in the developing national discourses, but may thus be viewed—in relation to the political significance of many Lithuanians deliberately *not* speaking Russian during the Soviet period—as a strong anti-Lithuanian signifier.[17] The criticism of the use of Russian in the market, seen in this light, may not only be aimed at 'the ethnic population', but rather at the Lithuanians in the market who are now speaking Russian.

Not only the use of Russian in the market, but also the lack of ethnic spatial organization and the prevalent 'locality' discourse of difference ('we are all locals') in the market have contributed to the creation of a conceptualization of the market as ethnic in the sense of 'trans-ethnic'. The 'ethnic' market cannot therefore be understood literally in the sense of a place dominated by non-Lithuanian 'others', but rather signifies a confusion of ethnic identities and a trespassing of ethnic (and national) boundaries. This confusion may be related to two main 'breaks' with the imagined cultural order, thus *bardakas*. The first may be related to the foundation of the Lithuanian national state, the collapse of national identities on an equal footing, and the establishment of a new form of formal ethnic hierarchy.

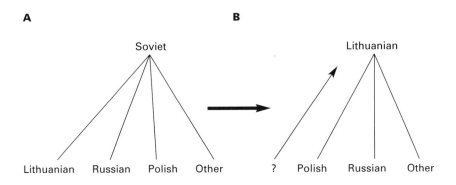

FIGURE 6.4. Changing paradigms of nationality and ethnicity

---

[16] Rūta, a history student from Vilnius University who was helping me with some of the surveys in the market, reported afterwards how traders had insisted on translating their Russian conversation into Lithuanian for her—although she, like most Lithuanians in Vilnius, speaks Russian fluently.

[17] In addition, the language dispute may not only involve a conflict of Lithuanian versus Russian, but may also be connected to 'bad' language, the slang being used in the market, something which both ethnic Lithuanians and local Russians in the market complained about. The language conflict seen in this light may therefore also involve a dispute between bad Russian and correct Lithuanian.

Although, as mentioned above, Soviet categories of nationality were in practice fairly flexible, the formalization of national differences, in passports, by quotas in various political representations, etc. made nationality an important basis for distinction. The stigmatization of the market may therefore be connected with a collapse of the 'national' as a classificatory category for both Lithuanians, local Russians, and local Poles. In Soviet times, and thus according to Soviet classifications, Lithuanian, Polish, and Russian were on an equal footing. Lithuanian independence has resulted not only in the category 'Lithuanian' becoming 'more national', but also in a change of status in relation to Russians and Poles, who have become sub-national ethnic minorities. This symbolic, political, and spatial reorganization promotes new forms of ethnic and national identities, not only for Lithuanians but especially for Russians and Poles, and for persons of mixed descent, who somehow have to cope with the shift in the formation of national relationships. Such a shift cannot be understood only as a substitution of former Soviet with Lithuanian nationhood, because it is the relative positioning of Lithuanians in relation to Poles and Russians that has changed from 'national' (A) to hierarchical (B). In 1995 it was no longer an easy task to talk about national difference, because the classificatory system of distinguishing had collapsed and therefore the meanings of the terms 'national' and 'ethnic' were becoming increasingly blurred. The way of overcoming the problem seems partly to have been solved (at least in Gariūnai) by the term 'locality', which not only connotes a common identity, but also refrains from evoking the categories of 'nationality' and 'ethnicity', which had become highly ambiguous and confusing.[18]

Secondly, and related to this, there has been a change in the status of what we can call 'practised ethnicity'. By this term I refer mainly to the flexible and ambiguous acknowledgement of national differences in Soviet society in practice. This change, which I contend did not only involve Gariūnai, can be viewed as one of the results of the 'formalization' of private practices, which the creation of the Gariūnai market both entails and signifies. The creolization and national trespassing that the Gariūnai trading signified was no longer only a social practice, because as the market itself had become more public, such inter-ethnic flexibility and disruption of formal categories of nationality had required a new and more formal status.

All in all, therefore, the stigmatization of the market as 'ethnic' revealed several related symbolic processes. First, the system of national identification was collapsing as a result of the removal of the Soviet umbrella identity. Second, a new set of formal principles of ethnic organization was emerging in the form of a Lithuanian majority and various local ethnic minorities. Finally, since a reorganization of the public and private domains was taking place as an inevitable consequence of making the market place more informal, private ways of dealing with ethnic differences were being transferred to a (relatively) public social space.

---

[18] In addition the internationalism of Gariūnai may further stigmatize the market by associating it with the Soviet ideology of internationalism.

7

Contested Images of Gender

The Gariūnai market as a non-Lithuanian space may be connected with several antagonistic ethnic discourses inside and outside the market as well as with changes in the principles for constructing national and ethnic differences after Lithuania's independence. However, the 'disorder' of the market can also be examined from another angle: images of gender, gender roles, and gender identities. Although discussions of 'gender' did not form a part of the public discourse of Gariūnai to the same extent as ethnicity and nationality, I believe that confusion about gender roles and blurred gender identities contributes to the general perception of the market as 'uncivilized' and 'out of order'. The reproduction of the marginality of the market can be related to what could be termed a transgression of boundaries between 'femininity' and 'masculinity'.

Such blurred gender roles are not confined to the market, but are most visible there. In consideration of the fact that the very establishment of the Gariūnai market may be viewed as a transfer of private activities to a legal and public place, it also follows that women's economic activities and a gender division in the economy become 'public' in the market. Furthermore, in Gariūnai, this blurring of borderlines between femininity and masculinity is not a recent phenomenon. An examination of gender borderlines in the market reveals that 'the transition' has not yet dramatically altered Soviet gender roles and identities. Rather than altering existing positions, market economy and new Western middle-class discourses on women seem to accentuate them. The disorder that Gariūnai has revealed in the area of gender is therefore to be related rather to the process of revealing conflicting images and practices of gender than to gender positions in the market.

The 'contestation' within the field of gender seems to be rooted in a fundamental tension within the Soviet division of labour. Actual gender roles in Soviet society were both ambivalent and in conflict with public discourses on equality. This involved women's double burden as 'mothers' and 'workers', men's lack of participation in, and responsibility for, the household, and the steady decline of the traditionally male-dominated public sphere in the last decade of Soviet rule.

All this has influenced men's and women's economic competencies differently. In the 'new economy', important areas such as *personal networks*, *former trading experiences*, and *economic responsibilities* therefore all appear to be 'gendered'.

WORKERS AND MOTHERS—THE DOUBLE BURDEN OF SOVIET WOMEN

The dual role or double burden (depending on the viewpoint) of women as both workers and mothers in the Soviet Union is a term frequently used to describe the position of women in Eastern and Central European societies under socialism (cf. Ostrovska 1992, Pilkington 1992a, Einhorn 1993, Toth 1993, Koval 1995):

> Under State socialism, women in Lithuania as well as in Eastern and Central Europe have been defined by policy makers as being child-bearers as well as economic producers. Women's roles as housewives were not questioned. Women were seen as mothers or potential mothers [and thus] as an essential element of the institution of the family . . . At the same time, the dominating State ideology increased emphasis on the role of women as economic producers. Women were encouraged to seek employment outside the domestic sphere . . . Legislation on working conditions for women had two main concerns: protection of women's health, especially of pregnant women and [nursing] mothers, and the improvement of possibilities to combine paid work and motherhood. (Kanopienė and Juozeliūnienė 1996: 224)

In reality, this dual role did not lead to the liberation of women, although Soviet emphasis on women's participation in the labour market resulted in very high employment figures for Lithuanian women.[1] However, despite the Soviet ideal of 'the woman on the tractor', Soviet women were usually engaged in what are generally regarded as more 'feminine' areas of work such as education, health, and culture (Pilkington 1992a). Although women formally occupied a position on the labour market equal to that of men, in reality women's incomes were lower, and they were often employed in administrative posts assisting male leaders rather than being leaders themselves (cf. Einhorn 1993 and Pilkington 1992a). This administrative role assisting male leaders (which is by no means unfamiliar to Western women) was also influencing women's participation in political institutions and decision-making. Although women were represented in political organizations such as the Supreme Soviet (Parliament), they were not involved to the same extent as men, nor did they participate at the highest political levels as representatives of the Politburo or the Central Comity (Pilkington 1992a: 216). It is important to note that the weak position of women at high political levels and women's general lack of interest in (or time for) political activities seem to have resulted in a high degree of masculinization of the nomenklatura networks. As such private connections play an important role today both politically and in connection with setting up a business, women are at a 'structural' disadvantage in this respect within the new economy.

At the same time, women's special responsibilities towards their family, household, and children (and often also towards their husband) were never

---

[1] Kanopienė and Juozeliūnienė state that in 1989, 81 per cent of Lithuanian women compared with 86 per cent of men (of working age) were active in the labour market (1996: 224).

really questioned.[2] Ostrovska (1992) refers to estimates of a Soviet woman's 'working week' totalling 88 hours as compared with a male average of 59 hours. More specifically, she quotes an investigation into the division of labour within Latvian families where 40 per cent of the responding women stated that their husbands never took part in *any* household task! (Although this investigation is based solely on data from Latvia, there is no indication that the situation was so very different in the rest of the Soviet Union.) As a result of the problems within the family during the last years of Sovietism, many women abandoned the traditional family pattern and lived alone with their children. Pilkington, for example, notes that by 1986 the divorce rate was one in three and most divorces were instigated by women (Pilkington 1992a: 213).

Not surprisingly, the result of women's 'double burden' was that they ended up struggling with a heavy workload and a feeling of responsibility for the upbringing of children and for the well-being of their family. These responsibilities furthermore meant that many women were very active within the Soviet underground economy, since this provided them with both an additional income and, during times of shortage, access to scarce resources. As mentioned in Chapter 2, many women currently involved in trade or small businesses in Lithuania today were previously engaged in such activities during the Soviet period. This 'femininization of responsibility', which then included responsibility for fulfilling the family's material needs, seems to have had a tremendous impact also in structuring the changes of gender-roles following 'the transition'. Thus, although according to Soviet ideology (before Gorbachev) women and men were formally equal and moreover held similar positions, this was a distorted image of gender roles in Soviet society. In reality, women's responsibilities have increased in scope within the latter half of the twentieth century. The traditional responsibilities for the family, for its proper conduct in moral and 'cultural' matters, have expanded into a participation in wage-labour, and also into a responsibility for the material well-being of the family, which could not always be ensured by a State-sector salary.[3] This development was especially visible in the last years of the Soviet empire, when Gorbachev publicly criticized women's participation in the labour market. Pilkington's account of the gender situation in the late 1980s illustrates this situation:

The devaluation of the public sphere—the ritualistic and unsatisfying nature of both the political and the economic spheres—has greatly reduced the traditional areas of the development of *masculine* identity. The widespread abuse of alcohol and the dependency on women that this includes has also led to a generally low regard for men among Soviet

---

[2] Although the question of women's emancipation was an important issue in State socialism (cf. Engels 1884, quoted in Pilkington 1992a), this never implied any serious discussion of the division of labour within the family, which continued to be considered the responsibility of women.

[3] In fact both Toth (1993) and Corrin (1992) mention that in Hungary during socialism they found that one of the main problems for women was this expanded feeling of guilt and lack of ability to fulfil the multiplicity of women's roles.

women. This weakening of the male 'role' has not led to more egalitarian relations between women and men but to a conservative retrenchment in which women take on many of the roles previously ascribed to men while espousing a desire to be more 'feminine', and men fail to pull their weight in the family while complaining that their wives are domineering and 'unfeminine'. (Pilkington 1992a: 220)

According to Pilkington, both female and male identities were becoming increasingly problematic in the last years of Soviet rule. There was a growing discrepancy between the official outlook on the dual role of women and women's actual experiences in the workplace, in their families, and as economic providers. Women's activities in the market not only highlight ambiguous gender roles, but the market also seems to have been instrumental in promoting women's economic activities.

THE TRANSITION AND GENDER RELATIONS IN LITHUANIA

In a recent article entitled, 'Gender Roles and Identity' (1996), two Lithuanian researchers, Vida Kanopienė and Irena Juozeliūnienė, make an interesting analysis of the transformation of gender identities in post-Soviet Lithuania. They contend that the 'transition' has altogether worsened the position of women economically, socially, and symbolically. Not only are women to a larger extent than men being pushed out of the restructured labour market, but the political discourse on femininity is also being redefined: 'Indeed, masculinity has increasingly become identified with the public domain, while freedom for women was mostly associated with freedom to "stay at home" and enact a traditional feminine identity' (ibid. 227). Kanopienė and Juozeliūnienė argue that since 1991 women have continuously formed a majority of the unemployed. They are not alone in their conclusion that women are increasingly becoming marginalized in society and being pushed back into their 'proper nutrient roles' (Verdery 1996), while men are, so to speak, recapturing their lost domain of public activities (cf. Einhorn 1993 and Bruno 1995). This 'reprivatization' of women is furthermore emphasized through the prevalent strong anti-socialist ideology, which has become an important post-Communist attitude. On top of this, political neglect of women's problems seems to have been the outcome of the present national 'quest for unity' in Lithuania. Politicians have shown little interest in the different and unfavourable position in society held by women compared with that held by men. But although political discourses on gender (especially on women) may be changing, I believe that the dual role of women has not been fundamentally altered. If anything, their workload has increased. I have found no indication that women's responsibilities to provide for their family have changed significantly. Furthermore, since at present even more money is needed in order to fulfil one's responsibilities as a breadwinner, I would contend that women are probably more economically active than ever.

After independence, significant changes in the labour market have taken place for women as well as for men, the most important being high inflation without higher wages, which has resulted in generally lower standards of living. In addition there has been a tremendous rise in unemployment. Official unemployment figures for Lithuania show that women are much more likely to lose their jobs than men (Kanopienė and Juozeliūnienė 1996, Gruževskis 1995). There are several reasons for this. First, women have traditionally been employed in 'non-productive sectors' such as education, service, culture, and health. The economic reforms have led to a dramatic decrease in salaries in these areas as well as to severe cuts in parts of the labour force. Second, it has proved much more difficult for women to obtain employment in the newly-formed private companies, which tend to prefer male employees. This tendency seems to be prevalent all over the former Soviet Union as well as in Eastern and Central Europe (cf. Einhorn 1993: 134 ff. and Bruno 1995: 75):

The increase in joblessness above all concerns women, who make up 80 per cent of the unemployed.[4] In the majority of cases these are people with higher or specialized education between the ages of thirty and forty-five. Unemployment has led to a sharp fall in living standards. (Koval 1995: 23)

But although women *officially* seem to have been pushed back into the domestic sphere of the family, I disagree with the conclusion reached by Kanopienė and Juozeliūnienė that this indicates a change in the scope of women's *actual* responsibilities. The change had mainly taken place at an ideological level and appeared as part of the anti-socialist reaction and probably also as an attempt to 'imitate' or appropriate Western middle-class models of men as breadwinners. However, the change did not reflect real changes in women's activities and responsibilities. In point of fact, women are as active in providing for their family as they were under the socialist regime. The difference is that now they are increasingly doing so within the (growing) informal economy.

The Lithuanian sociologist Gruževskis (1995) has attempted to estimate both hidden employment and hidden unemployment in Lithuania after independence. He suggests that although officially the rate of unemployment was only 3.4 per cent[5] (about 78,000 persons) in 1994, notably about 640,000 were 'missing' from the official figures. Since employers in Lithuania have to pay a dismissal benefit (between 6 and 36 months' wages), many have chosen not to dismiss their employees, but instead to send them on unpaid vacation. Although such persons are officially registered as employed, they are in reality unemployed, or may be employed elsewhere. The 640,000 figure is an estimate based on the decrease in the number of persons paying social security tax from 1991 until 1993 as well as on estimates of the decrease in production in industries and agricultural output. Gruževskis has supplemented this data by interviews in selected housing areas. These 640,000

---

[4] These figures are general for the Soviet Union.

[5] It has been reported that in Russia women constitute 70 per cent of the unemployed in general but 80 per cent of the unemployed in Moscow (Einhorn 1993: 129). If the same tendency prevails in Lithuania, women's unemployment in Vilnius may be considerably higher than the average for Lithuania as a whole.

people are therefore to be found either as economically active in the grey economy or as actually unemployed. As unemployment benefits are virtually non-existent it may be safe to regard most of them as economically active. The estimates made by Gruževskis furthermore imply that although women form a majority in the official unemployment figures, these explain very little about the 'gendering' of 'real' unemployment. He instead estimates real unemployment to be 13 per cent for women and 15 per cent for men (ibid. 11). An examination of the 'real' unemployment figures thus reveals that women are *less* likely to be unemployed than men! This means that although women have definitely disappeared from their official wage-employment, they are actually still contributing to the household economy, in fact to a slightly larger extent than their husbands.[6] In spite of a general ideological pressure on women (and men) to reorganize their division of labour, only a small number of 'privileged women' have actually stopped working. Instead, women are busier than ever, not only at attempting to cope with the family's financial problems, but also in dealing with 'the gap' between an image of femininity that includes a non-socialist emancipated woman with a husband who provides for the family,[7] and their own real situation, fully engaged in economic activities in the grey zones of the emerging private economy.

THE GARIŪNAI MARKET—GENDERED PRACTICES AND BLURRED BOUNDARIES

Basically, I suggest that gender roles in practice, enacted in the market, contrast with both Soviet and 'modern Lithuanian' discourses on gender, while they may be seen, not surprisingly, as a continuation of practised gender relations in Soviet society as well. However, since discrepancies between official discourse and actual practices were neither specific to the market nor in any way a recent phenomenon, this could not in itself account for the image of Gariūnai as *bardakas*. The difference between Gariūnai and many other areas in society was rather that by appearing in the market the contextualization of such practices had changed. Because the market had appeared as a (semi-) public and legal institution, conduct in it clashed much more openly with the public definition of gender identities and gender roles. I furthermore contend that such discrepancies between official discourses and actual practices on gender, although visible in the market and therefore given more importance by both men and (especially) women, epitomized conditions that were widespread in Lithuanian society. By looking at gendered practices in the market as well as traders' conceptualization of them we may thus form an idea of a more

---

[6] This is supported by data from Kanopienė and Juozeliūnienė (1996), since they too state that women more often than men are engaged in additional money-earning activities, yet they maintain, and here I do not disagree with them, that men's wages are generally higher than women's.

[7] See also an interesting discussion on love and marriage by Maj Olsen, 'Pure Relationships: The Search for Love among Hungarian Academic Women', *Anthropology of East Europe Review*, 14/1 (1996).

general transformation of gender roles in Lithuanian society and of the distur-
bance in, and contestation of, identities that this has entailed.

THE GENDERING OF MARKET TRADE

Although both women and men traded in the market during its early phase, the
early market was generally considered more masculine. For example, the engineer
Algis E., whose trading history I discussed in Chapter 3, stated: 'Sometimes wives
would help, but women could only be at Gariūnai with their husbands' (Algis E.
11.1). Although Rasa, for example, whose business history I also discussed in
Chapter 3, is an example of a woman who traded during the market's early phase,
many shared Jonas's view that in the early days Gariūnai was mostly for men. Even
goods were more masculine then:

In the beginning, when there was only one market, the most important goods were spare
parts for cars, hi-fi equipment and goods from the underground production in Kaunas and
Šiauliai. Today this business has almost ceased to exist. (Jonas 2.1)

Later, when the market grew bigger, a certain spatial diversification took place.
At the same time, the closing of the borders between Lithuania and especially
Russia made some forms of trade, particularly in Asian clothes, less profitable.
What happened instead was an increase in trade with Western second-hand cars
and the creation of a separate car market, which was moreover wholly dominated
by men. The car market, which was only open at weekends, regularly had between
5,000 and 10,000 cars for sale.[8] As more men have entered the car market, more
women have entered the (two) clothes[9] market(s). This enlargement of the market,
which was accompanied by a differentiation in trading incomes, furthermore
resulted in a spatial organization of the market that appeared to be gendered as
well. Figure 7.1 shows how the market had changed in terms of both gender and
prosperity. As profits decreased, men either left the market or moved upwards
within the internal structure, while women in increasing numbers filled the vacant
(marginal) positions in clothes.

Although the atmosphere in the clothes markets was distinctly feminine, I
found, much to my surprise, a majority of male traders in the survey I made in the
market of 137 traders. The male majority was furthermore larger in the New
Market than it was in the Old Market. My findings, however, may have been
biased since I only interviewed traders who were selling their wares from cars,
thus those engaged in the higher levels of trading. Because men usually occupied
better places in the market and had *larger profits* than women, men may have been

---

[8] It seems also that the car market is not regarded as a part of Gariūnai, and therefore is not stigmatized in the same way as the Old Market and the New Market. One informant had recently shifted
from clothes to cars. When telling me about this shift he said: 'I do not trade in Gariūnai any more.'
[9] Below I shall refer to the 'Clothes Market' as opposed to the 'Car Market'. The 'Clothes Market'
refers to both the Old Market and the New Market.

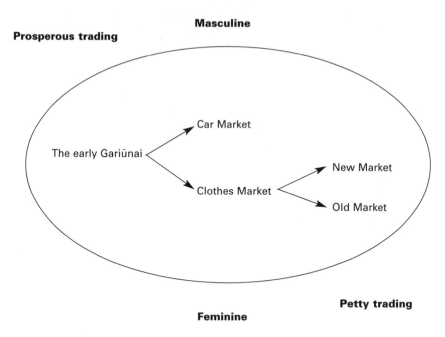

FIGURE 7.1. The gendered market space

over-represented in my survey. However, in spite of the increased number of women in the clothes business and the transfer of many men to the car market, there were apparently still many men in the clothes markets, and gender relations in them were far from being clear cut.

THE FEMININIZATION OF CLOTHES

The feminine atmosphere in the market was enhanced by the fact that the over-whelming majority of buyers were women (often middle-aged), and with a few exceptions the wares offered for sale were largely women's clothes, perfume, make-up, nylons—even wedding dresses. As a contrast to this there was a small section in the market that was decidedly masculine—here motor oil, spare parts for cars, and tools were being sold by men to men. As I had been told that this trade in spare parts had been much more important in the early days of the market, the small men's section appeared as a 'remnant' from this period that had now been pushed into a corner by the overwhelming femininity of the rest. But this only emphasized the process of femininization that may be said to have taken place in both the Old Market and the New Market. However, this increased number of women, as mentioned above, mainly resulted in an increased degree of commission trading. Because many of these women thus ended up occupying the least prestigious positions in the market, the effects on the market atmosphere was not unambiguous femininization. The 'gendered hierarchy' was partly reflected in the spatial organization of the market, since there would be almost exclusively men in the centre, occupying the best trading places, while some sections of the market, notably where the 'petty traders' were standing, were almost exclusively occupied by women. Such clusters of women could be found around the main entrances, where mainly pensioners were selling plastic bags on commission, or in front of the tables in *pastogė*, where a group of fifty to a hundred women would gather in the early mornings in the hope of selling a few home-made dresses, blouses, or skirts. A final indicator of women's position at the 'lowest levels of trade' was the fact that most buyers were also women. Since many buyers were small traders from other areas of Lithuania, Latvia, or Belarus, the prevalence of women buyers indicates that virtually no men were engaged in this small-scale trade. There are several reasons for women's lower position in market trading. Women's responsibilities for the family and their lack of extended networks were two serious obstacles for women traders compared to the group of male traders. In addition, the composition of the group of market women was rather different from that of men, especially as married women formed a larger proportion of women traders. For these reasons, there was a tendency for women to organize their trade differently from men.

Most of the women engaged in petty trading did so alone. If a woman was trading with a partner in the market (an indication of greater prosperity), this partner would usually be a man, and moreover either her husband or another close male member of the family. Regina, for example, one of the most successful female traders that I met in the market, traded with her son-in-law. She explained that she was divorced and thus had no husband to help her. Whereas unmarried (as well as married) men often traded with one or more friends, this was uncommon for women. There seemed to be several interconnected reasons. First, Soviet women lacked the extensive networks of friends that many men were a part of. As mentioned above, although women did have social networks, especially through family members and colleagues from their workplace, their 'double burden' had resulted in a reduced degree of participation in political and social activities outside the family. Men, on the other hand, seemed to have established more extensive networks of friends that they could draw upon, especially when starting their business. Jonas explained how, as a young man, he had developed his now quite profitable business:

My first business was . . . you know Šiaulai? It is the town of hand-knitting and sewing, underground factories. We were selling these goods in Gariūnai for the Russian market. After that I went to Korea and after that to Thailand. It was like this. Because we did not each of us have enough money to go to Korea and Thailand, instead we would pool money together, for example five persons, and send one person to Thailand to buy shirts and slippers. We went to Korea once and to Thailand twice by pooling money and after that I had my own money and I myself flew to the Emirates. That was two and a half years ago. Now I have my own business. (Jonas 2.1)

Thus we may even speculate that men's marginal position within the Soviet family also forced them to be more socially active outside the family and that in the long run this provided them with important social capital for future business activities.

Another reason for women's tendency not to trade in partnerships with female friends could be that women (and men) felt that women needed 'a protector' in the market. I suspect that this had been the reason why the above-mentioned Regina brought along her son-in-law, although she never said so directly. Women in the lower levels of trading seemed to be doing well alone, but they may also have been less vulnerable as they obviously had less money to carry around. Regina, on the other hand, who had a turnover which obviously exceeded even the 3,000 litai a week she herself mentioned, had a more urgent need for protection. Finally, I suggest that the age group represented by women in the market differed from that of men. Women were generally older, aged between 30 and 50.[10] Although several groups of young unmarried men were trading in the market, I met almost no young unmarried women. As men were also most likely to trade with friends when they were young and unmarried, the fact that women were older when they started trading may have further prevented them from using a network of friends as a starting-point. In any case, women more often started trading either with their husbands or alone. Although I met several men who had begun trading by pooling resources with a group of friends, I heard no such stories about groups of women. However, women also used their networks. Like Stasė in Chapter 3, for example, they would start trading together with a friend, or, like Irena, borrow money from a colleague in order to start in the market.

Women's limited access to extended networks moreover had economic consequences as it limited their opportunities to build up initial capital. But the most important difference, I believe, is connected with the fact that women in the market were generally using their income for the family, and were therefore less likely to be able to save money for future business activities. The fact that almost only married or divorced women, that is to say women with responsibilities for a family, traded in the market further emphasized this point.

VISIBLE WOMEN AND HIDDEN MEN

It may seem strange to talk about the femininization of the market, when in fact men occupy the most profitable positions and furthermore appear to be in the majority. As mentioned above, one reason for the overall feminine atmosphere in the market was the style of goods and overwhelmingly female buyers; however, the

---

[10] According to my survey, the average age of women in the market was five years higher than that of men. Since many married couples of around the same age were also trading, I suggest that the age difference resulted from the absence of any group of young women. It should be mentioned, however, that the survey is not representative of market traders, although it may give an indication of their composition.

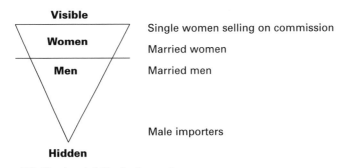

FIGURE 7.2. Gender visibility in the market space

fact that women traders were generally more active than men also contributed to making them more visible.

Figure 7.2 shows that men were generally less visible in the market than women. Some trading positions, such as the 'rich supplier' who either produced or imported large quantities of wares, were most often held by men. They usually employed other traders (often women) to sell for them and therefore did not appear in the market themselves. In this way the small 'market élite' by and large remained hidden, while the visible traders were predominantly women engaged in more petty forms of trade. Another example of such 'hidden masculinity' were the male racketeers, who as mentioned in Chapter 5 were becoming increasingly invisible as well as anonymous in the market. But the main reason why I suggest that femininity dominates the market is that many women are active in the 'middle layers' of trading, either in partnerships with their husbands or with other male family members. In such cases, it was notably the woman who was most active both in finding and selling the goods: 'I don't know why, but most people in the bus are women . . . going to Poland. Maybe it is easier for them to talk or to negotiate' (Teresa 16.1).

It was not only in the bus to Poland that most of the passengers were women. I was also told that women were predominant in the planes to Turkey and to China. In the case of Turkey this was confirmed by an article in the *Lietuvos Rytas* (1992)[11] by a journalist who had flown to Istanbul together with a group of traders. As these women were usually also the most active in selling the goods, I often talked with women traders in the market several times before I realized that they were trading together with their husbands. In several cases the man would only do the selling, while his wife was away buying new merchandise, which sometimes left him unable to remember what prices to charge. At most other times, the men in the market would either simply sit in the car and read a newspaper or stand passively nearby. Thus in cases where spouses were trading together, the woman was definitely more active and more visible in the market than the man. Also worth noting

[11] See Appendix (no. 12).

was the fact that women were believed to be better at dealing with racketeers, who were generally understood to be more polite towards women!

So although gender-specific hierarchies did exist in the market, they did not reflect any clear-cut gender roles. Because women were more active as traders than men, they also acquired more competencies and a more specific knowledge of trading and the market, especially compared with their husbands, who often did not have the necessary knowledge to travel and find goods abroad. Women's active role in market trading can furthermore be linked to their participation in underground production of clothes during the Soviet period. Women's 'traditional' position as providers of the needs of the family has in this respect given women trading competencies that many men lack. Consequently it was not surprising that I found several unmarried or divorced women, who had managed to reach the top levels of the trading hierarchy, including only imported goods and selling them on commission.[12] Interestingly, the former manager of the Old Market, who was murdered in the spring of 1995, was also a woman, which somehow contradicts the idea of the formal hierarchy in the market being exclusively dominated by men. It seems therefore that women's responsibilities for the family have promoted and at the same time hindered women's trading activities and thereby their acquisition of trading knowledge. Women with older children or women without children had a marked advantage. Women with small children relied on other female family members to help them with their trading as taking care of children appeared to be solely the responsibility of women:

I have two children and I have nobody to look after them. My brother also has to go to Poland, but his wife usually goes instead, because they are living with her mother, who looks after the children when their mother is away. (Teresa 16.1)

Teresa, who was living with her husband, did not consider for one moment leaving the children in his care while she was away getting new supplies of merchandise. The same point was made to me by the head of the Vilnius section of Women in Business. She pointed out that many women had difficulty in getting away from home if they had small children, and that this hindered their participation in business.

Still, some women did manage to combine their continual dual responsibilities in family life and trading by dint of creative thinking. Rasa, for example, the successful shop-owner I quoted in Chapter 3, had three small children and a husband. I believe that part of the reason why she ended up buying a café next to the shop she owned was because this would relieve her of the problem of providing hot meals for her unemployed husband.

---

[12] I suggest that the same principle applies to the gendering of economic areas outside the market, where most of the profitable positions are held by men, but where it is also not uncommon to see single women reaching very influential positions. One example of this is the establishment of the Godmothers' Club in Kaunas in response to the exclusively male organization called the 'Capitalists' Club'.

To sum up, I contend that 'femininization' could be linked to the fact that the markets to a certain extent appeared as a form of institutionalization of women's underground activities. The market has therefore made women's activities more visible. In addition, women's role as actual breadwinners has become highlighted as a result of the fact that more and more women have ended up in the market, in spite of the official political discourse that presented them as 'returning home'. At the same time this also questions the public discourse of transition, picturing the man as the main economic agent and provider within the family. Actually, as we have seen, women continue to be responsible for providing for the family, although in a different form, because they now occupy a position at the lowest levels of the emerging market instead of their State jobs.

I suggest that this has had consequences for the perception of femininity and women's identities as well as for the conceptualization of masculinity and male identities.

WOMEN'S LOSS OF SOCIAL STATUS AND THE MASCULINIZATION OF FEMININITY

Although women appear to be active both as traders and as buyers, their activities are regarded both by themselves and by others as 'shameful' and 'unfeminine'. The ambiguity of women's position in the market may be illustrated by the fact that women generally felt even more uncomfortable in the market than men, a fact emphasized by the stories related by Rasa and Stasė in Chapter 3. Both had particthem iapted in the Soviet underground economy and both had found it much more shameful to start trading in the market. This seems also to be related to women's roles as responsible for the family's moral and cultural status as well as for the general moral level of society (cf. Gorbachev quoted in Pilkington 1992a: 218). Another reason seems to be that women generally perceive their activities as less important than men's. In addition, although the market appeared to be feminine, the women I talked to in the market found their ability to express their femininity somewhat limited.

Towards the end of my stay in the market, while I was working with Irena, who was trading alone there, I experienced the lack of acknowledgement of their own activities that women expressed in the market. As I mentioned earlier, Irena was the head of a local kindergarten in Vilnius. One day a male trader asked her if she could change a 100-dollar bill. She could, but when he enquired, politely, how her business was going she answered: 'Oh this isn't business, it is too small to be business. What you're doing, that's business . . .'. Although she was probably making less money than he was, the difference was not that much, and she was definitely exaggerating it. This illustrates a more general difference in the way that men and women in the market perceived their own activities. Many of the other women as well as men that I talked to had the same idea about women's activities as not being 'serious', yet I met men who were definitely not more successful than Irena who would not hesitate for a moment to call their own activities 'business' (Vytalij, whose story I discussed in Chapter 3, is one example). The articulation of women's business activities presents women's activities as 'petty', as not being 'real business', and Irena's view of women's activities as less important than men's was shared by women in the Gariūnai market, although they were generally more active than the men. Thus in the numerous cases in which a married couple formed a partnership, and where the woman was in reality running the business, such gendered practice was not expressed as such by either of them. As the business talents of women remained 'unarticulated' practices, female and male traders alike had no ready explanation as to why the planes to Istanbul and Beijing were filled with women (although some, like Teresa, would mumble something about women's abilities to 'communicate').[13]

The tendency to disregard women's trading activities may of course have reflected an actual difference in income, but this can hardly be the only explanation. The above-mentioned local leader of Women in Business stated:

It is difficult for women to be in business, because of the mentality of men. They can't imagine that women can also be good partners. There is the opinion that women can be involved only in such business as cake-baking, etc. (Dalia Jurgaitytė)

This underestimation of women was emphasized by another successful businesswoman who owned a few companies in town. She told me she often managed to cheat men by pretending to be incompetent and then in the end managing to strike a good bargain. Generally, however, I believe that the shame many women felt in the market may be connected with their understatement of their own competencies. Although men too felt ashamed, their embarrassment was of a different nature. By conceptualizing what they did as 'business', they also emphasized that often they had aspirations to expand their business activities further and eventually get out of the market. Women, by contrast, failing to frame their own activities as professional, felt more responsible for the amoralitites of Gariūnai and their own participation in it. This again may be seen to reflect a traditional view of a woman in Lithuania that she is 'la gardienne de la moralité' (Greimas 1993: 62).[14] Women more often than men complained about the lack of solidarity in the market, and they would, I suggest, feel more concerned and more ashamed about trading in the market. The idea that women are more concerned with morality and act as guardians of society may also be illustrated by looking at the founding of a women's charity organization in 1993 by nine businesswomen in Kaunas. To start

---

[13] The same tendency for women to underestimate their potential is reported by Pilkington (1996) from the Moscow youth scene, where she found that girls were much less confident about their ability to carry their ideas through than their male counterparts. She suggests that this finding reflects a popular belief that women cannot survive in business because of the dangers associated with the business world in contemporary Russia.

[14] In this brief presentation of Lithuanian ethnology and culture, Greimas focuses on traditional peasant culture, but as most of the population was still living in the countryside until the 1970s, such peasant morality and general norms apparently also still influence life in the city.

with, even the name, the Godmothers' Club, epitomized women's special position. As the president of the Club explained, 'women feel more naturally a responsibility for the social problems that have followed Lithuanian independence'. This obligation was not only felt by women, but also ascribed to them by others. The president of the Godmothers' Club not only wanted to get involved in charity, but also felt obliged to share some of her wealth, for fear of incurring society's disdain. Although I know of Lithuanian businessmen who supported cultural or other non-economic activities, I know of no male equivalent to the above-mentioned women's charitable organization. To be rich was obviously a different experience for women than it was for men. As the head of the organization expressed it, 'successful businesswomen, more than men, need to use charity as a ticket to society'.

Finally, I found that both women and men were generally uncomfortable about women being in the market. As the manager of the Old Market put it: 'This is really hard work, it is not for women!' By this he was not only implying that the work was too physically demanding for women, but also probably thinking of the generally rough atmosphere of the market.

There are many different kinds of people in the market intellectually and education-wise . . . There are many very highly educated people, but there are also many who come as we say, 'from the dirt', meaning that they are very coarse. Sometimes it is even difficult to stay close to these people, especially if it is a woman who keeps cursing the whole time and being impolite. (Teresa 16.1)

In other ways, too, women in the market felt that what they were doing was contradictory to the ideals of 'femininity'. When I was trading with Irena in the market in November she had to wear warm, practical clothes, and although she made up her face carefully each morning she made a point of saying how terrible she looked. Women in Lithuania at the time were very concerned with clothes and often felt they had a moral obligation to be conscious of their appearance.[15] Lithuanian fashion was very feminine, including high heels, nylons, and dresses, in fact much more so than I was used to from Copenhagen. Compared with the way people dressed in Vilnius, the possibilities of expressing femininity in the market were therefore considered poor. Although some women in the market insisted on wearing high heels even when it was raining cats and dogs, the general dress code of the market was very different from the surrounding Lithuanian society. This difference was especially important for women. I had several discussions with my interpreter on the subject of rubber boots and femininity, for she considered them most unsuitable for women. All in all, therefore, the market in several ways epitomized ambiguities of female identity. The men, however, were not much better off.

---

[15] I witnessed a 17-year-old girl without make-up being scolded by her elder sister and mother because she was not paying sufficient attention to her appearance. See also Nordahl (1996) for a discussion of women's moral obligation to be beautiful in Romania.

MEN IN THE MARKET

As men generally made more money in the market and, as I have discussed above, were more inclined to acknowledge their professional competencies, they found it a little easier to accept their position as market traders. Furthermore, their activities as providers were more in accordance with the dominant discourse on masculinity.

Pilkington, quoted above, has reflected on the general decline and ritualization of the public sphere during the last years of Sovietism. In continuation of this line of observation, a totally different process of restructuring masculine identity in the market can be traced compared with the situation for women. While the 'disorder' of women's activities in the market developed because their private activities and responsibilities became more public, it seems that where men are concerned a development in the opposite direction has taken place. Thus the problem with masculine identities in the market was related to the fact that male market traders, by appearing in the market, showed that they were unsuccessful outside it. As the traditional male role was formed in the public sphere, the semi-private social space of the market represented a break with the traditional expressions of masculinity. As men tended to conceptualize their activities as 'business' rather than survival, they also positioned them more in comparison with the outside economic sphere. I suggest that the 'problem' for men trading in the market was therefore not so much their association with its uncivilized practices, the bad language and the criminality, but rather their inability to get out of it—to reconquer the public space.

Men reacted differently to this—from passive acceptance to violent counter-attack. The racketeers represented a form of hyper-masculinity and moreover quite a violent form. Racketeers used crude ways of obtaining control not only over women but also over other men in the market. The demand for power and the readiness to use it may be regarded as an attempt to re-masculinize society by capturing new territory. This aspect of the new post-Communist masculine identities has also been noted by Pilkington in an article on youth movements and gangs in Moscow (ibid. 1995).

But if racketeering was one extreme example of male strategies coming to terms with the feminine style of the market, there were other strategies as well and most men were, as mentioned above, somewhat passive in the market. Some attempted to disregard femininity completely, for example the successful male traders who sold brassières and underwear for women. Some of these men would sit in the central rows in the market, looking big and strong in their leather jackets, with these very feminine goods spread out everywhere as if this was a completely natural state of affairs. Unfortunately, at the time I did not approach these male traders, but I heard many jokes about men selling bras, both from women and from other men.

A last and even more passive male reaction could be found in the many cases, mentioned above, of married couples trading together in which the woman definitely took the lead. The weak position of men was further emphasized by the fact that it was the woman who would deal with the racketeers. This epitomizes the vulnerable state of male identity as it then appeared threatened by extreme masculinity (racketeers) and by the domination/protection of women alike.

CONCLUSION: A GENDERED ECONOMY AND DIVIDED FAMILIES

In public discourses on Gariūnai, the immorality of the market was and is based on its imagined 'roughness', uncivilized practices, non-Lithuanianness, and black trading. However, the focus on gender has revealed other problematic aspects of identity that are similarly highlighted in the market place. Relationships indicate a more general struggle over gender identities, although strangely enough each sex seems to be contending more with society and society's expectations rather than directly with the other. For women, the heavier and more public their workload has become, the more they have become involved in the market instead of staying at home in their proper (private) places. For men, on the contrary, the market epitomizes a change from dominance in an admittedly rather ritualized public space to a weak position within a semi-public low-status market. For both men and women, the changing contextualization of their economic activities has not only questioned Soviet discourses on gender, but popular (appropriated) Western ideals of the middle-class family inherent in transitional discourses as well.

This 'gender contestation' may be related to the institutionalization of Gariūnai and the emphasis placed on the market as a 'window' on existing gender roles in society and thus a sort of 'publication' of women's role as sole household providers in post-Soviet Lithuania. As the leader of the Godmothers' Club put it, 'the tradition of men as being responsible for the family was destroyed in Soviet times'. She continued: 'Women understand the troubles of the family, men here are somehow outside the family, they are not like men in the West!' In fact I met several women who were married and living with their husbands, yet did not share their economy with him.[16] The distinct differences in women's and men's positions and activities in the market not only seriously *questions the domestic role of women* prevalent in post-socialist rhetoric, but *also highlights the 'failure' of men* to provide for their families by indirectly exhibiting men's economic activities as unsuccessful. Viewed in this way, 'women's poverty' in the market emphasizes not only asymmetrical gender roles, but also reflects the *alienation* of men from their families, from their children, and, more symbolically, from their moral responsibility towards the community.

The different and more 'public' staging of their trading activities on the one hand emphasizes women's responsibilities as household providers, but at the same

[16] This tendency to 'split' families is also pointed out by Svendsen, in reporting on her research on women and beauty in Romania (Svendsen 1996). Corrin (1992) reports the same tendency in Hungary.

time renders them more vulnerable. Their femininity becomes questioned by their engagement in 'masculine' activities and their frequent absence from the family while travelling abroad to buy merchandise, and furthermore their role as market traders, contradicts their ideal role as guardians of culture and morality. Although the duality of women's role in Soviet society (as workers and mothers) may be seen to continue, the activities are changing and both roles are being challenged by the 'masculine style' of women's activities.

More generally, the market has epitomized the tendency for many women to live alone with their children as well as the 'femininization of responsibility' and 'demasculinization' of family life, a process which, although it was initiated during the Soviet occupation, seems to have escalated in recent years. While the majority of female traders are engaged in petty trading, only men or single women can manage to save and invest in more profitable activities. The problem as I see it lies not only in the establishment of new hierarchies of gender, but perhaps even more in the tendency towards a more fundamental diversion of 'large parts of generated incomes' away from the reproduction of families and thus more broadly speaking away from the 'community'. Women's activities in the market reveal blurred gender boundaries and point towards a growing gap between dominant discourses of traditional gender roles and the role of women as breadwinners. However, women's visibility in the market also implies that the more profitable areas of the new economy, within as well as outside the market place, are increasingly being controlled by men. This dominance takes place not only in terms of male control over the social space (for example, in the form of racketeering), but also—and this may, in the long run, be of more importance—in terms of masculinization of profits, femininization of poverty, and a divided society.[17]

---

[17] A parallel to this process of polarization can be found in Pilkington's account (1996) of the development of the Moscow youth scene. She describes not only a general re-masculinization of society in terms of racketeers, police, and other forms of male control, but also an absolute division of the sexes as violent male gangs dominate public areas and young women are pushed out of the public youth scene altogether.

8

Work versus Trading

The conceptualization of Gariūnai as *bardakas* may be further illuminated by turning to a third and final theme, the changes of practice and discourses of 'work' in Soviet society and in the recently established Lithuanian State. Although I have placed it last, the changing perceptions of work and related ideas of the workplace and unemployment that are being revealed in the market appear in many ways to be fundamental to the previous two themes as well. We saw this in relation to the discussion of women's role as workers, but it could also be related to the idea of the market as a non-Lithuanian space, since there is a high proportion of non-Lithuanian speakers among the unemployed as well as among traders in the market. Moreover, an analysis of 'work' shows in detail the wide scope of the consequences of the economic 'transition', socially and culturally, involving acknowledgement and symbolic classifications, morality, ideology, social interactions, social relations, and social prestige. The establishment of Gariūnai as a legal trading place (although not as a workplace, as we shall see below) symbolized and entailed processes leading to the development of a new economic field, and, in relation to this, a confusion in the conceptualization of 'work'.

The developing of a new field can be illustrated, as I mentioned in Chapter 2, by a change in terminology. The word *spekuliacija* (speculation) has been substituted by *prekyba* (trading). The same change may be found in the terminology of the 'place of action', as the word *talkučkė* (an illegal market) has been replaced by *turgus* (a legal market). But although the terminology has changed, old connotations remain. Thus, although 'trading' and 'market' were used to describe the scene in Gariūnai the negative connotations of 'speculation' and *talkučkė* remained. I would furthermore contend that when used about Gariūnai, the terms 'trading' and 'market' carry different and more negative meanings than the same words used about activities elsewhere in the developing market economy, although in practice the activities are not that different.

Part of the explanation for this difference may be found in the appropriation of 'Western transition discourses', in which the transition to market economy is assumed (automatically) to lead to increased prosperity (Aage 1995 and Hann 1992). Market trading, associated with economic marginality, questions such a goal. But Gariūnai was actually very profitable compared with State-sector incomes. Furthermore, as Rasa explained in Chapter 3, Gariūnai was much more profitable, yet less prestigious than the *mugė* (indoor market). Therefore it seems that money is not at stake here. Instead I suggest that the symbolic, moral, and social stigmatization of the market can be related to the specific 'staging' of trading activities there. I believe that such a difference may be related to the fact that the 'staging' of trading indoors may qualify it as 'work', whereas the same practice in the open-air market is conceptualized differently. I would also contend that by focusing not only on the changing terminology of trading but also on the conceptualization of work it may prove possible to reveal some of the mechanisms involved in the establishment of a new field as well as in the reproduction of certain forms of marginalization and social stratification.

WORK IN SOVIET SOCIETY

According to Marxist-Leninist ideology, work was one of the most important ideological and social activities in society. The individual's duty to work was stated in the programme of the Communist Party:

In the economic sphere the individual must 'respect work as the main basis of the communist personality, his social prestige' and observe 'the collectivist moral' which is 'incompatible with egoism, selfishness, and self-interest'. (Programma Kommunisticheskoi Partii, 1986, in Shlapentokh 1989: 19)

Stewart (1993, 1997), writing on gypsies and the work ethic in Hungary during socialism, emphasizes gypsies' lack of participation in wage-labour as the most important reason for their conflicts with the State. 'Within official ideology labouring was *the* activity which constituted one as a full member of society' and 'labour power was not a separable part of the human person, which one could choose to part with or not according to market conditions' (Stewart 1993: 191). Similarly, in Soviet society, 'Not only in the image of the ideal but also in the image of the good Soviet individual is work, based on the Marxist glorification of labour, presented as the crucial activity in a citizen's life' (Shlapentokh 1989: 37). Work therefore was not only important ideologically and politically, but morally, socially, and legally as well. The conceptualization of work can be related to a range of areas of a citizen's life.

Largely as a result of the low levels of efficiency and productivity of the economic system (cf. Verdery 1996, Humphrey 1995a), labour shortage was more of a problem than unemployment in Soviet society. The importance of work as compulsory therefore had consequences in several ways for the conceptualization of unemployment:

It was a crime, for which one could be imprisoned, to remain unemployed for any lengths of time. Unemployment was seen as an evil distinctive of capitalism. For this reason actual lack of work in the Soviet Union was camouflaged under a variety of other terms (non-occupation, labour in assignment, etc.). (Humphrey 1995a: 3)

Unemployment was thus not only illegal but also amoral. But although this was how work and unemployment were presented in the official political discourse, the changes in post-Stalinist society made room for an alternative conceptualization of work as well. In his book *Public and Private Life of the Soviet People* (1989), Shlapentokh discusses the general decline of the public sphere in post-Stalinist society. During the 1970s and especially the 1980s an increasing degree of 'privatization' of Soviet society took place, as a result of which participation in public events and adherence to socialist ideology became increasingly superficial and ritualized. This also had consequences for work and the work ethic since illegal practices such as pilfering from the workplace, and the illegal import and production of goods, became much more widespread. Although such activities gradually at the same time became more acceptable as a means of gaining access to consumer products, they still remained officially illegal. In the Soviet Union, legalization of certain forms of private enterprise in the form of co-operatives did not take place until 1986/87 (Shelley 1990). However, the increase in illegal sources of income did imply changing attitudes towards work as well as an increased demand for jobs in which it was easier to have access to 'additional' goods and services (Sampson 1987: 121). It is important to note, however, that the fact that people became increasingly involved in the black economy did not mean that participation in the official economy or wage-labour lost importance. What took place instead was the development of 'double morality' and an increased dependence on both a State-sector job and additional incomes (Bartusevičius 1993). As Shlapentokh explains it:

Only a minority of the Soviet people regard work as having no or minimal social significance. The majority still prefer to have work which they consider useful for the country and appreciate its social recognition. (Shlapentokh 1989: 43)

Wage-labour was important, not only because of the income it provided but also for a range of social, moral, and personal reasons. This continued social importance of wage-labour is also emphasized by Verdery. She describes the activities of some taxi-drivers in Romania (not localized more specifically) in 1991–2 (Verdery 1996). Most of the taxi-drivers were only driving a taxi as a sideline and had some other form of employment in the State sector. Although they could earn more money by driving a taxi, only one of them had left his State-sector job to become 'a fully private entrepreneur' (ibid. 215). The example shows that the main importance of a State-sector job may not be money at all:

Like the feudal estate, the socialist enterprise is not simply an economic institution but is the primary unit of Soviet society, and the ultimate base of social and political behaviour. This unit provided all manners of services and facilities for its labour force (housing, kindergartens, sporting and cultural facilities, clinics, pensions, etc.). (Verdery 1996: 206)

Although such multifunctionality seems to have been most prevalent on collective farms, urban jobs also generally provided access to housing, child care, and sometimes special consumer goods.[1] Access to such goods was often mentioned as

---

[1] As Humphrey (1995a) mentions, the farms were more like small villages, providing all kinds of services such as shops, hairdressers, and libraries. Even among those who were employed as farmers or

being of prime importance when considering a job. As in the example of the
Romanian taxi-drivers above, such additional functions of the workplace seem to
be continuing at least during the first few years of 'transition', as Humphrey
(1995a) reports from rural Russia, where, recently, even private plots of land were
being allocated through a person's place of work. The ideological and moral
importance of work in Soviet society was thus also related to the workplace,
because the choice of work had (and apparently still has) a direct bearing on other
aspects of one's life in various ways. Finally, professional pride also played an
important role. The high degree of specialization in many factories, as well as in
kolkhozes (collective farms), combined with access to employment in one's special
field as well as relatively low 'job turnover', resulted in a very specialized and
professional workforce, but also one with a low degree of flexibility. Work was not
important merely as work, but as a specific professional activity for which one had
been trained.

THE SOCIAL MEANING OF WORK

In addition to the material considerations mentioned above, the choice of work and
workplace, quite apart from the economic benefits, had social implications. In a
situation of scarce consumer goods and limited means of investment, money was
not in a general sense—as in the West—a means of acquiring social prestige
(Taliūnaitė 1996). Although, as mentioned above, money and material well-being
became increasingly important in the last decades of Soviet society, the ideological
stress on the social importance of work and the moral obligation attached to it have
resulted in an alternative 'hierarchy of prestige'. The point I wish to make is that
work was a means of achieving both material well-being and social prestige, yet the
two were not interconnected in any simple way. What is particularly interesting in
order to understand the contemporary evaluation of market trading is the apparent division between 'prestige' and income. Thus, while higher education and
intellectual work carried the most prestige, such work was considered economically
unprofitable in an economy which was increasingly becoming based on barter and
bargaining power as a condition for obtaining the necessities of life. In the mid-
1980s, a survey of Soviet teenagers showed that they considered black marketeers
as having the highest income and regarded hairdressers, sales-girls, prostitutes, and
taxi-drivers more economically successful than professors, actors, and pilots. This,
however, does not mean that such occupations were more prestigious in social
terms (cf. Fisher-Ruge 1993). The privatization of Soviet society during the last
decades before its dissolution, although indicating that money had become more

agricultural labourers there was a high degree of specialization which meant that, for example, a tractor driver would not know any other forms of agricultural work very well. The high degree of specialization therefore led to a 'narrow' conceptualization of one's profession. Apart from making it
problematic for many people to find a new job, this might also result in a lack of recognition of 'other'
work as 'real' work.

important, did not therefore fundamentally alter the division between prestigious professions and profitable ones. This duality of work in Soviet society has prevailed.

GARIŪNAI—MARKET TRADING IN A SOCIAL VACUUM

For a variety of reasons, trading activities in Gariūnai may be regarded as antagonistic to the above-mentioned notion of 'work'. Partly as a result of the understanding of trade as 'speculation' and thus illegitimate according to Marxist-Leninist ideology, the conceptualization of market trading as morally and socially problematic may also be related to the fact that such activities were not (yet) regarded as an *occupation* and therefore not recognized as 'real work'. Activities in the market may therefore just as well be understood in terms of what they are *not* rather than what they *are*, as illustrated by the following statement by Teresa:

Earlier all traders in the market would be called 'speculators' and *they would go to the market because they didn't want to work*—meaning they would be 'speculators', because at that time there were jobs to be had, employment to be found, but they somehow preferred to go and trade in the market. Trading has a bad reputation in this sense. (Teresa 16.1, my italics)

Following this line of thought it is not so much the actual activity of 'speculation' that seems to be the problem as the fact that 'speculators' refused to 'work'. As Teresa suggests, trading in Gariūnai, being conceptualized very much like former 'speculation', was likewise regarded as 'anti-work' or parasitism. There are several indications that market traders acknowledged this problem and that they had various ways of solving it. Irena's job as a leader of a kindergarten in Vilnius gave her an income of less than 280 litai a month ($70). Her activities in the market gave an 'additional' income of 400 litai a month, even though she only traded two or three days a week in order to be able to spend some time in the kindergarten as well. For her it would have been more profitable to skip the kindergarten completely and concentrate on her Gariūnai activities, but she would not dream of doing so. Although she too found her activities in the market problematic, the fact that she had a job made a difference, precisely because her market activities could be conceptualized as 'additional'. Her working identity was not seriously altered by the fact that she traded in the market, especially because she made a point of concealing this from everybody except close friends. However, although the strategy of 'double jobs' seems to have been important during the first few years of the market's existence, the situation changed as a result of the increasing level of unemployment. I was often told that during the first few years (1989–91) most traders in the market would also have a job elsewhere:

Around 1989/90 people usually had another job and they were trading only on the side to earn some money on Saturdays and Sundays. Only now it is becoming a main business for the people. And 50 per cent of them would probably be happy to get back to their jobs now. (Mikhail 5.1)

The increasing level of unemployment after independence was followed by an increase in the number of people who started trading in the market. Growing unemployment in the State sector had made market trading all the more important socially and morally, because trading had ceased to be 'additional' and was instead becoming 'work'. Trading thus also became evaluated according to a discourse of 'work', including all the connotations and functions of 'work' in Soviet society. Market trading had become an 'occupation'. This had altered the focus of criticism and increasingly placed the evolving market as a 'work-like institution', yet without the conditions normally associated with work and earning money. The result is a change (and confusion) in the conceptualization of what is 'real work', 'prestigious work', and 'hard work'.

HARD LABOUR BUT NO WORK

The form of trading carried out in Gariūnai involved hard and heavy labour. The need to carry large bags of goods together with having to arrive between 4 and 5 a.m., six days a week, resulted in most traders suffering from a chronic lack of sleep. Working at Gariūnai therefore was considered to be *juodas darbas* (literally 'black work', but in the Lithuanian sense of hard physical labour). As one trader explained it:

You fly to Turkey, buy half a ton of goods and pack them in boxes, 50–60 kg in each. Then you take them to the hotel and then to the airport and then through customs and then to your home. Next morning at 4 o'clock you get up and go to the market with two or three bags. Eventually you come home again at about 3 o'clock. Some days it may be cold and on others it may be terribly hot and sunny. (Vytenis 3.2)

Vytenis told me that he actually changed his activities from clothes to cars because of heart trouble resulting from *juodas darbas*.

Apart from the resultant fatigue, many traders felt that the physical hardships also reflected the low prestige level of their activities. Especially for the many intellectuals in the market, the loss of prestige connected with the physical labour seemed to intensify their low regard for the market. As mentioned above, however, since most people were 'specialists' in their former jobs, the lack of prestige in market trading may also be related to the fact that no special training seemed to be needed in order to trade at Gariūnai.[2] As indicated above, one of the important aspects of 'work' in Soviet society was being 'a specialist' capable of performing particularly well in a job that was useful to society. The general low regard for physical labour (and, related to this, the idea that 'anyone can do it') was in itself an 'image' problem for many traders in Gariūnai.

But the image of trading as *juodas darbas* was not the only way of conceptualizing it. Parallel to this was the idea that market activities did not really constitute

---

[2] As I have specifically emphasized in Chapter 3, one did actually need training and experience, but market traders seemed to be unaware of their own resources.

work at all. Thus, in spite of all their hard labour and fatigue, traders generally felt that they were not really *doing* anything.

Not everybody here knows how to work. They just *sit* here! (Jurij 12.1, my italics)

Trading in the market has nothing to do with business. Business is if you are producing something. *We just sit here.* (Stasė 13.2, my italics)

Stasė here contrasts 'business' with 'market trading' and opposes 'production' to 'trading', and reaches the conclusion 'we just sit here'—in other words being passive. This idea of trading as something passive may be connected to the Marxist-Leninist view of work as primarily production. But why is market trading considered to be more passive, or a less suitable form of 'work', than, for example, selling from a shop or a company office? For instance, Teresa says:

If somebody tomorrow would offer me to start working for 800 litai per month in my special field I would have no doubt at all. I would start working there immediately and stop trading. It would be nicer to *sit* in your job being warm and doing a nice job. (Teresa 16.1, my italics)

Teresa also talks about sitting, but in a rather more positive sense. If one has a job then it is apparently acceptable just 'to *sit* there'. It seems, therefore, that the negative evaluation of such passivity is closely connected to the market, whereas in other contexts it is apparently more acceptable. However, it is not only market trading that may be viewed as representing a break with the idea of work as employment, for the same is true for other entrepreneurial activities. But although these were similarly condemned, it was apparently for different reasons.

BUSINESS VERSUS TRADE

Generally, people would regard their activities inside the market as 'trading', and outside it as 'business'. However, the categories 'trader' and 'businessman' were not mutually exclusive. There were traders in the Gariūnai market, and traders outside it, businessmen in the market and businessmen at various economic levels outside it. Some of the more affluent traders attempted to classify their activities as 'business', but it was generally believed that 'real' businessmen were to be found outside the market, although many of them were believed to have started in the market during its early period, when profits were high. People would not always agree on the positioning of their own or other people's activities, but there was a consensus of opinion about the main topological differences. According to the Marxist-Leninist outlook on the creation of wealth, only production could qualify as business, while trading and services could not be included. Business was a broader concept than trade. Furthermore, the difference seemed to be directly related to the size of profits.[3] Businessmen were rich—traders were poor.

---

[3] One Lithuanian–American businesswoman actually complained quite a lot about this direct association of money with business. According to her it resulted in a business environment in which people

This difference between 'business' and 'trade' and the higher regard for business can be related to their different classifications in terms of 'work'. To be a businessman was almost regarded as an 'occupation' and therefore as a kind of work:

Business is not only trade it is also service, construction, mechanics (car fixing) and for that it is not necessary to know how to trade. *You have to know how to work well.* (*Nesutinku*, Lithuanian television programme about Gariūnai, April 1995)

It follows from this statement that trading was not in itself regarded as work. Thus the image of traders as 'not knowing how to work' and as passive was emphasized here as well. The distinction between trading and work was also linked to the temporary nature of trading, as market-traders regarded their activities as a temporary source of income pursued until some better alternative showed up. In short, trading was not regarded as work and even less so as a career. The temporary, on-and-off involvement in the market likewise signalled a 'break' with the idea of trading as an occupation. A 'real' occupation, often in line with one's special field, would have to be of a much more permanent nature.

This distinction between trading and business was also connected with the idea of business as employment. As market trading was not, it followed from this that traders would sometimes view themselves as 'unemployed'. This point can be illustrated by the difficulties encountered by the Lithuanian socialist Gruževskis (1995).

Gruževskis attempts to estimate hidden unemployment in Lithuania, as for various reasons the official figures are rather illusory. He operates with two categories outside the official statistics: 'hidden unemployment' and 'hidden employment'. But as unemployment benefits are low (maximum 96 litai per month), most unemployed persons tried to earn an additional income, as did all the 'employed' on unpaid vacation and others not officially registered as unemployed. The distinction between who is 'unemployed' and who is 'employed' in such a situation is difficult to make—empirically as well as analytically. Gruževskis mentions how, for example, persons who previously worked on a State farm, and who later, after the land reforms in the beginning of the 1990s, had started cultivating the land as independent farmers, often categorized themselves as 'unemployed'! The change from 'hired rural labourer' to 'farmer' was therefore not conceptualized as a *change* of job, but as a *loss* of job! The same applied to the urban population, where Gruževskis found that even small entrepreneurs who managed to maintain an income considerably higher than that of a monthly State-sector job salary would similarly categorize themselves as 'unemployed' (Gruževskis 1995: 11–12). It follows that privately earned income, although an important means of survival, did not qualify as an 'occupation'. Much the same seems to be the case in Gariūnai, where traders, although often earning considerably more than they did in their former State-sector jobs, considered themselves as 'unemployed'.

Finally, although both the trader and the businessman or businesswoman are

were only interested in short-term profits and not in long-term investments. 'People in Lithuania are not interested in doing business,' she complained, 'they are only interested in the money.'

confronted with the classification of their profits as 'unearned income' (Verdery 1996), the 'businessman' is regarded as being more in line with the expected development of a free market, not only because of his higher income, but also because of his more 'civilized' activities:

Yes, trading is business of course, but every kind of business should be civilized and we don't see much of this civilization in Gariūnai. Other traders, who sell in shops, in kiosks, from a counter, they pay something to the State: profit tax, value added tax. Traders in Gariūnai don't pay anything for the *Sodra* (social security). They don't care about the rest of society, they only care about themselves. (Television debate, *Nesutinku*, 1995)

Here the image of entrepreneurs outside the market was contrasted with the Gariūnai trader, and traders outside Gariūnai were regarded as somehow more conscious of their social responsibilities, because they paid taxes. In practice, however, there seemed to be little difference in the willingness (or unwillingness) to pay taxes among various groups of traders and entrepreneurs. I did not meet any businessman or businesswoman in Lithuania who paid all the taxes they were supposed to. Bribery and tax evasion were fairly normal in all businesses regardless of their size. Nobody attempted to deny this at all. The distinction between the two categories 'businessmen' and 'traders' (inside as well as outside the market) was mainly the result of differences in social networks. Those who had the right networks had no need to bribe their way through quite as openly as those who were unable to make use of their personal connections. Although such strong private networks were often referred to as 'Mafia' and generally criticized, businessmen who could make use of their connections were able to promote a more civilized business style, often because their activities were never made public.[4] In 1995 the business environment in Lithuania was dominated by such groups of networks structured by personal connections and contacts with administrative units. In order to enter a profitable business niche one was totally dependent on connections. Thus a rather different picture of the people in Gariūnai is emerging:

In Gariūnai there are people who are not able to establish their own private company, who are not in high positions, who have no uncles and aunts somewhere, and who had to start with a bottle of beer or a packet of cigarettes. (*Nesutinku*)

Traders in the market were very aware of this situation, where money was not enough to 'break out' of it. The very marginalization of Gariūnai can be regarded as a sign of this economic conflict, where other, more influential 'Mafias' struggle to monopolize important economic niches within the national economy.[5] As Jonas, a fairly successful market-trader, explained:

---

[4] In addition, this division may go back to Soviet morality, where everybody would make use of connections, but where bribery and black-market practices involving money were considered more morally problematic.

[5] Most shops in Vilnius also paid 'protection money' to racketeers, although I have no way of knowing whether these were the same groups as those operating in Gariūnai. The term 'Mafia' was often used in this way by traders themselves when describing the Lithuanian economic environment.

We can't do business outside Gariūnai. If I wanted to buy a shop in Vilnius . . . it's easy to find premises—no problem. But it's difficult to open a shop because, for example, if I wanted to open a shop in Vokiečiu Street and wanted to start trading in jeans, traders, or people from, for example, Londvil, who are also trading in jeans, simply wouldn't let me do so. It's because of corruption . . . big corruption. They have friends in the economic police or in the Fire Brigade . . . They would find a reason to close my shop. I would have big problems—they would come and check my business. Of course I would like to open a shop, because the prices in town are much better, but I can't handle this kind of business. (Jonas 2.1)

As Lithuanian legislation was then complicated and often contradictory, it was always possible to detect some violation of the law. Newcomers without connections would be unable to bribe or negotiate their way out again. Seen in this light, economic practices in Gariūnai did not seem fundamentally different from or more criminal than those of more 'established' businesses outside the market. The Gariūnai market would appear to be, not 'blacker', but rather a different shade of black compared with more prestigious businesses in Vilnius. Such successful businessmen might use their connections not only to keep others out of profitable branches, but also to 'cover' their very doing so, and they would therefore appear more 'civilized' and less corrupt than, for example, the market traders.

To sum up, the actual practices of traders and businessmen, although different in scope, seemed to be rather similar. Yet 'business' was categorized more as work than the 'petty trading' in the market. The importance of this difference, I suggest, can be connected with the importance of the workplace in Soviet society. This is because although the owner of, for example, a clothes shop may be no less of a trader than somebody selling jeans in the market, the staging is completely different.

THE IMPORTANCE OF THE WORKPLACE

When I made my survey of traders in Gariūnai (see Chapter 6), I also asked traders about their former occupation. Interestingly, a large number answered this question not in terms of 'I was a plumber' or 'I was an engineer' (although some of them did) but in terms of *where* they used to work. In many cases, the workplace was seen as more important than the kind of job they were doing there. Thus I got answers such as: 'I worked in the Post Office', 'In the Police', 'In the Soviet Army', or sometimes, 'In the "Dovana" factory'. One trader wrote: 'Worked in Ministry of Agriculture', without mentioning whether he was employed as the minister or as a secretary (although he probably would have mentioned it if he had been the minister). In short, when asked about former activity, *the place* of this activity was emphasized, in many cases to such an extent that the actual 'specialization' was not even mentioned. The workplace therefore must be understood to have played an important part in one's social identity—and seemed at least in some cases even more important than professional specialization. I suggest that this social importance of the workplace might have contributed to the marginalization of market trading, as the Gariūnai market could not provide traders with the institutional, social, and administrative framework that used to be part of one's 'work'. This might also further have strengthened the image of market traders as unemployed. If the idea of 'employment' was not only connected to receiving an actual wage and performing a specific job, but in addition meant access to child care, housing, pensions, etc. and generally formed an important identity-making role, it follows that work which is cut loose from all this may strictly speaking fail to qualify as 'real work'. The importance of the workplace, administratively, legally, and socially, and the complete lack of institutional framework in the market, sheds new light on the social stigmatization of market trading. In broader terms, this might involve a change in the relationship between work and identity.

The importance of the institutional frame of work can also be seen in the difference in image between an open-air and an indoor market (*mugė*). The difference is to be found purely in the way trading is staged, as both the goods and the actual activities are similar.[6] Another example of this is that Lithuanian open-air markets are generally regarded as being less civilized than similar markets in Poland. However, I was often at a loss when confronted with the complaint about the 'uncivilized' and 'uncultured' pattern of trading in Gariūnai compared with the Polish markets, because the actual differences in terms of variety and style of goods, profits, and style of trading seemed very small. The main difference was that the Polish markets were under roofs or even placed inside large hangars and thus appeared more like indoor markets.[7] Indoor markets, although by no means regarded as the most prestigious form of activity in Lithuanian society either, were more likely to be classified as 'shops' and those trading in them came closer to being considered 'shop assistants'.[8] At any rate the degree of institutional framework seems to play a very important part in establishing the status of trading and the social position of traders. Even within the internal hierarchy of the market, traders with a regular position with a tent or a van were considered to be more 'civilized' and 'cultured' than those trading from the ground or from 'uncovered cars'.

Paradoxically, while many traders take part in a symbolic struggle to make their trading more acceptable, for example by emphasizing the risk and hard labour involved, it seems that their reluctance in naming market trading as their occupation counteracts their own efforts to improve the market's image. Although a businessman may have trouble transferring his economic capital to influence his

---

[6] The one section in the market that is under a 'roof', *pastogė*, was considered to be more civilized than the rest of the market.

[7] It should be mentioned that some traders moreover found the language used in the Polish markets more polite than that in Gariūnai. Although there may have been more differences, I believe that these were all epitomized in the different staging of market trading in Poland, mainly as a result of being conducted under a roof.

[8] As mentioned in Chapter 7 in connection with femininity, I suggest that as a shop assistant one could permit oneself to be more elegantly dressed, and thus could further alienate oneself from the 'roughness' and 'uncivilized' character of the outdoor market.

position in the symbolic and social hierarchies (cf. Sampson 1993), he still seems more likely to succeed in doing so than the market trader. (One possible way for the businessman could be, as noted in the last chapter, to get involved in charity or other cultural activities.)

The market might provide an income, but nothing else in terms of social, moral, and professional respect. In the words of Mikhail, trading at Gariūnai seem to be a compromise between social prestige and money:

I don't know anybody who likes it. People would gladly have a *normal job* but they have no opportunity. Nowadays any job is just a waste of time because you can't earn enough at it. (Mikhail 5.1)

Thus, although neither business nor market trading may easily be accepted as an 'occupation' or 'employment' in accordance with post-socialist concepts of work and workplace, business is still closer to being a profession in terms of staging and style. Moreover, as many such economic activities are carried out in a marked Western style—at least on the surface—this, combined with the resultant prosperity, makes them more in accordance with transitional discourse and local expectations of the transition to a free market.

THE FORMALIZATION OF 'ADDITIONAL INCOMES'

As the Soviet system expected everybody to be committed to the well-being of the State, Soviet ideology gave priority to the individual's public role and duties over any form of private activity or interest. However, as an ironic result of the obvious widespread manipulation and control of cultural production and mistrust of the State, a large 'underground space' was created in which everybody was busy living their own lives as well as establishing their own truths and norms. Although views have varied as to the extent of public control over individual and private lives, duality as a structuring principle in Soviet-type societies has prevailed (e.g. Kenedi 1981, Mars and Altman 1983, Sampson 1987, Shlapentokh 1989, Bartusevičius 1993). Life in Soviet-style societies seems to have been characterized by the ability to deal with an ambivalence between rigidly separated communal and individual moralities. This seems to have had a tremendous influence on the conceptualization of work, because although engagement in all sorts of underground money-earning or bartering activities appears to have been widespread, the social, cultural, and administrative importance of work as a social and moral obligation and as a means of achieving prestige remained. By way of contrast, Gariūnai is associated with pure 'money-making' without the identity and social recognition that was previously supposed to be a part of 'work'. The fact that the market is legal does not have any positive effect on the evaluation of the market expressed by my informants. On the contrary, it seems that the very establishment of the market as a place, without being a workplace, places vendors in an even more dubious social and moral position than if they had been able to carry out their activities in secret.

The development of the market as a legal and public place has therefore not only resulted in a 'formalization' of the earlier hidden means of obtaining an additional income—thus moving this activity from one social context to another—but is also an example of a new kind of 'work', which has an almost exclusively economic function. Moreover, as unemployment has increased, more and more traders are involved in the market on a full-time basis and are deprived of their former social position based on employment in, and identification with, a morally and culturally invested workplace. Viewed in this light, market trading at Gariūnai cannot provide an alternative job, but only function as a source of income, and many traders as well as non-traders regard 'Gariūnai people' as unemployed. The stigmatization of market trading has, in this sense, less to do with a negative evaluation of the actual activity of trading than with the social and administrative functions that are absent in it.

The economic and political changes in Lithuania since independence was proclaimed in 1990 have had several drastic consequences for the structure of the labour market and for the possibility of earning a living and have furthermore encouraged new economic activities. In practice, the blurring of boundaries between 'work', 'employment', and 'unemployment' can be related to a fundamental transformation of the labour market, including new forms of money-earning activities and a reorganization of the principles of social stratification. This is, moreover, a much more general phenomenon in all Eastern European societies. As noted by Sampson in a recent article about the *nouveaux riches* in Romania and Hungary, not only do new social and cultural categories emerge but, more importantly, the 'basic principles for constructing these categories are changing' (Sampson 1993: 10).

Although in some ways at a social pole opposite to that occupied by the *nouveaux riches*, Gariūnai traders exemplify and face the same kind of 'symbolic consequences' of this fundamental social revolution.

CONCLUSION: *BARDAKAS* AS SYMBOLIC TRANSGRESSION

In the last three chapters I have discussed the 'disorder' of Gariūnai in the areas of ethnicity, gender, and work. In all three cases the disorder associated with Gariūnai could be related to much more widespread consequences of 'the transition'. Viewed in this light, the marginalization of Gariūnai seems to be connected with a reconceptualization of fundamental societal norms, cultural categories, and social identities. Parallel to the moral marginalization of the market, all three areas therefore reveal a process of boundary-remaking as a direct result of the institutionalization of market activities, the opening of Soviet borders towards Asia, and generally changing possibilities of means of survival. This means that the disorder in Gariūnai should not be understood solely as a departure from normative 'common sense', but additionally, since a fundamental reconstitution of these boundaries is taking place, as a challenge to existing hegemonic discourses on 'nation', 'gender', and 'work'.

However, it should be clear from the above discussions that within all three areas, ambiguities and antagonistic discourses also existed during the Soviet period. Furthermore, such discrepancies increased dramatically in the post-Stalinist period, especially in the last two decades of Soviet rule. But although neither ambivalence nor change is a recent phenomenon in Lithuania, transition, exemplified by the widespread disorder within fundamental social and cultural categories, has led to an intensification of 'the symbolic contest' after Lithuania's independence. It seems that the transition has resulted in the 'transgression' of earlier more or less accepted national, personal, political, and social boundaries. 'The transition' may here be viewed as a series of social and symbolic movements.

First, it may be seen as a movement from 'a locality' to several 'globalities', leaving out 'nationality' completely. The nation state hardly counts for anything here except as an obstacle in the form of regulations and taxes personified by the police and the customs at the border. Since national identity is a highly debated political area in Lithuania (as well as elsewhere in the former Eastern European bloc), this is difficult to tackle politically as well as symbolically in a nation that has recently become independent. Thus parts of the 'disorder' involve 'national transgression', since the 'national space' of the market is in practice occupied by traders who, in various ways, disregard Lithuanian national borders, as well as hegemonic cultural boundaries. This is visible at the national borders where the national 'gate-keepers' (customs officials) are bribed.

In the area of gender the direction of the movement is less obvious, yet I suggest that both women and men are transgressing the established boundaries of gender. The fundamentally feminine character of the market suggests that the territorial masculinity (see also Verdery 1996: 62–82) is being undermined. Although men still control the market territory, women's increasing influence on the market and their expertise in trading are challenging male dominance. Furthermore, although most women are still operating at the lower levels of trading, they travel physically long distances while their husbands stay at home. The independence and abilities that women acquire may also dispute gender boundaries. Finally, the very concept of 'femininity' is changing and becoming more masculine, so in a sense the market is undermining boundaries of femininity from within.

Regarding the final example, the changes that have taken place in 'work', there is also a series of movements involved. The most important is a transfer of wage-earning activities from a workplace to a place of heavy physical labour. The social, moral, and identity-making functions of the 'normal' workplace were lost in Gariūnai, the most important symptom being that the institutional framework is lacking (cf. Olwig 1990 for a discussion of the interrelationship between status and institution-building). Another indicator of this is the fact that relations between colleagues were partly being substituted and confused by competition.[9] Moreover,

---

[9] Since colleagues held an important social as well as economic function in Soviet society, the introduction of competition does have a serious impact on social relations in the market.

'making oneself and one's trading public' was perhaps the most important 'passage' for traders in Gariūnai as it included a reversal of the fundamental conceptualizations of the division between 'public' and 'private' conduct in Soviet society. The transgression involved here, which is inherent in the very establishment of the market, takes the form of moving one form of conduct from where it is 'tolerated' (in private) to where it is forbidden (in public). This movement has had consequences for the basic dualities of public and private social spaces in Lithuanian society and has resulted in a conceptual confusion of social identity and cultural orientation. The creation of a cultural grey zone in the market place indicates a re-establishment of cultural boundaries. Some of these changes epitomize changes in basic cultural categories and means of identity-making. 'The transition', therefore, may be most fruitfully understood by investigating such areas of boundary-making.

9

Remaking Boundaries

THE POST-COMMUNIST CONDITION AND NEW FORMS
OF DISTINCTION

Ever since Fredrik Barth's famous introduction to *Ethnic Groups and Boundaries* in 1969, boundaries and boundary-making have occupied an important place within anthropological theory. However, despite the well-known general critique in recent years of 'culture' as something homogeneous and bounded, anthropology has been 'preoccupied with boundaries between cultures' (Cohen 1994: 123), rather than with the analyses of boundaries that separate and divide. In my analysis of the changes in Lithuanian society after independence, boundaries have appeared to be crucial in many different ways and at various analytical levels. 'Transition' in the form of the establishment of new institutions such as the market place may be viewed as a kind of reterritorialization—also metaphorically—thus indicating changes in symbolic and social boundary-making as well. By focusing on society's 'internal' boundaries and their transformation, starting with those between the Gariūnai market and surrounding society, I have attempted to utilize anthropological fieldwork to go beyond the image of the market as an isolated yet homogeneous cultural entity. At a more general level, such an analytical framework presents society and culture[1] as diverse and stratified and therefore aims at an investigation of differences and how these are being reproduced rather than pursuing any kind of coherence or logic of a shared system of meaning. Consequently, the aim has been to investigate the complexity and ambiguity of 'transitional culture' by focusing not on the market itself but on its marginal social position and on the processes involved in reproducing a negative moral image of the market which consequently position the market as being outside and opposed to Lithuanian society. By studying forms of marginalization and exclusion, I have given analytical priority to processes of social hierarchization and symbolic struggle as well as power relations and social identities in the making.

The 'transition', involving new means of survival, new social identities and

---

[1] I have almost entirely refrained from using the word 'culture' throughout the book, precisely because it connotes boundedness and homogeneity. Instead I have frequently used the term 'discourse', which although by no means an unambivalent term, emphasizes power relations, ambiguity, and positioning, and thus in the words of Abu-Lughod, 'works against the assumption of boundedness, not to mention idealism of the culture concept' (Abu-Lughod 1991: 148).

social roles, has made boundary-making an essential social strategy in post-social-ist society. Not only do we find an increased need to affirm social and cultural distinctions in a situation of social reorganization, but since the need to reaffirm boundaries is accompanied by rapidly changing social conditions and symbolic capital, a strong sense of ambiguity has emerged within the social field. This has pushed the whole process of boundary-making even further into the focus of attention. In the Lithuanian context, the establishment of Gariūnai in the first place, and the continuous process of its moral exclusion, epitomize processes of symbolic struggle and (re)making of boundaries within the new economic field.

In Chapters 1 and 2 I argued that the moral stigmatization of market trading, although anchored in Soviet ideology of trading conceptualized as speculation, cannot be understood solely as a remnant of socialist thinking. Although the market was clearly conceptualized as originating from the Soviet underground markets, *talkučkė*, and although formally the stigmatization of *talkučkė* in Soviet times was used as an explanation of the uneasiness about the Gariūnai market, the individual trading histories in Chapter 3 reveal that such stigmatization had increased rather than decreased since the establishment of the market as a legal trading place. Rather than viewing the attitudes towards market trading as a 'remnant' of socialist thinking, I found therefore that the marginalization of the market could be related to the establishment of a legal and public institution as well as to the terminological shift from 'speculation' to 'trading'. In other words, marginalization cannot be understood as a continuation of tradition, but has to be seen in relation to the specific conditions under which it is currently being repro-duced. According to Bourdieu, such attitudes may be regarded as a complex mixture of past and present:

because they tend to reproduce the regularities immanent in the conditions in which their generative principle was produced while adjusting to the demands inscribed as objective potentialities in the situation as defined by the cognitive and motivating structures that constituted the *habitus*, practices cannot be deduced either from the present conditions which may seem to have provoked them or from the past conditions which have produced the *habitus*; the durable principle of their production. They can therefore only be accounted for by relating the social conditions in which the *habitus* that generated them was consti-tuted, to the social conditions in which it is implemented, that is, through the scientific work of performing the interrelationship of these two states of the social world that the *habitus* performs, while concealing it, in and through practice. (Bourdieu and Wacquant 1992: 56)

Throughout the book my aim has been to uncover the social conditions in Soviet society and in post-Communist Lithuania that are relevant to an under-standing of the differences within the specific market field (or sub-field) as well as the differences that appear related to the social seclusion of the market as a place and as a social and symbolic space in society, in practice as well as in discourse. After Chapters 2 and 3, where I attempted to trace the market place and market practices back to conditions in Soviet society, I presented in Chapter 4 an analysis of the conditions and trading practices in the 'transitional' market. There I found that the most important feature of the market was its continuous but rapid process of being 'in the making'. Buyers and sellers needed constantly to be on the alert and to seek new knowledge of seasonal changes in goods, prices, and trade routes. The rapid institutionalization of certain forms of trading and the collapse of others made the ability to seek reliable information the main prerequisite for being successful in the market. But the conditions of 'transitional society' were also mirrored in the Asian trade routes and Asian commodities in the market, combined with an overall attempt to Westernize this merchandise. Here again, boundary-making becomes important, because the specific links with Asia combined with the attempted Westernization create a very specific and unplanned trans-national space, which in political discourses as well as in folk models is presented as excluded from Lithuanian culture and thus from the imagined Lithuanian community. I shall return to this matter below.

Perhaps the idea of reterritorialization has become most evident in Chapter 5, where I dealt with another aspect of the transitional society, the influence of racketeers and new forms of violence. Moreover, the analysis of the power struggle and the development of new forms of discipline and control which I embarked on quickly forced me to include a discussion of forms of communication and communicative style. The crude strategies of control in the market and their opaqueness have promoted forms of communication in 'half-words', a technique that seems to have evolved during Soviet rule. This specific form of communication furthermore functions as a symbolic boundary between insiders and outsiders in the market.

Already at this point I therefore had to go beyond the economic field (to use Bourdieu's term) since the reproduction of the boundaries in the market as well as between the market and the outside world seemed to include rather different cultural and social domains in addition to the economic ones.

In Chapters 6, 7, and 8, I further developed this non-economic aspect, following the processes of social and cultural change that the market epitomizes by discussing three social domains: ethnicity, gender, and work. Here I argued that the image of the market as 'out of order' may be closely related to the recontextualization of practices within these domains. Many of these changes were initiated during the last decade of Sovietism. The discrepancy between official discourse and actual practices, which seemed so problematic in all three cases, is therefore not entirely a recent phenomenon, although it has both accelerated and changed in form. By establishing the market place as a public institution, such discrepancies have become visible and more difficult to ignore. Furthermore, since we are dealing here with key cultural domains, the crisis that has been revealed becomes crucial, because it involves questioning basic social identities, moral responsibilities, and ultimately the very reproduction of society. Here I would like to point out that I have not intended to argue that the only change that is taking place is a transfer of activities from one sphere to another, but rather to emphasize that the present cultural ambiguity is only partly a phenomenon of the transition.

Furthermore, I contend that the specific contextualization of such ambiguities in the market is an important factor when discussing the marginalization of the market.

What has emerged from the above-mentioned discussion and manifested itself generally throughout the analysis is that the moral marginalization of Gariūnai seemed to be closely connected to boundary making and remaking in a variety of ways, and at several levels of abstraction. I shall now investigate some of these boundaries and the recontextualization that has followed in the wake of the political and economic changes introduced after Lithuanian independence. Although I have argued that socialist ideology cannot in itself account for the present stigmatization of trading and especially market trading, the moral economy of Marxism-Leninism has of course had a marked influence on present attitudes to money and wealth as well as on general criticism of the strategies involved in social mobility. Thus the moral economy of socialism, combined with the very transformation of economy from what was an at least formally controlled economy of redistribution to an at least formally free market, will therefore be my starting-point in a concluding discussion of the relation between the market, moral economy, and marginalization. This discussion will prove to be directly related to that of boundary-remaking in general and the ambiguity of recontextualization that I have mentioned above. As I have continuously argued throughout the book, the imagined differences between the market and other forms of trading are notably larger than the differences 'in practice'. We need to understand why. We may start by asking why it was and is necessary to seclude this segment of traders physically, morally, and socially from surrounding society. And we may also ask, who benefited from this?

COMMODITIZATION AND MORALITY

Moral uneasiness and condemnation of market exchange as well as of the people engaged in it is by no means a specifically Lithuanian or recent phenomenon. Within anthropological literature there are numerous empirical examples of negative moral evaluations of money and market-related activities, commonly termed commoditization (cf. Appadurai 1986). Such reactions have shown a remarkable similarity in various parts of the world. Moreover, as Helgason and Palsson have noted in a very enlightening paper entitled *Contested Commodities: Mapping the Moral Landscape of Exchange* (1996),[2] there is a similarity in the metaphors used to express this moral uneasiness and resistance.

This process [of commoditization] involves the eradication and homogenisation of extant social relations and significations that govern the movement of things in exchange and the expansion of a single, universally commensurable standard of value. Interestingly, such

---

[2] This paper was presented at the EASA conference in Barcelona in 1996 in the session on 'The Duality of Economic Life'.

objections are commonly manifest as condemnations of profit-oriented motives, laden with metaphors of danger, greed and immorality. (Helgason and Palsson 1996: 2)

A few cases will serve to illustrate this. One of the best-known examples of the cultural effects of commoditization is Taussig's analysis (1980) of two ethnographic settings in South America (Bolivia and Colombia). Here he shows how the metaphor of entering a contract with the Devil was evoked when peasants were 'entering the market economy' in the form of wage-labour in the mines (ibid.). As Bloch and Parry have discussed at length in their introduction to *Money and the Morality of Exchange* (1989), such disruptive power is furthermore often attributed (also by Western scholars) to money itself. Thus commoditization may lead to a differentiation in the conceptualization of money *within* the same society, as Verdery (1996) has shown in the case of Romania at the beginning of the 1990s, where a pyramid scheme known as Caritas had emerged. During the first three years of its existence it managed to make large parts of the Romanian population invest their savings in the expectation of getting an eightfold return on their money after three months. According to Verdery this 'easy' way of making money led to a conceptual differentiation: money became divided into 'Caritas money' and 'other money', or 'their money' versus 'my money'. In passing we may note a similarity in the Lithuanian context, where money made in the market was also perceived as 'unearned', because people were not really 'working' to make it. In the Romanian case, the distinction was carried further into the field of morality as 'their money' was increasingly being conceptualized as 'unearned money' or 'dirty money' as opposed to 'my money' as being 'earned' and morally neutral (Verdery 1996: 168 ff.). It should be noted, however, that the cultural reaction to Caritas was not only a negative evaluation of 'evil money' but also a development of a whole new conceptual world of money based on ideas of 'faith', 'trust', and 'hope' (ibid. 189 ff.). Finally, Zelizer (1979) has studied the moral evaluations of commoditization in Western societies. Part of the virtue of her study is that she cements the notion of commoditization as a continuous process and not a singular 'event' where commercial products, money, and commercial exchange are introduced. She analyses the cultural reactions to the development of life insurance in the United States in the nineteenth century and finds that reactions are often ambivalent if not directly hostile. The idea of making money out of life and death, both domains associated with religion, was regarded as improper and the money was often regarded as 'dirty' (Zelizer 1979; see also Helgason and Palsson 1996).

As indicated by the above example from Romania, in post-socialist Eastern Europe in particular (although market economy as an ideology is often readily appropriated here) there is still a certain amount of moral uneasiness and condemnation of trade and wealth. This is further emphasized by Sampson in his analysis of the *nouveaux riches* in Romania and Hungary (Sampson 1993). Sampson analyses how the newly rich engage in a symbolic struggle in order to transfer their economic capital into a symbolic or cultural one, since their wealth of economic capital is supposed to be matched by 'wealth of cultural capital' (ibid.). But one common condition of the post-Communist societies in Europe is that the social and moral discourses in which the new entrepreneurs operate are complex and often conflicting. As old status systems have broken down, the need to signal one's new position in society increases, yet this is evaluated as improper. An example of this is reported by Kryshtanovskaya (1994) from Russia, where the newly rich attempt to hide the ways in which they have made their money while at the same time exhibiting signs of their wealth by buying expensive cars and building large new houses.

As we have seen in Lithuania, when the social consequences of commoditization become visible, the moral outcry increases and hostility and accusations of fraud, criminality, and theft become widespread. In his introduction to *Contesting Markets: Analyses of Ideology, Discourse and Practice* (1992), Dilley also discusses moral evaluation of the market and market trading. In his view, the moral discourse is a result of the processes of contestation that are inherent in changing exchange relations, as well as a product of the particular socio-cultural environment:

> The relationship between morality and commerce cannot simply be derived from the structure of a peasant ideology. Moral evaluations, whose forms are always culture specific, result from the processes of contestation within, and over, exchange relations. In the hands of exchange partners—perhaps for the lack of any other means—morality is a weapon in the attempt to address potential imbalances of power relations which arise from and are articulated throughout the extension and development of 'market' relations. (Dilley 1992: 6)

According to Dilley, moral condemnation is therefore a weapon in the hands of the weak, the losers in the struggle for influence in the emerging market. But although contestation is certainly a part of the problem, changes in moral economy should not solely be understood as a question of domination and power struggle.

More often, however, the Durkheimian view of market exchange as destroying solidarity by disrupting moral bonds is inferred—or referred to—in anthropological studies of commoditization. The same line of thinking can be found in analyses focusing on commodity versus gift exchange, where negative moral evaluations are seen as a reaction to the substitution of personal and altruistic gift exchange with impersonal, but profitable, commodity exchange. Such ideas are moreover widespread in local Eastern European evaluations of the emerging market, since Marx has been one of the most influential critics of the market and its destruction of moral bonds and social obligations (for a survey, see Bloch and Parry 1989: 8 ff.). But, as Appadurai has shown (1986), the radical opposition between the two kinds of exchange is dubious, and furthermore more likely to be the product of their separation in Western economic thinking. Bloch and Parry, who share his view (although proposing an entirely different framework), moreover point to several empirical exceptions to the gift/commodity dichotomy in the non-Western world, where the two kinds of exchange often coexist quite unproblematically. Taking as their starting-point the view that since the meaning of money and commodities not only varies cross-culturally but also appears to be contextualized and continually changing, even within distinct social settings, Bloch and Parry look for other ways than the idea of the 'corrupting market' in order to understand the apparent similarities in the moral responses to commoditization throughout the world. Instead they focus their attention on the existence of different exchange spheres of value (exemplified by Bohannan's analysis (1955) of the Tiv economy) and especially the transfer that takes place between such spheres. Boundary-making and the negotiation of boundaries form an important part of such an approach; according to Bloch and Parry (also Helgason and Palsson, who have attempted to expand this framework) it is not trading or money itself that causes the condemnation, but the collapse of the boundaries between various formerly separated spheres of exchange:

The study of commoditization . . . presents an example of transformation within the moral economy of things. Thus, as things and classes of things gravitate towards the commodity sphere of market exchange, boundaries are rearranged, equivalencies in exchange are homogenised and social relations and significations are transformed. (Helgason and Palsson 1996: 15)

Bloch and Parry then continue to extract two basic spheres of exchange, which seem to be coexisting in a range of different social settings: a long-term transactional order, concerned with the reproduction of the cosmic and/or social order, and 'a sphere of short-term transactions concerned with the arena of individual competition' (Bloch and Parry 1989: 24). The long-term order would typically be religious donations, or gifts to community leaders or elders. Now, these 'orders' are of course generally to be kept separate so as to ensure the reproduction of society and especially to ensure the domination of the long-term order over the individual one. It seems furthermore that diversions from the short-term order into the long-term order are considered positive (as, for example, one could note in the case of charity), but a flow in the opposite direction (an example would be all forms of corruption) is bound to cause very negative moral evaluations. An illuminating example is the Brahman who receives a religious donation and keeps it for himself without 'passing it on'. 'The consequence is not only the belief that he himself will rot with leprosy and suffer the torments of hell', but also that he will bring misfortune to the donors of the gift, since he is 'blocking the channels of purification' (ibid. 27). Another example is the moral condemnation of life insurances described by Zelizer, where the commoditization of life and death, which may be viewed as belonging to the sphere of reproduction of society, was being condemned. The above approach is highly suggestive in an Eastern European context. I therefore suggest that the coexistence of several spheres of transaction and the decontextualization of such spheres form a relevant framework in order to understand the changes in moral economy in Eastern Europe and thus in my empirical context of Lithuania after the transition. I would like to emphasize, however, that we need to outline such spheres of exchange by looking at actual practices and not, as Bloch and Parry in fact do, by focusing solely on economic discourses. The difference may be illustrated by the following statement:

While we believe that the pattern [the existence of two separate transactional orders] we have identified as common to all our case studies is typical of a wide range of societies, it is arguable that the mature ideology of capitalism would be an example of something entirely different. By a remarkable conceptual revolution, what has uniquely happened in capitalist ideology, the argument would run, is that the values of the short-term order have become elaborated into a theory of long-term reproduction. (Bloch and Parry 1989: 29)

Bloch and Parry continue to suggest that we may describe capitalism as 'a theory in which it is only unalloyed private vice that can sustain the public benefit' (ibid.) According to this line of thought, what is happening in Eastern Europe after 'the transition' is not only an *expansion* of the short-term exchange spheres, which have apparently caused moral condemnations of money in a range of Third World contexts, but an even more radical *substitution* of two opposed systems of transactional orders. Socialist society, where the economy may be formally understood as a system of redistribution, can then be described as the other extreme case—the antithesis to capitalism, because, as ideology, it allowed no space for the existence of a short-term, individually oriented transactional order at all. The framework is enlightening, yet by this last leap it seems to fall into the dichotomy trap again, as in this form it moves dangerously close to the commodity/gift dichotomy that it itself attempted to criticize. Instead of focusing on various separated exchange contexts *within* societies, we are back at discussing economic differences *between* societies. But if we instead focus our attention on economic practice models, the framework of recontextualization among various transactional orders, as it has been outlined by Bloch and Parry, seems highly illuminating in an analysis of economics and morality in post-Communist societies.

THE MARKET AS IMAGERY AND PRACTICE

Although often presented as such in Western political and economic discourses, the transformation of the Eastern European economies cannot simply be termed 'a transition' from a planned economy to a market economy. Soviet-style economies, as shown by, for example, Sampson (1987), Verdery (1991), Humphrey (1991), and Gerner and Hedlund (1994), could not simply be understood as planned. Black economic practices were widespread, and bribery and 'informal networking' resulted in a general diversion of resources away from their proper channels of distribution. Underground production was closely connected to and dependent on the official economy as this was the only place to get the resources necessary to engage in any production at all. Actually existing socialist economy may rather be viewed as a coexistence of three typologically different exchange systems: plan (redistribution), market (commercial exchange), and gifts (reciprocity).[3] Moreover, when speaking about socialist economies in Eastern Europe, distinctions between these sorts of transactions were by no means easy to make. As Sampson (1987), among others, has pointed out, underground economic practice could neither ontologically nor analytically be separated from the formal economy. For example, gifts seem to have played an important role in the everyday lives of people in the former Soviet Union, being commonly used to obtain access to basic services such as education, housing, or hospitals. A Lithuanian–American businesswoman stated:

> In English there are not different words for a 'business gift' and a bribe. But 'business gifts' always existed in Lithuania. You gave something as a sign of gratitude. But the huge bribes of today—that is something different. (Rita, Vilnius businesswoman)

Such gifts could be viewed more as a kind of 'forced obligation to repay them' than as a gift in the sense of an altruistic and 'non-economic' object of exchange (Bartusevičius 1993). In practice, therefore, the actual transition of the Soviet and Soviet-style economies has as its starting-point an economic system that may be said to have contained several economic spheres of exchange, separated by their contextualization rather than by name or type. Although space limitations prevent me from elaborating this point here, the image of the 'end product of transition' (a free market) in Western Europe may likewise be problematized by analysing actual economic conduct and market structure as it has been done, for example, by Alexander (1992). An example could be the European Union's subsidization of the agricultural sector, which actually resembles 'plan' considerably more than 'market'.[4] The most important point here is the failure to distinguish between ideology and practice, or, more broadly, ignorance of the differences between economic models as 'models of' and 'models for', expressed by Gudeman and Penn (1982) as 'local models' and 'universal models'. Indeed, Gerner and Hedlund (1994) have seriously criticized Western political discourses and Western aid to the former Soviet Union for building politics on a neo-classicist economic *vision* in which (as mentioned above) 'only unalloyed private vice can sustain the public benefit', without taking into account the actual limitations of the 'free market' in Western Europe. Gerner and Hedlund use the development of a wild bazaar economy in post-Communist Russia as an example of how Western economic experts and politicians have failed to give their Eastern European counterparts adequate assistance. They are therefore on the whole highly critical of what they conceive as

---

[3] Feher, Heller, and Markus in *Dictatorship over Needs* (1983) have also characterized the Soviet-style economies as consisting of 'three economies': command economy, second economy, and informal networking.

[4] Moreover, although the Western markets are ideally speaking market economies, there are many things that have still not been commodified. Such items as donor organs, and more generally people (although professional football players come close), may still not be bought and sold. At the margins of the market there is a changing set of items that may be sold, but are not considered 'nice' to sell, e.g. sex, weapons, pesticides, and the Crown Jewels, to mention but a few. The Western markets are therefore obviously limited by morality as well.

an unrealistic project of transforming the former Soviet Union into an ideal model of late American capitalist society, their main argument being that modern versions of the neo-classicist economic paradigm completely ignore the historical foundation of the economy in the West. Gerner and Hedlund maintain that the whole project of rapid systemic transformation in Eastern Europe was totally unrealistic from the outset. There is no single ready-made version of Western society, and even if there were, it would be unrealistic to assume that it could be easily transferable to a radically different socio-cultural context (ibid.).

On the other hand, if we combine the knowledge of economic practice models with the framework of transactional orders, we obtain an interesting framework for understanding the marginalization of trading, including market trading in post-Communist Lithuania. First, the development of a market place as a continuation of black-market practice during Sovietism may be understood as a form of commoditization of network-based barter. The very establishment of a distinct place of exchange literally separates commercial exchange from other social relations. In addition, place-making, or siting of commercial exchanges, may also be viewed as another kind of recontextualization as illegitimate forms of exchange become visible and 'a trader' becomes a new social role. This is especially important in the Lithuanian case, since the 'peaceful coexistence' of black economic practices and the formal economy in the Soviet period was apparently dependent on social and feigned public ignorance of the black-market trade. By focusing on practice, the physical visibility of traders, money, and markets in post-Communist societies therefore indicates not only a break with Marxist-Leninist definitions of trade as illegitimate and amoral, but a break with the established strategies of dealing with the market and commercial exchange. The process of recontextualization here has rather taken the form of separating transactional orders, which were earlier closely connected and integrated. But although the overall process of reconstructing Soviet transactional orders definitely plays a part in the overall marginalization of market trading, the approach does not adequately explain why new private shops are not conceptualized as morally problematic to the same extent as are the open-air markets. In order to understand such a distinction, I shall turn to the common conceptualization of 'the transition' as a 'return to Europe.

TRANSITION AND THE 'RETURN TO EUROPE'

In Lithuania (Bartusevičius 1993), Poland (Buchowski 1994), and Czechoslovakia (Holy 1992), the phrase 'to return to Europe' is an important way of expressing the goal of transition. The phrase denotes an image of the West as 'cultured' and 'civilized'. Moreover, 'to return to Europe' indicates in all three cases a return to an imagined 'normal order' based on personal freedom, market economy, and democracy (in that order). Eastern European countries compete as to who is most 'European', as for example when Czechs position their country as 'the heart of Europe' while Lithuanians present 'the geographical centre of Europe' as a tourist attraction. However, the idea of European culture, democracy, and the market is often rather vague. Bartusevičius (1993) has discussed this critically by looking at Lithuanian discourses on 'transition'. He maintains that the symbolism in the phrase 'return to Europe' resembles old Communist slogans, lacks specific political content, and therefore can be used to manipulate and criticize rather than as a starting-point for real changes. Nevertheless, the ideal of a European, civilized, prosperous market forms an important part of Lithuanian discourses of 'the transition'. I suggest that this has influenced evaluations of Gariūnai and market trading in general and plays a part in the different moral evaluations of various aspects of the emerging market.

In a television programme an interviewee expressed his criticism of the Gariūnai market as follows: 'Try going to a civilized country like Denmark, which is really an example for Lithuania, and then try to pay in dollars!' (*Nesutinku*, April 1995) Paying in dollars is a symptom of the uncivilized nature of market trading as it is contrasted with national currencies in Western countries. It is interesting to note here that in Lithuania in 1995 it was common to pay for expensive commodities like cars and housing in dollars as well, yet dollars used in these situations were to my knowledge not conceptualized as 'uncivilized' in the same manner as dollars in the market. By using dollars fairly openly in Gariūnai, traders not only demonstrated the illegal aspects of their trading but also (and this I believe is the basic difference) made their international trading routes 'public' by trading in dollars. The 'uncivilized' use of dollars in Lithuanian markets was often contrasted with the situation in Polish markets, where in the mid-1990s it was rare to use dollars as a currency. Since most of the Polish commodities at the time were produced in Poland, Polish traders had no need of dollars and thus they disappeared as a currency. On the other hand, in Lithuania, where home production was limited (although generally increasing) in comparison with the Asian commodities in the market, dollars prevailed as market currency. Moreover, in spite of the overall attempt to Westernize commodities, the Asian aspect of the trade was obvious and widely known. The prevalence of dollars in the market, as well as the existence of fake Western commodities, epitomize therefore a discrepancy between the imagined 'return to Europe', and the actual Asian influences. The market not only appeared then as a non–Lithuanian global space, but also as a symptom of a rather different kind of internationalization that was both expected and wanted. Although, as Kryshtanovskaya (1994), among others, has shown, travel and internationalism were important signs of status in Soviet society, such 'internationalism' was almost solely understood as 'Western'. The kind of market Lithuania aimed for was one that fitted the image of 'returning to Europe'. This was a Western functioning of the market principle with nice, clean shops and Western goods and not a Middle Eastern bazaar. The difference between 'market' as principle and as place is important here, since, as mentioned above, and also by Kryshtanovskaya, the various negative moral evaluations of commercial exchange have led to strategies by businessmen and the newly rich with the aim of *hiding their actual activities* while at the same time *demonstrating their wealth*. Open-air markets thus not only contradict the imagined direction towards Western Europe by being Asian rather than American, but also by exhibiting commodities and trading and thus the means of making money rather than the wealth itself.

The importance of such images when analysing moral reactions to the market has likewise been expressed by Holy (1992) in the case of Czechoslovakia where, as in Lithuania, there appeared to be a close relation between the idea of a return to Europe, national identity, and moral condemnation of 'the wrong kind' of economic agents:

The self-image of the Czechs as a cultured and civilized nation is invoked in the moral condemnation of the money-changers and emerging private entrepreneurs. As they offer their services mostly to foreigners who do not know their way around, they destroy the reputation of the Czechs as a cultured nation and create the undesirable image of Czechs as cheats, swindlers and profiteers. In doing so, they hamper the Czechs' return to Europe: 'Would Europe really want us if we are not able to behave in a civilized manner?' is regularly the bottom line of moral reprehension about the activities of the private entrepreneurs. (Holy 1992: 240)

If we return for a moment to the 'blurring of boundaries' between the transactional spheres of exchange, discussed above, we find that such a framework, although enlightening in terms of showing a general struggle within the field of economy, is inadequate if we want to comprehend the different moral reactions that have taken place. We have to transcend the field of economy and look for 'other boundaries' in order to depict the specific position of the market place in post-Communist Lithuania.

REJECTING LIMINALITY

The relation between the market place and society ('society' understood here both geographically as the town of Vilnius and figuratively as 'the accepted social order') is therefore rather complex. Viewed from the point of view of official political discourses, the market is clearly separated and demarcated from society, physically, socially, and morally, yet according to my analysis of the production of this marginal position, the market, in terms of both practice and discourse of the 'disorder', seems closely bound to central cultural and social domains of Lithuanian society. The 'connection' can be defined as a double bind. We can define one part of the 'bind' as a direct social connection and a second connection as a form of 'symbolic othering'. Regarding the first, there are obvious similarities between trading practices in the market and economic practices outside it. This was shown in areas such as the use of dollars, Asian commodities, black money, bribery, and so forth. Another aspect of this direct connection was the fact that traders were oriented socially towards society at large (as we saw in Chapter 3, often hiding their activities in the market) and therefore their conduct and motivation can only be analysed in terms of both the market and everyday life in general. Finally, regarding the 'social connection', traders are involved with a range of society's institutions when crossing national borders. One important aspect of their occupation is negotiating with the customs and another is their relationships with the police. Both 'meetings' must be understood as partly reflecting the 'working principles' of the State institutions.

In addition we have seen the market used as a 'significant other' in a range of contexts and this can give us important clues as to the imagined symbolic order in society. As Douglas expresses it:

If we can abstract pathogenicity and hygiene from our notion of dirt, we are left with the old definition of dirt as a matter out of place. This is a very suggestive approach. It implies two conditions: a set of ordered relations and a contravention of that order. Dirt, then, is never a unique, isolated event. Where there is dirt there is system. Dirt is the by-product of a systematic ordering and classification of matter, in so far as ordering involves rejecting inappropriate elements. The idea of dirt takes us straight into the field of symbolism and promises a link-up with more obviously symbolic systems of purity. (Douglas 1995 (1966): 36)

As a final move we may therefore rephrase the question of the marginality of the market and ask instead: What can the study of the marginalization of Gariūnai tell us about the making of present and future economic, social, and cultural boundaries in Lithuanian society?

MAKING 'OTHER' BOUNDARIES

Although I do not know the exact circumstances that eventually led to the establishment of a market 10 km outside Vilnius, is seems clear that the removal of traders from the town centre added a physical boundary to the already existing social boundary between market traders and large parts of the surrounding community—Vilnius itself. Because trading was perceived as morally and legally problematic, the act of 'collecting traders' and positioning them at one place seemed partly to be aimed at freeing society from 'this evil'. Instead of having traders 'everywhere around the corners',[5] the uncivilized nature of market trading was (supposedly) being secluded from Lithuanian society. However, the process of establishing such a market had far-ranging unforeseen and unplanned consequences. Not only has 'petty trading' become more visible, socially and economically, but establishing the market as a 'window' has furthermore exposed various other contested domains. As I have argued above (see Chapters 6, 7, and 8), 'siting' market trading therefore framed the social consequences of 'transition' and thereby illuminated a general confusion within key cultural domains. Thus, ironically, the establishment of physical boundaries between market trading and society has added to the moral uneasiness and condemnation connected with it, because it

---

[5] *Nesutinku*, April 1995.

has revealed other contested fields. The result has been that traders and commercial exchange have moved from a more or less anonymous existence to occupying a place and a cultural space in the centre of a range of symbolic, political, and economic struggles following independence and the economic and political changes. Market trading appeared to be more important in the mid-1990s, several years after the legalization of such forms of trading, both economically and in terms of national as well as social identity-making.

The focus on boundary-making combined with an emphasis on practice has led me to look beyond the official picture of the market as marginal and temporary. It appears neither as an isolated place, nor, if the social and symbolic consequences are included in the analysis, as just a temporary phase in 'the economic transition'. The social and symbolic marginalization of the market is connected just as much with the remaking of boundaries that cross-cut such a division of 'the market versus society'. I am therefore no longer concerned (nor have I been for some time) with the market, but with understanding the reproduction of society by analysing areas where spatial, social, and symbolic boundaries are being made. This is an illuminating approach to what I have so far termed 'the transition', not only because it provides a framework for conceptualizing the key areas of change, but also because the concept of 'boundary' demands clear definitions of the groups or categories involved as well as their mutual positions. According to Cohen (1994) we may define boundaries as follows:

boundaries are the subjects of claim based on a perception by at least one of the parties of certain features which distinguish it from others. Whether it refers to a collective condition, such as ethnic group identity, or to something as ephemeral as 'personal space', boundary suggests contestability, and is predicated on consciousness of a diacritical property. (Cohen 1994: 122)

Boundaries are socially constructed and strategically invested and manipulated. They may be negotiable and soft, or they may be fixed and unavoidable. Finally, they may be changed, destroyed, remade, and diverted from their original meaning. In short, they may be challenged and often reveal points of social and symbolic contestation. An analysis of boundary-making thus involves a focus on social agents and their practices. I would furthermore contend, following Douglas above, that boundaries are not only, as emphasized by Barth (1969), mainly strategic and instrumental, although these are of course important aspects too. As Cohen has emphasized: 'When we consult ourselves about who we are, that entails something more than the rather negative reflection on "who we are *not*" ' (Cohen 1994: 120). By focusing on boundary-making within groups and on what boundaries aim at keeping in (or keeping out) it becomes necessary to acknowledge processes of change within the fields of symbolism, identity, and meaning. In addition, the focus on the remaking of boundaries, viewed in this light, enables us to follow new social groups and new identities in the making. Pellow has briefly discussed the relationship between spatial and conceptual boundaries in her short introduction to *Setting Boundaries: The Anthropology of Spatial and Social Organization* (1996). The material presented here has shown that it may be fruitful to keep different kinds of boundaries analytically separate, and make their (changing) relationship an analytical focus. Pellow mentions specifically the relationship between physical and social boundaries as particularly interesting. In the case of the Lithuanian market, it was quite clear that the physical and social boundaries by no means coincided. Although the establishment of a physically bounded market place did reflect some social boundaries as well, it also revealed changes in social and symbolic boundaries which cross-cut the physical and visible social division. Changes in physical and spatial boundaries, although enlightening, may in some ways always be socially manipulated and invested with new meaning.

Another point of importance here is the boundaries between various kinds of status hierarchies. An analysis of the market in Lithuania has not only revealed a process of separation between formerly closely integrated economic exchange systems (redistribution, commercial exchanges, and gifts), but also a general separation of various status systems. As new means of social stratification are combined with old status systems, we find an increasing discrepancy between a person's economic, social, and cultural capital. Ambiguity within the social domain was also inherent under Sovietism, apparent for example in the high status of intellectuals within the official socialist discourse and their low ranking in more pragmatic 'private discourses of consumption'. However, as new status hierarchies become more visible and economic capital outweighs its cultural and social counterparts, social boundaries may appear more bitterly contested. This may result in new categorizations and new forms of social seclusion, such as the market place at Gariūnai. An example of such contestation and its social consequences can be found if we turn to changes in ethnic boundary-making.

Although there appeared to be several 'floating' discourses of ethnicity in Lithuanian society in the mid-1990s, the establishment of the market place and thus the physical and social creation of a boundary between the market and society resulted in a process of transformation. New forms of trans-ethnicity appeared, based on the use of the Russian language as well as on trans-national mobility. By examining processes of boundary-making inside the market place, as well as those made between the market and surrounding society, I was forced in this way to look at other social distinctions as well as make room for a reconsideration of ethnic boundary-making in general. Such a focus revealed that ideas of *bounded* 'ethnicity' and 'nationality' were being partly substituted by *forms of trans-ethnicity* as well as trans-nationality. Although these new forms of local yet trans-ethnic (instead of ethnic) identities were built on older Lithuanian traditions of identity-making, especially from Vilnius, their 'reinvention' and social importance were definitely accelerated by the establishment of the market. Forms of trans-ethnicity which reappeared in this way were not, however, readily accepted, and thus in turn reinforced the already existing boundary between the market and society. In addition, as the competition within the economic field as a whole increased, the 'losers' started to appear in the market. Ironically, the market place became the locus of agents and activities that had been pushed out of the emerging market economy. This further reinforced the market's marginality. Viewed over a longer time span, the moral condemnation and social seclusion of the Vilnius Jews of the early markets at the beginning of the century had developed into a seclusion of 'those without social connections', the Russian-speaking minorities, intellectuals, and increasingly women.

In this way the possibility of studying a place bounded by shifting forms of 'moral condemnation' has given me a methodological and epistemological advantage. Acknowledging the changing negatively invested place has created a dialogue between various Lithuanian social positions. The naming of otherwise silent attitudes and practice has revealed new interpretations of 'transition'. This choice of an analytical focus on marginalization has, as mentioned above, resulted in a 'dialogue' between several Lithuanian voices. It has sharpened my focus on boundary-making *within* Lithuanian society. Thus, in addition to the ever prevalent dichotomy of anthropologist versus 'anthropologized', I have added another level of 'othering' among the 'anthropologized'. Apart from making the whole research process considerably more complicated in this way, I have also (luckily) found that the approach has yielded additional insight into the contestation, stratification, and social and symbolic reterritorialization which, to my mind, is what 'the transition' is really all about. Moreover, although I do not contend that I have found the solution to the theoretical and political problems of reflexivity in anthropology, I do maintain that by adding additional positions we may escape the dichotomy and direct 'exoticism' prevalent in much anthropology.

Finally, one of the most consistent images in the West in recent years has been the image of the 'fall' of the Berlin Wall. More generally, 'the transition' has been conceptualized as a consequence of the destruction of this borderline. What the investigation of the remaking of boundaries around the Lithuanian market place revealed was not only a strong sense of an actual rebuilding of the wall to the West, but, more surprisingly, a strong criticism of the 'building of walls' *between* the former Soviet republics. For traders, who had previously travelled and 'exploited deficits and price asymmetries among the respective countries' (Konstantinov 1996), this was regarded as a highly problematic and absolutely unexpected outcome of the 'transition'. In addition, the result was that large amounts of Asian merchandise were imported into Lithuania (and here I do not speak only of the market) and increasing numbers of entrepreneurs oriented themselves towards Asia. The expected 'return to Europe' was at the time therefore not being fulfilled.

Now that almost fifteen years have elapsed since the 'fall' of the Berlin Wall, and the Baltic states along with Poland, Hungary, the Czech Republic, Slovakia, and Slovenia are on the brink of EU membership, we should be able to see the contours of such a 'return'. However, although this in some ways promotes processes of economic and legal 'homogenization', such a development may still be rather 'uneven' as it is not likely that all areas of the economy will be affected at the same rate, nor that all changes will take the same direction. One needs only to glance at the differences between the present EU members, many of whom have been subject to processes of EU 'standardization' for years. I suggest, furthermore, that the open-air markets may be one of the phenomena that will persist and retain a distinctive character for the foreseeable future. If we turn to the Gariūnai market, trading continues in spite of the fact that most people regarded it as 'dying' in 1995, and the market has already developed into a more permanent institution.

In a recent paper, Aidis (2003) describes the situation in Gariūnai in December 2000. Although it is difficult to 'count' the exact number, Aidis's material suggests that the number of traders in the market (estimating this to be between 2,000 and 8,000 depending on weekdays) has at any rate not markedly decreased since 1995 (see Chapter 2). Furthermore, she describes recent developments in the market, which suggest that the process of institutionalization of trading practices in the market has continued rather than ceased.[6] At present, therefore, there seems to be no indication that the Gariūnai market will disppear, although it has of course changed both shape and style in recent years.

What are we then to make of the millions of people who cross the borders of their countries in order to pursue mainly Asian-produced consumer products to be sold in the large open-air markets all over Central and Eastern Europe and the former Soviet Union? Are these markets a sign of the dysfunction of more formal trade regulations and institutions of retailing? Does the 'black' trading and corruption that these activities entail suggest an anti-authoritarian ethos and a continuation of former second-economy conduct? Although some may be purely transitional phenomena, how many will turn into more permanent institutions— and what distinctive character will they form? Finally, how are we as anthropologists analytically equipped to interpret the significance and the future of a specific market phenomenon such as open-air markets?

EVALUATING THE SIGNIFICANCE OF OPEN–AIR MARKETS

Burawoy and Verdery (1999) highlight a few analytical guidelines for understanding contemporary Eastern European societies in their introduction to *Uncertain Transition*. First and foremost, they emphasize (along with most other anthropologists) the importance of contextualizing economic and political features of development socially and culturally. Second, and in continuation of this, acknowledging the vast differences not only between but also within countries in the region, they suggest that the changes in Eastern Europe should be conceived as 'transformation' rather than 'transition', since the process is not 'a unilinear one of moving from one stage to the next, as projected in neoliberal plans'. Rather, the processes of transformation are unevenly affecting different regions, and within regions

---

[6] For example she describes how garage-like concrete stalls, a restaurant, and even a hotel have been built in the area (Aidis 2003).

different sectors at different rates (ibid. 14–16). Third, they caution against denoting various economic changes to be either 'regressive' or 'progressive', since such contradictory dynamics may perfectly well exist simultaneously. Needless to say, this is also true of features which may appear as 'remnants' of post-Communism. In both cases such phenomena must be analysed with regard to their contemporary meanings, roles, functions, and importance. An empirical example of such a semantic change is Woodruff (same volume), who identifies the (continuous) widespread use of barter between enterprises in Russia, despite the fact that the meaning and social significance of barter has completely changed in recent years. 'Whereas in the previous system the expansion of barter signified affluence and surplus products, it now signifies bankruptcy' (Burawoy and Verdery 1999: 9). Far from being just a remnant of socialist economy, barter may in this case be regarded as a much more salient and persistent activity connected to the specific processes involved in creating the Russian market. Finally, Burawoy and Verdery state that 'we should be very explicit about the comparisons we draw between post-Communist and other countries'. They emphasize the danger of comparing the post-Communist countries with ideal-typical conceptions of the West, that is textbook notions of the free market, since economic features of post-Communist societies are then viewed only in terms of their deficits without considering their distinctiveness (ibid.)

This last point may serve as a starting-point for understanding the continuous existence and significance of Gariūnai and other open-air markets. The development of such huge markets and the widespread shuttle trading that sustains them has proven to be a rather unexpected phenomenon of transition from the point of view of most 'transitologists'. Even after the existence of such markets had to be politically recognized (reluctantly in the West as well as in the East) they are often disregarded as transitory and insignificant, contributing nothing to the construction of 'real' markets. For example, Scase (2000), in a publication from the United Nations University World Institute for Development Economics Research, distinguishes between what he terms 'proprietors' and 'entrepreneurs' in Russia, suggesting that only 'real entrepreneurs' may be regarded as promoters of transition (and hence worth supporting politically and financially). However, according to his definition of 'entrepreneurs', almost no one involved in small-scale business in Russia qualifies to fit the category, and subsequently most business activities are regarded as unimportant. Scase's definition of a true 'entrepreneur' is based on Weber, who defines an entrepreneur as 'a miser who sacrifices personal consumption for the longer term goal of expanding the entrepreneur's activities' (Weber 1992 (1930)). However, Humphrey (2002), among others, emphasizes that consumption patterns of the 'New Russians' are fundamentally different from consumption patterns in the West. In Russia, she argues, conspicuous consumption is to a large extent associated with the 'amount' of, i.e. 'style is denoted in quantity' (ibid., p. xxv). Viewed in this light it becomes highly inadequate to identify Russian entrepreneurs by comparing their ethos with the one described by

Weber, which, although presented as textbook economy, is closely related to the Protestant ethic of the West (Weber 1992 (1930)). From an anthropological as well as an ethical point of view this is obviously highly inadequate and would be both a misleading and a sad conclusion. As the analysis of Gariūnai as well as anthropological studies in Russia, Hungary, Poland, Bulgaria, Azerbaijan, Kazakhstan, and elsewhere in the region show, there are—and continue to be—millions of traders who not only earn a living from shuttle trading—selling their wares in open-air markets—but also contribute to the reproduction of society by engaging in these activities and thereby establishing social practices, social roles, images of market conduct, and also of course economic capital (cf. Hann and Hann 1992, Konstantinov 1996, Bruno 1997, Czako and Sik 1999, Humphrey 1999, Sik and Wallace 1999, Wallace, Shmulyar, and Bedzir 1999, Farideh Heyat 2002, Aidis 2003).

Although most shuttle trading can be viewed as 'survival strategies' it is analytically inadequate to interpret these as 'a meaningless last resort' (Humphrey 2002). Although markets are certainly regarded differently among citizens of the same country and between countries, they cannot be termed 'insignificant' just because they seem to epitomize economic dynamics that are unexpected and unfamiliar in the West and unwanted in the East. Rather, traders (and most often it is women who are the agents in this business) create new social forms and cultural images. In this way traders contribute to 'altering the contours of the previously familiar world' (Humphrey 2002).

Appendix:
Selected Lithuanian Newspaper Articles
about Gariūnai Market 1989-1995

Komjaunimo Tiesa (now Lietuvos Rytas)

1. 16/8/1989: 'Dar ne agonija'
2. 22/12/1989: 'Suvažiavimas turguje' (At the time: *Komjaunimo Tiesa*)
3. 11/9/1990: 'Į ką žvalgosi mūsų spekuliantai?'
4. 15/9/1990: 'Rinką—ne Gariūnuose, O Gedimono prospekte 30'
5. 29/9/1990: 'Trys Paros—ir į rojų'
6. 17/11/1990: 'Šūviai Gariūnouse'
7. 7/1/1992: 'Vokietijos televizija rodo Gariūnus'
8. 22/1/1992: 'Vidurnakčio kaubojai teisiami dieną'
9. 237/5/1992: 'Visus Lietuvos bankus pralenkia . . . Gariūnai'
10. 16/6/1992: 'Gariūnų kasdienybė: prekeivius apvaginėja ir reketuoja, bet ji nerėkia'
11. 10/7/1992: 'Vilniaus policija Gariūnaų reketininkams paskelbė karą'
12. 26/8/1992: 'Oro tiltas Lietuva-Turkija: aukštesniuosius turgaus komercijos kursus Stambule lenkai jau baigė, lietuviai dar tik įpusėjo'
13. 27/8/1992 'Oras tiltas . . .—tęsinys'
14. 22/12/1992: 'Nelegalus svetimšalių turgus Vilniuje: keletą talonų taupydami, keliskart rizikuojame?'
15. 4/4/1993: 'Balandžio ryto staigmena Gariūnouse: Policija uždejo antrankius reketininkū vadams'
16. 13/1/1994: 'Plešikų Jaimikis Gariūnų turgavietėje—daugiau kaip 30 milijonų rusų rublių'
17. 27/5/1994: 'Gariūnouse reketininkai įbagino ne visus'
18. 21/7/1994: 'Moksleiviai atostogauja Gariūnų dulkėse'
19. 26/7/1994: 'Gariūnai: pigios ir prastos prekės ir didėjantys prekybos plotai'
20. 2/8/1994: 'Lietuviškieji 'blusų turgūs' seniai okupavo kultūros ir pramogų centrus'
21. 8/8/1994: 'Nelegali darbo rinka: be mokesčių ir socialinių garantijų'
22. 24/8/1994: 'Viliaus ekonominė policija prieš Gariūnų patvoriu prekeivius'
23. 6/9/1994: 'Lietuvoje kas dešimtas žmogus be darbo, tačiau oficiali statistika tai neigia.
24. 3/11/1994: 'Garsioji, "Vilnius brigada": kur driekiasi nusikaltimų pėdsakai?'
25. 5/11/1994: 'Vakar Gariūnų turguje dirbo išminuotojai'

26. 30/11/1994: 'Pareigūno užpuolimas susijęs su Gariūnais?'
27. 13/12/1994: 'Sprogimai ir kulkų švilpimas tapo Panevežio kasdienybe'
28. 16/3/1995: 'Po šūvio namo kieme—mirtis ant operacinio stalo'
29. 9/6/1995: 'Policininkai reketavo Gariūnų prekiautojus'

Respublika

30. 28/3/1990: 'Juodojoje rinkoje?'
31. 27/7/1990: 'Pirkimo aistros'
32. Spring 1990: 'Tegyvuoja spekuliacija!'
33. 16/3/1995: 'Nušauta Gariūnų turgavietės vedėja'
34. 9/6/1995: 'Policijos Gariūnai'

Lietuvos Aidas

35. 28/7/1995: 'Turgus—ne laikraščiams skaityti'

Pirmadienis

36. 23/1/1995: 'Gariūnai: didybė blėsta'
37. 3/7/1995: 'Bus šeimininkas, bus tvarka'
38. 17/7/1995: 'Visi keliai—Į Gariūnus'

BIBLIOGRAPHY

AAGE, HANS (1995), 'The Language of Economic Ideology', Paper presented at the conference 'Soviet Civilization: New Interpretations?', Odense University.

AALTEN, ANNA (1989), 'The Accidental Businesswoman: Gender and Entrepreneurship in the Netherlands, 1950–1975', J. Boissevain and J. Verrips (eds.), *Dutch Dilemmas: Anthropologists Look at the Netherlands* (Assen/Maastricht: Van Gorcum), 153–64.

ABU-LUGHOD, LILA (1991), 'Writing against Culture', in Richard G. Fox (ed.), *Recapturing Anthropology: Working in the Present* (Santa Fe, New Mexico: School of American Research Press), 137–61.

AIDIS, RŪTA (2003), 'Officially Despised yet Tolerated: Open-Air Markets and Entrepreneurship in Post-Socialist Countries', in *Post-Communist Economics* (forthcoming).

ALEXANDER, PAUL (1992), 'What's in a Price?', in Roy Dilley (ed.), *Contesting Markets: Analyses of Ideology, Discourse and Practice* (Edinburgh: Edinburgh University Press), 79–96.

ALISAUSKIENE, RASA, and BAJARUNIENE, RITA (1993), 'Economic Values and Attitudes to the Economic Reform of Lithuanian People', Paper presented at ESOMAR seminar, Budapest.

ANDERSEN, ERIK ANDRÉ (1995), 'Arbejdsløshed blandt russere i Estland', *Nordisk Østforum*, 2: 34–9.

APPADURAI, ARJUN (ed.) (1986), 'Introduction', *The Social Life of Things* (Cambridge: Cambridge University Press), 3–64.

—— (1990), 'Disjuncture and Difference in the Global Cultural Economy', in Mike Featherstone (ed.), *Global Culture: Nationalism, Globalization and Modernity* (London: Sage Publications), 295–310.

—— (1991), 'Global Ethnoscapes: Notes and Queries for a Transnational Anthropology', in Richard D. Fox (ed.), *Recapturing Anthropology: Working in the Present* (Sante Fe, New Mexico: School of American Research Press), 191–210.

Baltic Observer, 9–15 March 1995.

BARTH, FREDRIK (1969), 'Introduction', in Fredrik Barth (ed.), *Ethnic Groups and Boundaries: The Social Organization of Culture Difference* (Boston: Little, Brown).

—— (1989), 'The Analysis of Culture in Complex Societies', *Ethnos*, 54/3, 4: 120–43.

BARTUSEVIČIUS, V. (1993), 'Socializmo Liekanos Lietuvos Zmoniu Santykiuose', *I Laisve*, 117 (Nov.) 30–49.

BLOCH, MAURICE, and PARRY, JONATHAN (1989), 'Introduction: Money and the Morality of Exchange,' Maurice Bloch and Jonathan Parry (eds.), *Money and the Morality of Exchange* (Cambridge: Cambridge University Press), 1–32.

BOHANNAN, PAUL (1955), 'Some Principles of Exchange and Investment among the Tiv', *American Anthropologist*, 57:

BOURDIEU, PIERRE 1992 (1980), *The Logic of Practice* (Stanford: Stanford University Press), 52–65.

—— and WACQUANT, LOIC J. D. (1992), *An Invitation to Reflexive Sociology* (Chicago: Polity Press).

BOYM, SVETLANA (1994), *Common Places: Mythologies of Everyday Life in Russia* (Cambridge, Mass.: Harvard University Press).

BRIDGER, SUE, and PINE, FRANCIS (1998), 'Introduction: Transitions to Post-Socialism and Cultures of Survival', Sue Bridger and Francis Pine (eds.), *Surviving Post-Socialism: Local Strategies and Regional Responses in Eastern Europe and the Former Soviet Union*, Routledge Studies of Societies in Transition (London: Routledge).

BRUNO, MARTA (1995), 'In Search of Difference: Gender and Stratification in Russia', in David Anderson and Francis Pine (eds.), *Cambridge Anthropology* 18/1: 73–82.

—— (1997), 'Women and the Culture of Entrepreneurship', in Mary Buckley (ed.), *Post-Soviet Women: From the Baltic to Central Asia* (Cambridge University Press).

BUCHOWSKI, MICHAEL (1994), 'From Anti-Communist to Post-Communist Ethos: The Case of Poland', *Social Anthropology*, 2/2: 133–48.

BULOFF, JOSEPH (1991), *From the Old Marketplace* (Cambridge, Mass.: Harvard University Press).

BURAWOY, MICHAEL, and VERDERY, KATHERINE (1999), 'Introduction' in Michael Buraway and Katherine Verdery (eds.), *Uncertain Transition: Ethnographies of Change in the Postsocialist World* (Lanham: Rowman & Littlefield).

CHAVEZ, LEO R. (1991), 'Outside the Imagined Community: Undocumented Settlers and Experiences of Incorporation', *American Ethnologist* 18/2: 257–79.

COHEN, ANTHONY P. (1994), *Self Consciousness: An Alternative Anthropology of Identity* (London: Routledge 1994).

CORRIN, CHRIS (1992), 'Gendered Identities: Women's Experience of Change in Hungary', in S. Rai, H. Pilkington, and A. Phizacklea (eds.), *Women in the Face of Change: The Soviet Union, Eastern Europe and China* (London: Routledge), 167–85.

CROLL, ELISABETH (1987), 'Short Term Field Investigation in China: A Personal View', *China Information*, 11/1: 17–26.

CZAKO, AGNES, and SIK, ENDRE (1999), 'Characteristics and Origins of the Comecon Open-Air market in Hungary', *International Journal of Urban and Regional Research*, 23: 715–37.

DE CERTEAU, MICHEL (1988), *The Practice of Everyday Life* (Berkeley: Berkeley University Press).

DEMIRDIREK, HULYA (1996), 'The Painful Past Retold: Social Memory in Azerbaijan and Gagauzia', Paper presented at the conference 'The Anthropology of Post-Communism', University of Copenhagen.

DILLEY, ROY (1992), 'Contesting Markets: A General Introduction to Market Ideology, Imagery and Discourse', in Roy Dilley (ed.), *Contesting Markets: Analyses of Ideology, Discourse and Practice* (Edinburgh: Edinburgh University Press), 1–34.

DOUGLAS, MARY (1995 (1966)), *Purity and Danger: An Analysis of the Concepts of Pollution and Taboo* (London: Routledge).

EINHORN, BARBARA (1993), *Cinderella Goes to Market: Citizenship, Gender and Women's Movements in East Central Europe* (London: Verso).

FARIDEH HEYAT (2002), 'Women and the Culture of Entrepreneurship in Soviet and Post-Soviet Azerbaijan', Caroline, Humphrey and Ruth Mandel (eds.), *Markets and Moralities: Ethnographies of Postsocialism* (Oxford: Berg).

FEATHERSTONE, MIKE (ed.) (1990), *Global Culture: Nationalism, Globalization and Modernity*, London: Sage Publications).

FEDOSEYEV, P. N. *et al.* (1977), *Leninism and the National Question*, (Moscow: Moscow Progress Publishers).

FEHER, FERENC, HELLER, AGNES, and MARKUS, GYÖRGE (1983), *Dictatorship over Needs* (Oxford: Basil Blackwell).

FISCHER-RUGE, LOIS (1993), *Survival in Russia: Chaos and Hope in Everyday Life* (Boulder: Westview Press).

FRIEDLAND, R., and ROBERTSON, A. F. (1990), 'Introduction', in R. Friedland and A. F. Roberson (eds.), *Beyond the Marketplace: Rethinking Economy and Society* (New York: Aldine de Gruyter).

GANS, HERBERT J. (1979), 'Symbolic Ethnicity: The Future of Ethnic Groups and Cultures in America', *Ethnic and Racial Studies*, 12/1: 1–20.

GEERTZ, CLIFFORD (1963), *Peddlers and Princes—Social Development and Economic Change in Two Indonesian Towns* (Chicago: University of Chicago Press).

—— (1979) 'Suq: The Bazaar Economy in Sefrou', in C. Geertz, H. Geertz, and L. Rosen (eds.), *Meaning and Order in Moroccan Society* (Cambridge: Cambridge University Press).

GERNER, KRISTIAN, and HEDLUND, STEFAN (1994), 'Homo Oeconomicus Meets Homo Sovieticus', *Idäntutkimus: The Finnish Review of East-European Studies*, 1: 8–26.

GOFFMAN, ERVING (1959), *The Presentation of Self in Everyday Life* (Garden City, NY: Doubleday).

GREIMAS, ALGIRDAS JULIEN (1992 (1979)), *Of Gods and Men: Studies in Lithuanian Mythology* (Bloomington: Indiana University Press).

—— (1993), *La Lithuanie: Un des pays baltes* (Vilnius: Baltos Lankos).

GRUŽEVSKIS, BOGUSLAVAS (1995), 'The Trends of Employment and Labour Market Policy in Lithuania', Paper presented at the confererence 'Demographic Processes and the Socio-Economic Transformation in Central and Eastern European Countries', Warsaw.

GUDEMAN, STEPHEN (1992), 'Markets, Models and Morality', in Roy Dilley (ed.), *Contesting Markets: Analyses of Ideology, Discourse and Practice* (Edinburgh: Edinburgh University Press), 279–94.

—— and PENN, MISCHA (1982), 'Models, Meanings and Reflexivity', in D. Parkin (ed.), *Semantic Anthropology*, ASA Monograph 22 (London: Academic Press), 89–106.

GUPTA, AKHIL, and FERGUSON, JAMES (1992), 'Beyond 'Culture': Space, Indentity, and the Politics of Difference', *Cultural Anthropology*, 7/1: 6–24.

HANN, C. M. (1992), 'Market Principle, Market-Place and the Transition in Eastern Europe', in Roy Dilley (ed.), *Contesting Markets: Analyses of Ideology, Discourse and Practice* (Edinburgh: Edinburgh University Press), 244–59.

—— (1994a), 'Fast Forward: The Great Transformation Globalized', in C. M. Hann (ed.), *When History Accelerates: Essays on Rapid Social Change, Complexity and Creativity* (London: Athlone Press), 1–22.

—— (1994b), 'After Communism: Reflections on East European Anthropology and "The Transition" ', *Social Anthropology*, 2/3: 229–49.

—— and HANN, ILDIKO (1992), 'Samovars and Sex on Turkey's Russian Markets', *Anthropology Today*, 8/4: 3–6.

HANNERZ, ULF (1987), 'The World in Creolization', *Africa*, 57/4: 546–59.

—— (1990), 'Cosmopolitans and Locals in World Culture', in Mike Featherstone (ed.), *Global Culture, Nationalism, Globalization and Modernity* (London: Sage Publications), 237–52.

—— (1992), *Cultural Complexity: Studies in the Social Organization of Meaning* (New York: Columbia University Press).

HASTRUP, KIRSTEN (1992), 'Introduction', in Kirsten Hastrup (ed.), *Other Histories* (London: Routledge), 1–14,

—— and OLWIG, KAREN FOG (1997), 'Introduction', in Karen Fog Olwig and Kirsten Hastrup (eds.), *Siting Culture: The Shifting Anthropological Object* (London: Routledge), 1–14.

HELGASON, AGNAR, and PALSSON, GISLI (1996), 'Contested Commodities: Mapping the Moral Landscape of Exchange', Paper presented at the EASA conference, Barcelona, 12–15 July 1996. A later version of the paper is published as 'Contested Commodities: The Moral Landscape of Modernist Regimes', *Journal of the Royal Anthropological Institute* (incorporating *Man*), 3/3: (1997) 451–71.

HOLY, STANISLAV (1992), 'Culture, Market Ideology and Economic Reform in Czechoslovakia', in Roy Dilley (ed.), *Contesting Markets: Analyses of Ideology, Discourse and Practice* (Edinburgh: Edinburgh University Press), 231–43.

HUMPHREY, CAROLINE (1991), ' "Icebergs", Barter and the Mafia in Provincial Russia', *Anthropology Today*, 7/2: 8–13.

—— (1995a), 'Introduction', in David Anderson and Francis Pine (eds.), *Cambridge Anthropology*, 18/1: 1–13.

—— (1995b), 'The Politics of Privatization in Provincial Russia: Popular Opinions Amid the Dilemmas of the Early 1990s', in David Anderson and Francis Pine (eds.), *Cambridge Anthropology*, 18/1: 40–61.

—— (1999) 'Traders "Disorder", and Citizenship Regimes in Provincial Russia', in Michael Burawoy and Katherine Verdery (eds.), *Uncertain Transition: Ethnographies of Change in the Postsocialist World* (Lanham: Rowman & Littlefield).

—— (2002), *The Unmaking of Soviet Life: Everyday Economics after Socialism* (Ithaca: Cornell University Press).

—— and MANDEL, RUTH (2002), 'The Market in Everyday Life: Ethnographies of Postsocialism', Caroline Humphrey and Ruth Mandel (eds.), *Markets and Moralities: Ethnographies of Postsocialism* (Oxford: Berg).

HYLLAND-ERIKSEN, THOMAS (1995), *Kulturelle Veikryss: Essays om kreolisering* (Oslo: Universitetsforlaget), 5–43.

KANOPIENĖ, VIDA, and JUOZELIŪNIENĖ, IRENA (1996), 'Gender Roles and Identity', in Meilute Taliūnaite (ed.), *Changes of Identity in Modern Lithuania* (Vilnius: Social Studies), 223–39.

KARKLINS, RASMA (1986), *Ethnic Relations in the USSR: The Perspective from Below* (London: Allen & Unwin).

KASPARAVICIENE, VIDA (1996), 'Ethnic Composition of Vilnius Residents, National Relations and Estimations', in Meilute Taliūnaite (ed.), *Changes of Identity in Modern Lithuania* (Vilnius: Social Studies), 262–9.

KENEDI, JANOS (1981), *Do it Yourself: Hungary's Hidden Economy* (London: Pluto Press).

KOBECKAITE, HALINA, *et al.* (eds.) (1992), *National Minorities in Lithuania* (Vilnius: Centre of National Researches of Lithuanian).

KOLSTØ, PÅL (1995), 'Nasjonsbyggning i Eurasia', *Nordisk Østforum*, 1: 39–54.

KONSTANTINOV, JULIAN, KRESSEL, GIDEON M., and THUEN, TROND (1996) 'Outclassed by former Outcasts: Engagement in Petty Trading in Varna', Unpublished manuscript.

KONSTANTINOV, YULIAN (1996), 'Patterns of Reinterpretation: Trader-Tourism in the Balkans (Bulgaria) as a Picaresque Metaphorical Enactment of Post-Totalitarianism', *American Ethnologist*, 23/4: 762–82.

KOVAL, V. V. (1995), 'Women and Work in Russia', in V. V. Koval (ed.), *Women in Contemporary Russia* (Oxford: Berghahn Books), 17–33.

KRAG, HELEN (1992), 'Det baltiske dilemma, minoritetskonflikt i Estland', in Erik Andre Andersen (ed.), *Minoriteternes situation og rettigheder i de baltiske lande* (Copenhagen: ICØ), 10–37.

KRYSHTANOVSKAYA, OLGA (1994), 'Rich and Poor in Post-Communist Russia', *Journal of Communist Studies*, 10/1: 3–24.

KÜRTI, LASLO (1996), 'Homecoming', *Anthropology Today*, 12/3: 11–15.

LARSEN, PERNILLE (1995), 'Hebben Nederlanders dan geen cultuur? Een beschouwing over Nederlands onderzoek naar "etnisch ondernemerschap" ', *Tien Jaar Migrantenstudies*, 1: 30–8.

LIEVEN, ANATOL (1993), *The Baltic Revolution: Estonia, Latvia, Lithuania and the Path to Independence* (New Haven: Yale University Press).

MARCUS, GEORGE E. (1995), 'Ethnography in/of the World System: The Emergence of Multi-Sited Ethnography', *Annual Review of Anthropology*, 24: 95–117.

—— and FISHER, MICHAEL M. J. (1986), *Anthropology as Cultural Critique* (Chicago: University of Chicago Press).

MARS, GERALD, and ALTMAN, YOUCHANAN (1983), 'The Cultural Basis of Soviet Georgia's Second Economy', *Soviet Studies*, 35/4: 546–60.

MILKALKEVIČIUS, ALGIRDAS, and STANISLOVAS, ŠIKUNAS (1992), 'Ideology and Alcohol Problems in Lithuania', in Jussi Simpura and Christoffer Tigerstedt, (eds.), *Social Problems around the Baltic Sea*, Helsinki: Nordic Council for Alcohol and Drug Research (NAD) Publication no. 21: 53–69.

MILOSZ, CESLAV (1975), 'Vilnius, Lithuanian: An Ethnic Agglomerate', in George de Voss and Lola Romanucci-Ross (eds.), *Ethnic Identity: Cultural Continuities and Change* (Palo Alto, Calif.: Mayfield Publishing Company), 339–52.

MISIUNAS, ROMUALD J. (1989), 'The Baltic States: Years of Dependence 1980–1986', *Journal of Baltic Studies*, 20/1: 65–87.

—— and TAAGEPERA, REIN (1993 (1983)), *The Baltic States: Years of Dependence 1940–1990*, rev. edn. (London: Hurst).

MOORE, SALLY FALK (1987), 'Explaining the Present: Theoretical Dilemmas in Processual Ethnography', *American Ethnologist*, 14: 727–36.

MØRK, YVONNE (1995), 'Kulturel kompleksitet og empiri-brocolage: Refleksioner over et projekt om etnisk minoritetsungdom og multikulturalisme', *Tidskriftet Antropologi*, 31: 121–31.

NORBORG, ÅKE, 'Song Festivals and Politics: The Manipulation of National Symbols in Lithuanian', Unpublished manuscript.

NØRGAARD, OLE, *et al.* (eds.) (1994), *De baltiske lande efter uafhængigheden. Hvorfor så forskellige?* (Aarhus: Politica).

OLSEN, MAJ (1996), 'Pure Relationships: The Search for Love among Hungarian Academic Women', *Anthropology of East Europe Review*, 14/1: 15–21.

OLWIG, KAREN (1990), 'Cultural Identity and Material Culture: Afro-Caribbean Pottery', *Folk*, 32: 6–22.

—— (1997), 'Cultural Sites: Sustaining a Home in a Deterritorialized World', in Karen Fog Olwig and Kirsten Hastrup (eds.), *Siting Culture: The Shifting Anthropological Object* (London: Routledge), 17–38.

—— and HASTRUP, KIRSTEN (eds.) (1997), *Siting Culture: The Shifting Anthropological Object* (London: Routledge).

ORTNER, SHERRY (1984), 'Theory in Anthropology since the Sixties', *Comparative Studies in Society and History*, 26: 126–66.

OSTROVSKA, ILZE (1992), 'Grænser for udholdenhed: Om mænd og kvinder i Letland', *Nyt forum for kvindeforskning*, 2: 16–22.

PAHL, RAY, and THOMPSON, PAUL (1994), 'Meanings, Myths and Mystifications: The Social Construction of Life Histories in Russia', in C. M. Hann (ed.), *When History Accelerates: Essays on Rapid Social Change, Complexity and Creativity* (London: Athlone Press), 130–60.

PELLOW, DEBORAH (1996), 'Introduction', in Deborah Pellow (ed.), *Setting Boundaries: The Anthropology of Spatial and Social Organization* (Westport: Bergin & Garvey), 1–9.

PILKINGTON, HILARY (1992a), 'Russia and the Former Soviet Republics: Behind the Mask of Soviet Unity: Realities of Women's Lives', in Chris Corrin (ed.), *Superwomen and the Double Burden* (London: Scarlet Press), 80–235.

—— (1992b), 'Whose Space is it Anyway? Youth, Gender and Civil Society in the Soviet Union', in S. Rai, H. Pilkington, and A. Phizacklea, *Women in the Face of Change: The Soviet Union, Eastern Europe and China* (London: Routledge), 105–29.

—— (1995) 'Farewell to the Tusovka: Masculinities and Femininities on the Moscow Youth Scene', Paper presented at the conference 'Soviet Civilisation—New Interpretations', University of Odense, December.

—— (1996), ' "Youth Culture" in Contemporary Russia: Gender, Consumption and Identity', in Hilary Pilkington (ed.), *Gender, Generation and Identity in Contemporary Russia* (London: Routledge).

PINE, FRANCIS (1994), 'Privatization in Post-Socialist Poland: Peasant Women, Work, and the Restructuring of the Public Sphere', *Cambridge Anthropology*, 17/3: 19–42.

PRESTON, PETER (1992), 'Modes of Economic-Theoretical Engagement', in Roy Dilley (ed.), *Contesting Markets: Analyses of Ideology, Discourse and Practice* (Edinburgh: Edinburgh University Press), 57–75.

RAUN, TOIVO U. (1994), 'Ethnic Relations and Conflict in the Baltic States', in W. R. Duncan and G. P. Holman, Jr. (eds.), *Ethnic Nationalism and Regional Conflict: The Former Soviet Union and Jugoslavia* (Boulder: Westview Press), 155–82.

REDDY, WILLIAM M. (1986), 'The Structure of a Cultural Crisis: Thinking about Cloth in France before and after the Revolution', in Arjun Appadurai (ed.), *The Social Life of Things* (Cambridge: Cambridge University Press), 261–85.

ROEPSTORFF, ANDREAS (1996), 'Form og Indentitet eller That national Thing. Et studie i historie, narration og national identitet i Litauen', ethnographical dissertation, Moesgaard, Aarhus Universitet.

RUUTSOO, REIN (1993), 'The Transformation of Estonia into a Nation-State and the Search for a new Identity', in Ilkka Alanen (ed.), *The Baltic States at a Crossroads: Preliminary Methodological Analysis* (Jyväskylä: University of Jyväskylä), 95–106.

SAHLINS, MARSHALL (1985), *Islands of History* (London: Tavistock Publications).

SAMPSON, STEVEN (1987), 'The Second Economy of the Soviet Union and Eastern Europe', *Annals of the American Academy of Political and Social Science*, 493: 120–36.

—— (1991), 'Is There an Anthropology of Socialism?', *Anthropology Today*, 7/5: 16–19.

—— (1993), 'Money without Culture, Culture Without Money: Eastern Europe's Nouveaux Riches', *American Journal on European Cultures*, 3/1 ('World View, Political Behaviour and Economy in the Post-Communist Transition'), 7–31.

SCASE, RICHARD (2000), 'Entrepreneurship and Proprietorship in Transition: Policy

Implications for the Small- and Medium-Size Enterprise Sector', Working Papers no. 193, The United Nations University, World Institute for Development Economics Research (WIDER), August.

SENN, ALFRED ERIC (1990), *Lithuania Awakening* (Berkeley: University of California Press).

SHELLEY, LOUISE I. (1990), 'The Second Economy in the Soviet Union', in Maria Los (ed.), *The Second Economy in Marxist States* (London: Macmillan), 11–25.

SHLAPENTOKH, V. (1984), *Love, Marriage, and Friendship in the Soviet Union: Ideals and Practices* (New York: Praeger).

—— (1989), *Public and Private Life of the Soviet People: Changing Values in Post-Stalin Russia* (New York: Oxford University Press).

SIEVERT NIELSEN, FINN (1994), 'Rapport fra Forskerkurset: Continuity and Change in Post-Soviet Societies', *Antropolognytt*, 2. http://mac18.anthro. ku.dk/~sivert/oeur/1nor/Tromsoe-1994.htm

SIK, ENDRE, and WALLACE, CLAIRE (1999), 'The Development of Open-Air Markets in East-Central Europe', *International Journal of Urban and Regional Research*, 23: 697–714.

STEWART, MICHAEL (1993), 'Gypsies, the Work Ethic, and Hungarian Socialism', in C. M. Hann (ed.), *Socialism: Ideals, Ideology, and Local Practice*, ASA monograph 31 (London: Routledge), 187–203.

—— (1997), *The Time of the Gypsies* (Boulder: Westview Press).

SVENDSEN, METTE NORDAHL (1996), The Post-Communist Body: Beauty and Aerobics in Romania', *Anthropology of East Europe Review*, 14/1: 8–15.

TALIŪNAITĖ, MEILUTE (1996), 'Social Groups and the Growth of Social Dislocation', in Meilute Taliūnaitė (ed.), *Changes of Identity in Modern Lithuania* (Vilnius: Social Studies), 300–25.

TAUSSIG, MICHAEL T. (1980), *The Devil and Commodity Fetishism in South America* (Chapel Hill: University of North Carolina Press).

THUEN, TROND (1997), 'Borders as Resource and Impediment in East European Transition Processes'. Later published in Cristina Papa, Giovanni Pizza, and Filippo Zerilli (eds.), *Incontri di etnologia Europea* (*European Ethnology Meetings*), II/1 (Naples: Edizion i Scientifiche Italiane, 1998).

TOTH, OLGA (1993), 'No Envy, No Pity', in Nanette Funk and Magda Mueller (eds.), *Gender Politics and Post-Communism: Reflections from Eastern Europe and the Former Soviet Union* (New York: Routledge), 213–23.

TURNER, VICTOR (1969), *The Ritual Process: Structure and Anti-Structure* (New York: Aldine Publishing), 94–131.

VAKNIN, SAM (2002), 'Trading from a Suitcase: Shuttle Trading', *Business & Economics Desk*, United Press International, http://www.upi.com/print.cfm? StoryID=03042002-121843-3501r

VARDYS, STANLEY (ed.) (1965), *Lithuania Under the Soviets: Portrait of a Nation 1940–65* (NewYork: Praeger).

—— (1990), 'Litauen—Sovjetrepublik mod sin vilje: Udviklingen siden 1994', *Estland, Letland, Litauen: Den Syngende Revolution i Baltikum*, SNUs documentation series, 69–82.

VERDERY, KATHERINE (1991), 'Theorizing Socialism: A Prologue to the Transition', *American Ethnologist*, 18/3: 419–39.

—— (1996) *What was Socialism and What Comes Next?* (Princeton: Princeton University Press).

WALLACE, CLAIRE, SHMULYAR, OKSANA, and BEDZIR, VASIL (1999), 'Investing in Social Capital: The Case of Small-Scale, Cross-Border Traders in Post-Communist Central Europe', *International Journal of Urban and Regional Research*, 23: 751–70.

WEBER, MAX (1992 (1930)), *The Protestant Ethic and the Spirit of Capitalism* (London: Routledge).

WEDEL, JANINE R. (1986), *The Private Poland* (New York: Facts on File Publications).

—— (1992) (ed.), *The Unplanned Society: Poland During and After Communism* (New York: Columbia University Press).

—— (2001), *Collision and Collusion: The Strange Case of Western Aid to Eastern Europe* (New York: Palgrave).

WOLF, ERIC (1982), *Europe and the People without History* (Berkeley: University of California Press).

WOODRUFF, DAVID (1999), 'Barter of the Bankrupt: The Politics of Demonetization in Russia's Federal State', in Michael Buraway, and Katherine Verdery (eds.), *Uncertain Transition: Ethnographies of Change in the Postsocialist World* (Lanham: Rowman & Littlefield).

ZASLAVSKY, VICTOR (1982), *The Neo-Stalinist state: Class, Ethnicity and Consensus in Soviet Society* (New York: Sharpe).

ZELIZER, V. ROTMAN (1979), *Morals and Markets: The Development of Life Insurance in the United States* (New York: Columbia University Press).

INDEX

Note: **emboldened** page numbers indicate chapters